Big Skies, White Hoods

Big Skies, White Hoods

THE 1920s KLAN AND A HISTORY OF HATE IN MONTANA

Christine K. Erickson

UNIVERSITY OF OKLAHOMA PRESS : NORMAN

Publication of this book is made possible in part through the generosity of Edith Kinney Gaylord.

Library of Congress Cataloging-in-Publication Data

Names: Erickson, Christine K., 1959– author.
Title: Big skies, white hoods : the 1920s Klan and a history of hate in Montana / Christine K. Erickson.
Description: Norman : University of Oklahoma Press, [2025] | Includes bibliographical references and index. | Summary: "Explores the little-known history of the Ku Klux Klan in Montana, revealing what this twentieth-century incarnation of the KKK in the American West had in common with its post-Civil War antecedents in the Deep South, how it differed from the Klan's reappearance elsewhere in the 1920s, and what it might tell us about the current resurgence of white nationalism in Montana and across the West"—Provided by publisher.
Identifiers: LCCN 2024038943 | ISBN 9780806195377 (hardcover)
Subjects: LCSH: Ku Klux Klan (1915-) | White nationalism—Montana—History—20th century. | African Americans—Violence against—Montana—History—20th century. | Racism—Montana—History—20th century. | Montana—Race relations—History—20th century.
Classification: LCC HS2330.K63 E75 2025 | DDC 322.4/209786—dc23/eng/20250111
LC record available at https://lccn.loc.gov/2024038943

The paper in this book meets the guidelines for permanence and durability of the Committee on Production Guidelines for Book Longevity of the Council on Library Resources, Inc. ∞

To my parents, Ron and Nancy

Contents

Acknowledgments

It has been a long journey and I have incurred many debts along the way. I would first like to thank the Department of History at the University of Montana in Missoula, where I received my Master of Arts degree, especially the department chair, William Farr, for his willingness to admit a student of science into the graduate program, and David M. Emmons, whose assent to share his discovery of an archive on the Ku Klux Klan at the Eastern Washington Historical Society provided the topic for my master's thesis and the beginning of a lifelong interest in nativism in general and the Ku Klux Klan in particular. My adviser, Michael S. Mayer, patiently guided me through the program and the successful completion of my master's thesis on the Butte Klan. His enthusiasm for history was contagious.

Many thanks to the Department of History at Purdue Fort Wayne (formerly Indiana Purdue Fort Wayne), especially Richard Weiner and Ann Livschiz for their helpful advice and unwavering support. I received institutional support as well, including several sabbaticals, two Summer Faculty Research Grants, and a New Frontiers Exploration Traveling Fellowship Grant from Indiana University, which allowed me to travel across Montana one summer visiting historical societies and public libraries. The Office of Research and External Support provided funds to place an advertisement in over sixty Montana newspapers seeking information on the 1920s Klan. Many thanks to Dean Janet Badia for creating The College of Liberal Arts Faculty Summer Research Camp, which provided a welcoming space to work.

Thanks go to the excellent staff at the Montana Historical Society Research Center in Helena, who were always helpful in discovering new treasures. In the days before ancestry.com and other internet sites, the Silver Bow Archives in Butte gave me my first taste of archival research. A meeting with Travis McAdam at the Montana Human Rights Network office provided the key link between the Klan of the 1990s and the Klan of the 1920s. A long list of staff at public libraries and historical museums in towns across the state provided help in seeking out the stories on paper that could only be found on bookshelves and in cabinet drawers. Many thanks to the staff at *Montana: The Magazine of Western History* for their guidance and support, which resulted in the publication of two articles on the Montana Klan, parts of which appear in *White Hoods.*

Other individuals deserve my deepest appreciation, including Dave Walter, dedicated and enthusiastic research historian at the MHS, who passed away too soon in 2006. My appreciation also goes to Tim McCleary in Hardin and Tim Schaff in Roundup, both of whom willingly shared their research about the MacLeod and Gilmore shootings in Hardin and the Roundup Klan respectively. Thanks to Chris Boe for his generosity in sharing sources and to Daniel Gardiner, for his assistance with the Masonic membership in Montana. Many thanks to the reviewers of the manuscript for the University of Oklahoma Press (OUP), who offered their honest assessments and advice. Thanks also goes to OUP acquisitions editor Joe Schiller, OUP managing editor Steven B. Baker, and copyeditor Stephanie Marshall Ward. Their careful edits and suggestions greatly improved this work.

My parents, to whom I dedicate this book, passed away in 2022 and 2023. Without their love and encouragement, my journey as a historian would have been far more difficult. Finally, I thank my daughter, Avery, who arrived when I was in graduate school and whose curiosity about the world and sense of adventure continue to inspire me.

□　□　□

Author's note: Readers will find several instances of quotes from racists and homophobes that might be triggering, especially in the epilogue.

Introduction

I guess you've heard of the K.K.K.,
But if you haven't say!
I want to tell you 'bout them;
We cannot do without them
If you are one hundred per cent,
Then you are just the gent
So come and join today,
Be a Klansman right away.
                    "Come Join the Knights of the Ku Klux Klan (fox trot)," 1923

In late March 2006, a fifty-three-year-old Montanan named Bill called me on my office phone. He hesitated when he discovered I was a woman, and after a long pause, he said in an accusatory tone, "You should have told me you were a lady." I had recently received some funding from my university to place an advertisement in Montana weekly newspapers, in which I provided my contact details and expressed my interest in information about the 1920s Ku Klux Klan. Several residents generously responded by postal mail with helpful insights, but it was the phone conversation with Bill that stuck with me.

He was "not ashamed" to hang the Confederate flag in his home, as he told me what he knew of the Civil War and the first Ku Klux Klan, which was created, he confidently stated, to drive the Yankees out of the South and to champion the rights of southern whites who, according to Bill, were not

allowed to vote during Reconstruction. He proclaimed his membership in the
Sons of the American Revolution and the Sons of Confederate Veterans and
revealed that he was "turning anti-Catholic" in response to the "immigration
problem" and "too many Mexicans and illegals." As it became clear that Bill
did not know much about the 1920s Klan, I asked him about the Klan that
appeared in Montana during the 1990s. He scoffed and said that they were "a
bunch of buffoons—troublemakers, neo-Nazis, young kids from Seattle" with
no larger purpose and no idea what they were doing or what they wanted.
"They were nothing."[1]

Grand Dragon Lewis Terwilliger would have been dismayed to hear it.
The leader of the Montana Realm was one of the Ku Klux Klan's proudest
members. Three to four million men joined the nativist white supremacist
organization during the 1920s—it was hardly "nothing," as it dominated
American politics and society during that decade. Dismayed too, would have
been the over 5,100 men in Montana who paid their dues, including the "three
hooded riders in full regalia" who galloped on horseback down the streets of
Hamilton one summer evening in 1922, skidded to a stop at a local newspaper office, and slid a note under the door declaring that the Ku Klux Klan
had arrived in Ravalli County. Before astonished witnesses could react, the
hooded Knights had pivoted their horses "back toward the hills." Elsewhere
across the state during that spring and summer, reflecting the massive surge
in membership across the country during the early 1920s, the Klan organized
in at least forty-six communities in Montana. *Big Skies, White Hoods: The
1920s Klan and a History of Hate in Montana* tells that story for the first time
in book-length detail.

Sparsely populated though it was, the Big Sky country offered Imperial
officials a potential source of revenue and an opportunity to increase the
Klan's political clout. It was in that spirit that on September 16, 1923, Imperial
Wizard Hiram Wesley Evans welcomed the Realm of Montana into the Invisible Empire. Complete with appropriate "herewiths" and "hereby ordereds,"
the official charter briskly divided Montana into four provinces, appointed
Hydras and Great Titans to assist in governing, and laid out the financial
responsibilities of the Montana Klan to the Imperial Palace, headquartered
in Atlanta, Georgia. The future appeared promising to the newly anointed
Grand Dragon of Montana, Lewis Terwilliger. In his first official circular, an
optimistic Terwilliger pronounced that Montana Klansmen were "now ready
to get into the harness and operate as a real Realm organization."[2]

It would not be easy. Western Realms encountered multiple challenges to recruiting and retaining members. Two main exceptions were Oregon and Colorado, whose urban centers provided ample recruiting grounds for the Klan. Around 25 thousand men paid allegiance to the Realm of Oregon, over half of them located in Portland, and 35–45 thousand joined the Klan ranks in Colorado, with almost 17 thousand in Denver alone. Denver's proximity to four other major Colorado cities offered even more opportunities for membership drives.[3] This was not the case in many other western states. As the Grand Dragon of Wyoming explained in 1923, the thinly spread population and the immense distances required for travel ("a day or hours" to attend the Klavern) in western Realms tested the commitment of even the most dedicated Klansman. But "noble" Knights, he quickly added, were diligently working to overcome the adversities of geography and "studying to improve" themselves in the ways of Klankraft.[4] The Grand Dragon was spinning the situation as best he could. Much of the West continued to be difficult hunting grounds for the Ku Klux Klan. Nevada's Klan was mostly "invisible," as David Chalmers states, while Wyoming's faithful could not even muster a respectable number of attendees or a meeting hall for a proposed visit to Casper by Imperial Wizard Evans.[5]

In *The Invisible Empire in the West*, Shawn Lay suggests the West might not be "the ideal region" for a general evaluation of the Klan because of its relatively low profile.[6] Yet the essays in Lay's anthology reveal that Klan activity flourished in sections of Colorado, Oregon, California, Texas, and Utah. Moreover, those essays and other recent studies agree that the Klan was infinitely more complex than earlier assessments that had painted the hooded order as an aberrant and violent fringe group, attractive only to the rural, irrational, and uneducated. Scholars have rightly dismissed this one-dimensional view of the Klan, demonstrating not only the Klan's chameleon-like ability to adapt its program to the prejudices of local communities, but also that the order's interests often overlapped with those of the mainstream, such as Prohibition and immigration restriction.[7] As Linda Gordon states in *The Second Coming of the KKK*, even if most Americans did not join the hooded order, its agenda "seemed ordinary and respectable to its contemporaries."[8] "There was," Thomas Pegram adds in *One Hundred Percent American*, "an ordinary, everyday quality to the Klan's presence in the still-dominant white Protestant America of the 1920s."[9] State and regional studies confirm that Klansmen moved with ease in the local white Protestant culture, reflecting the fact that much of the larger society thought as they did.[10] That was often the case in Montana, with some notable exceptions.

Big Skies, White Hoods, however, does not tell an exhaustive history of each of the forty-six communities where the Klan organized. The availability of archival materials determines the story that can be told. Most of the primary source documentation comes from Kontinental Klan No. 30 in Butte, the only Montana Klan to leave behind minutes from meetings and letters from Kligrapps (local secretaries). The original archives of the Butte Klan are located at the Eastern Washington Historical Society, and microfilmed copies are housed at the Montana Historical Society, which later acquired membership receipts for the Wheatland Klan in Harlowton. Butte's records include lists of members, Terwilliger's official circulars and letters, minutes from the Butte meetings and Kloreros (state conventions), correspondence from the Imperial Wizard and various Klansmen throughout the state, and financial records. I have also relied on documentary evidence from the Montana Historical Society, the Butte Silver Bow Archives, local Montana public libraries and historical societies, newspapers, interviews (conducted by the Montana Historical Society and by me), and a wide variety of sources from Montanans I met during my travels around the state, including a membership list of the Roundup Klan that achieved wide circulation at the time. Most Klan documents from the 1920s are missing, of course. Especially grievous are the boxes of Realm papers from Lewis Terwilliger's attic, which, according to an audience member at the 2014 Montana History Conference, Terwilliger's son burned in the backyard. Also missing, except for one copy, are issues of the short-lived *Montana Klansman.*

Rich as these sources are, they do shape the kind of story that can be told about the Montana Klan in the 1920s. *Big Skies, White Hoods* is largely about the ambitions, preoccupations, interests, and challenges Klan leadership faced in growing their Montana Realm. It confirms what other recent studies on the Klan have revealed, such as the hooded order's organizational structure, recruiting methods, political interests, and membership. It also confirms that it reflected the white Protestant culture in which it operated. Yet, unlike most other Realms, the Montana Klan faced the insurmountable difficulties of organizing in a vast state where weather and geography dictated the Klan's ability to network, and where no large urban centers existed in which to build a strong base for recruitment. The task for Grand Dragon Terwilliger, and it was no small challenge, was to bring those small, isolated Montana communities together for a common cause: to keep the levers of power firmly in the hands of white Protestants.

That isolation Terwilliger had to contend with has attracted the contemporary radical right. This is where the significance of the Klan's presence in Montana rests, in the geographic and demographic makeup of the state itself, and this is where the story diverges from and adds to the broader narrative. While some Montanans in the 1920s undoubtedly hoped that the state's population would continue growing and that their respective towns would become centers of commerce and industry, the reality is that vast sections of the state would remain sparsely populated well into the twenty-first century, with many communities losing population across time. That relative isolation and the white demographics of Montana have been key for the successors of the Klan of the 1920s. Beginning in the 1980s and continuing to the present day, white nationalists have moved into Montana by choice, hoping to create a white ethno-state far away from multicultural urban centers. They have even invoked the 1920s Klan and Terwilliger's name as inspirations. At the same time, just as the Klan had to contend with some pushback from those in Montana (especially in Butte) who objected to the Klan's religious and ethnic bigotry so, too, do the white nationalists who are confronted by organizations such as the Montana Human Rights Network and other concerned citizens. The story of the 1920s Klan is century-old history that still reverberates.

One of the many echoes is the importance of charismatic leadership, at least as far as those leaders on the right have positioned themselves to give their movements a respectable face. In the 1920s, that leader was Lewis Terwilliger. Declaring that the Klan was "the moral, spiritual and patriotic standing army of America" engaged in "high and holy work," the Grand Dragon, whose anti-Catholicism was second to none, was a true believer. His efforts to transform Montana into a 100 percent Realm of which the Imperial Palace would be proud was his greatest challenge, but he never stopped trusting in the potential power of the Klan to enact political and social change in the state. While Terwilliger drives the narrative, a second theme involves the Imperial Palace's, the Realm's, and the local Klans' shifting misconceptions about the Klan's mission and Knights' responsibilities. Thomas Pegram also discusses this internal strife within the Invisible Empire and notes that each entity often held different expectations of their respective obligations, which contributed to the national Klan's eventual demise.[11]

This study is organized both chronologically and topically. The first chapter sets the historical stage for the arrival of the Klan in Montana, including the impact of the American Protective Association (APA), the virulent anti-Catholic organization, and the legacy of World War I, especially that of the notorious Montana Council of Defense. Thus, Kleagles (recruiters) found fertile ground for the order as they made their way across the state in the early 1920s, heeding the instructions of Imperial headquarters to establish Realms across the country. Hoping to tap into that potential source of profit, Imperial Wizard Evans chose well-known fraternalist and successful businessman Lewis Terwilliger of Livingston to lead the Realm. Chapter 2 examines an area of inquiry that has not been adequately explored—the connection between the Klan's version of secret fraternalism and its political ambitions. While the Grand Dragon belonged to many secret fraternal orders—the Masons chief among them—only the Klan offered him the comforts of traditional secret fraternalism combined with a hardcore commitment to militant Protestantism and white supremacy and a path to political power and influence. Terwilliger was certain that Klankraft—the exclusive, secret fraternal knowledge of Klan mysteries, rituals, and degrees—would provide Montana Knights with a solid foundation to understand the threats facing the country and lessons on how to repel those threats.

Chapter 3 takes a chronological approach to Terwilliger's and the Klan's battles against enemies, especially the Roman Catholic Church. The church was the source, Terwilliger believed, of almost all threats facing Montana and the United States. Knowledge and understanding of Klankraft was a critical first step in battling America's enemies, as examined in chapter 2. Now Terwilliger wanted to see his Knights implement those lessons at the state and local levels. Chapter 4 explores the presence of the Klan in Butte, Harlowton, and Roundup, the only communities where membership lists are known to exist. Each section discusses the larger social, political, and economic context of the community to understand the Klan's success, or lack thereof, in attracting members and implementing its program.

Chapter 5 takes a topical approach and focuses on the relationship between local communities and the Klan across the Realm with particular emphasis on the threat of violence. Connected with this theme of violence are a variety of hoaxes, ranging from anonymous threatening letters to kidnappings, perpetuated by non-members who clearly understood the Klan's well-deserved reputation for terror and wished to frighten or intimidate local residents for their own purposes. Chapter six discusses the downfall of the Klan in Montana. As the conclusion to this study, it explores the gap between Terwilliger's expectations of success and Knights' inability or unwillingness to transform his plans into action, which became too great to overcome. Finally, the epilogue examines the various strands of white nationalism that form the connecting thread between the 1920s Klan and the resurgence of right-wing activity in Montana, especially during the 1990s and the first decade of the twentieth century, and the Make America Great Again movement (MAGA) in the 2010s and 2020s.

CHAPTER 1

The Klan Comes to Montana

Lo! there's a man with a hooded face,
Wearing a cloak with a princely grace,
Cares not for gold or the lure of fame,
And from all he's withholding his name;
He's silent when tongues of the harsh condemn
And bears it all for his countrymen;
But glad in his heart that all patriots rejoice,
To see him come and to hear his voice.

"He's a Knight of the Ku Klux Klan," 1924

Lewis Terwilliger, the newly anointed Grand Dragon for the Realm of Montana, wanted very much for Montanans to "rejoice" when the Ku Klux Klan arrived, and, most certainly, he wanted them to "hear his voice." Throughout his tenure, during which he vigorously championed the ideals of the hooded order, Terwilliger offered doses of encouragement and praise to Montana Klansmen balanced with reprimands and pleas to remind them of their commitment. His first official document to Klansmen, in the fall of 1923, expressed confidence that Knights would take their oaths seriously and that the Montana Realm would make the Imperial Palace proud.[1] The gap between Terwilliger's expectations and the reality of Klansmen's inconsistent dedication to the cause was not apparent at first. It soon would be. In the beginning, however, Terwilliger had good reason to be optimistic that his efforts to make Montana a 100 percent Realm would work.

Kleagles (recruiters) for the Ku Klux Klan found fertile territory in Montana during the early 1920s. The anti-Catholic agenda pursued by the American Protective Association (APA) and the hyperpatriotism encouraged by World War I seeped into the postwar period and provided an opening for the kluxing of the state, in which Kleagles established chapters in at least forty-six communities. Besides appealing to nativist bigotry, Kleagles capitalized on other inducements, such as entrance into a new secret fraternal world, promises to establish law and order, and claims that the best and the brightest of civic minded professionals and businessmen were already rushing to join local Klans across the country. As Klaverns quickly multiplied around the state, they celebrated their entry into the Realm of Montana with demonstrations and cross burnings, while local communities, some watchful and others curious, wondered what would happen next.

Setting the Stage in Montana

Most of the men who joined the Ku Klux Klan arrived in the state in the 1890s–1910s, the vast majority from the Midwest.[2] Some journeyed as children with their parents; more moved as young men seeking new opportunities and adventures. One Knight, reflecting upon his youth before the Harlowton Kiwanis Club in 1927, for example, remarked that "things got too tame" in Minneapolis so he made his way west to Montana in 1888.[3] Another ventured to Montana with a friend in 1914 on the Milwaukee railroad. Harlowton was supposed to be a temporary stop, but the future Klansman liked his job at a grocery store and decided to remain.[4]

It was the expansion of the Homestead Act in early 1909, however, which doubled the land a homesteader could own from 160 acres to 320 acres, that enticed prospective settlers, and the change in the residential requirement from five years to three.[5] Montana was the state of choice.[6] Immigrants, "attracted to Montana by the lure of inexpensive land and the promise of golden wheat," streamed into the state by the thousands before 1920.[7] The "go-west" urge, as another resident put it, also convinced young men to seek their fortunes in the untamed West.[8] Ranchers, boosters, businessmen, and local newspapers further extolled the wonders of living in Montana. As the editor and founder of the *Musselshell News* asserted in 1906, "At the present time there is much talk, newspaper and otherwise, about 'boosting Montana.' We can scarcely pick up a paper without seeing something about a meeting held to consider steps to induce emigration to the state."[9] The advertising worked. The phenomenal growth of eastern Montana as 1920 approached demonstrated the attraction of the homesteading. Between 1909 and 1917, almost 157,000 settlers filed homesteads in the state. Close to 22,000 applications were filed in 1910 alone.[10] Census numbers reflect the homesteading boom as the rural population in the state jumped by over 134,000 between 1910 and 1920.[11]

The propaganda enticing settlers to move proved hard to resist. Railroads' and the state government's publicity pamphlets skillfully imparted shame upon the readers if they did not immediately take advantage of such splendid opportunities. As asserted by the Montana State Department of Agriculture and Publicity: "Thus the men and women who came, and are coming, to make their homes on Montana farms are not the failures, the derelicts or the ne'er-do-wells of other lands. Instead, they are . . . the strong and the self-reliant, [and] the educated and cultured."[12] The Chicago, Milwaukee, and St. Paul Railway agreed: "The ideal settler for Montana and the one we are trying to reach is the man who has made a moderate success in the East, but who is too ambitious to be satisfied with slow progress and too wise to overlook the great opportunities in the West. . . . What is perhaps more important than money [to start a new life], is brains, enterprise and grit."[13]

Many future Klansmen were convinced by this rosy picture of a prosperous beginning—at least twenty-six members of the Harlowton Klan filed homestead claims between 1900 and 1914. Of the 180 Harlowton Klansmen for whom occupations were found, fifty-four had some connection with the land—they made their living from farming or growing stock, started out with a homestead and sold it, or maintained their investment while pursuing other jobs.[14] The percentage of known homesteaders was smaller in Roundup, but there were still plenty of Klansmen who worked on farms. More found employment with the growing coal industry and railroads. The vast and rapid growth of the railroads that crisscrossed the state—the Northern Pacific, Union Pacific, Great Northern, Montana Central, Burlington Route, and Milwaukee Road had laid tracks in the Treasure State by World War I—was integral to both homesteading and the mining industry. They helped create new cities and towns in their wake and transported grain, stock, and ore to points east.[15] As one settler recalled, "the western expansion of the Milwaukee railroad" was what brought the family to Montana.[16] Almost all local Klans lay close to one of those lines.

Once settled, new arrivals discovered that Montana was a state in flux. Large corporate interests, especially the Anaconda Copper Mining Company, vied for political and economic power in the state while local civic boosters sought power in the counties. The latter received support from a willing state legislature, which went on a county-splitting binge between 1910 and 1925 and carved out twenty-eight new counties from old ones. Most of this activity occurred in the northern, central, and eastern sections of the state.[17] Many charter members of the Wheatland Klan, for example, were founding fathers of the new county and Harlowton, the county seat. If homesteaders settled in the northeastern section of the state, they would find the radical voices of the Nonpartisan League rallying to support farmers, and in the west, they would encounter labor activism in the timber fields and mines, much of which was supported by the Industrial Workers of the World (IWW).

Two of the most influential factors that would lay the foundation for the Montana Klan were the lingering hostilities of the viciously anti-Catholic APA and the hyperpatriotism that swept across the state during World War I. While the APA and World War I were separated by two decades and different points of emphasis—targeting Catholics and targeting critics of the war—their commonalities, mainly intolerance and suspicion toward those who did not fit into preconceived notions of what it meant to be an American, would spill over into the postwar period. Elements from both eras wove their way into the Realm in the 1920s.

Speaking in Chicago, Illinois, in early 1923, former Kansas governor Henry J. Allen declared that the Ku Klux Klan was simply "the old A.P.A., plus hatred of the negro plus hatred of the Jew, all rolled up in the American flag labelled [sic] 100 per cent and sold for $10 apiece."[18] He had a point. Before William Joseph Simmons re-created the Klan in 1915, the APA was setting new standards in anti-Catholic vitriol across the country. Henry F. Bowers, a Scottish Rite Mason, founded the APA in 1887, and it quickly became the most powerful anti-Catholic organization of the era. The APA launched a crusade against the perceived Catholic threat in politics and the public schools, warning Protestants that minions of the Pope were conspiring to control the country and hand it over to Rome.[19] This fear of "papal power" dominated the APA's rhetoric and convinced approximately one million Protestants to join (although the APA's *Examiner*, headquartered in Butte, Montana, optimistically claimed 3.5 million in the beginning of 1896).[20] Membership in states with high numbers of Catholics soared.[21] By the early 1890s, the APA's "initials were already being used to identify the whole program of anti-Catholicism and nonsectarianism."[22]

For the APA and other nativist groups, Catholics provided a convenient scapegoat for challenges facing the country during the late nineteenth century. Labor militancy, with its corresponding union activities and strikes that swept through the industrial sector, was, to the APA, just another weapon in the Catholic arsenal to rip apart the social fabric.[23] Economic uncertainty and the high rate of unemployment were also blamed on Catholics, who had presumably stolen jobs from native-born Americans under orders from the Pope.[24] One Montana farmer expressed alarm with what he saw as the prominence of the "flannel mouthed Irish mick" in police uniform and in city governments.[25] APAers' suspicion of a Catholic agenda correlated not only with the escalation of Catholic immigrants into the country—the number of Catholics in the United States had increased by 70 percent between the late nineteenth century and World War I—but also with the growing prominence of Catholics in politics and education. As Donald Kinzer states, "Probably nothing was so important in explaining the growth of the [APA] as the fact that Catholics were taking a more active part in national and local affairs."[26] The number of parochial schools, dioceses, and Catholic newspapers multiplied rapidly in the late nineteenth century—in Montana, the Diocese of Helena was created in 1884—while major New England cities chose Irish Catholic mayors for the first time in the early 1880s.[27] By the 1890s, Catholic political strength had surfaced in national elections. Adding fuel to the fire, the incendiary "Pastoral Letter" made the rounds in anti-Catholic circles.[28] The fraudulent document, similar to the bogus oath of the Knights of Columbus, two decades later, that worried Klansmen pointed to as proof of Catholic treachery, advocated "the formation of a papal political party" and encouraged "the faithful to exterminate all heretics" in the United States.[29] Catholics, then, as seen through the nativist lens, were on the offensive.[30]

To combat the perceived threat, the APA often looked to political solutions. Passage of an immigration restriction act was at the top of the APA's list—the organization argued that America was turning into "Europe's cesspool"—and although it failed to secure legislation to check immigration, its successor, the Klan, succeeded.[31] The APA relied on the ballot to defeat politicians who presumably honored the Catholic church above all else. Its "willingness to take part in political contests" set it apart from the other nativist organizations, a characteristic it shared with the Klan.[32] It insisted members cast aside their allegiance to political parties and accept without question the order's recommendations. The bottom line, claimed the APA, was "loyalty to true Americanism," a quality that evidently only the APA and, later, the Klan could identify. "We care nothing for the names republican and democrat" cried the *Examiner* in 1896, and, indeed, when it reported the results of a city council election, it identified the winners as either "Americans" or "Romanists."[33] By 1892, the APA had gravitated toward the Republican Party, a not altogether surprising move since Catholics, notably the Irish, tended to land in the Democratic camp.[34] In Denver, Colorado, for example, the Republicans and the APAers were "virtually interchangeable."[35] During the tenure of Colorado governor Albert W. McIntire (1895–1897), "no Catholic was permitted to hold any state office or job, however menial."[36] The political lines were not as clear-cut with the Klan, as both Democrats and Republicans joined (and the Klan, unlike the APA, asked potential candidates their party affiliation), but Klansmen outside the South tended to favor the GOP, including most Klansmen in Montana.[37]

Regardless of which political party APAers and Knights called home, rescuing the West from Catholic hands was seen as vital. In 1886, prominent reverend Josiah Strong declared that only a surge of Protestant activism in the western United States could thwart the growing peril of the Roman Catholic Church. Strong warned that Rome was "concentrating her strength in the western territories. As the West is to dominate the nation, she [Rome] intends to dominate the West."[38] Taking that message to heart, the APA established itself in Montana soon after a visit from President William J. Traynor, who assumed the helm from Bowers in 1893.[39] APA councils were scattered throughout the state, but the heavily Irish Catholic city of Butte emerged as the focal point of activity. *The Examiner*, whose rhetoric was matched only by the Ku Klux press two decades later, targeted all who "wore the chains of Romanism" but saved its most potent venom for priests and the "Dago at Rome."[40] According to the *Examiner*, Butte was home to "one of the healthiest [councils] in Montana."[41] The *Examiner*'s estimate of "10,000 APAs" in Montana in 1895 was surely wishful thinking, but there is no question of either the APA's enthusiasm or the opposition's reaction, especially in Butte, where a riot erupted in 1894 between Irish Catholics and APA supporters that left one person dead and hundreds injured.[42]

Two years after the "APA Riot," the organization was on the verge of collapse.[43] It was being torn apart by "internal squabbling," which included accusations of putting political party before Americanism and arguments about whom to support in 1896. (The *Examiner*, like other western APA outlets, championed silver and "the boy orator of Nebraska," William Jennings Bryan.)[44] The APA limped along to the turn of the century, never again to regain its former influence. But even as the APA receded, worries about a Catholic agenda and Catholic political power continued to simmer in the state and across the country, and the fear of Catholic uprisings and papal schemes endured well into the postwar period.[45]

Besides a lingering suspicion of the Catholic Church's intentions, the legacy of World War I in the state helped lay the groundwork for the arrival of the Klan by legitimizing extralegal activity, creating an atmosphere of intolerance toward those who failed to vigorously support the war effort, and defining who was an American and who was not.[46] "No state in the union engaged in quite the same orgy of book burning, inquisitions of suspected traitors, and general hysteria," observed K. Ross Toole.[47] "Montana," a spokesman for the National Council of Defense remarked in admiration, "possesses a vital spirit of patriotism not found excelled anywhere."[48]

That enthusiasm found expression in newly formed local chapters of the American Defense Society, the Montana Loyalty League, and, of course, the Montana Council of Defense and its attendant County Councils of Defense.[49] Besides pressing the state legislature to enact the repressive Montana Sedition Act of 1918 (which formed the template for the Federal Sedition Act that same year), the Montana Council of Defense encouraged the crushing of anti-war dissent and the purging of all German influence in the state.[50] Among other orders, the Council prohibited the speaking and teaching of German, demanded the names of all students in German classes, and mandated the removal of German books from public and private libraries.[51] Harlowton public schools, for instance, had stopped teaching German by early April 1918.[52] The Harlowton school board, on which sat two Klansmen, including the future Grand Kligrapp (secretary) of the Realm of Montana, took the Council's directive one step further, as did other school boards across the state, and ordered the burning of all German textbooks. At least several Klansmen served on the local defense councils—and likely even more participated, as a letter to the chair of the Wheatland council indicated in April 1918: "With fifteen hundred members now enrolled . . . Wheatland County [could], in the near future, have the largest patriotic association there is in the state."[53] In Roundup, the chairman of the Musselshell County Council of Defense wrote to a member of the State Council of Defense, asking if the Council could hire "a good detective" to root out "an organization of German sympathizers and possibly spies." He was willing to pay half of the cost, if necessary.[54]

Montanans felt free to express their hostility toward those who did not support the war effort, and they did so with little restraint. One of the main targets of self-proclaimed patriots was the radical labor organization the Industrial Workers of the World (IWW), which, because of wartime repression, would be decimated by the war's end. If the IWW opposed the war, it stood to reason (according to Montana patriots) that it was pro-German.[55] The most vehement of war critics were quite often the voices on the left—the IWW and the Socialist Party, both of which were active in Montana, argued that the war was a capitalist plot geared toward enriching the armaments industry and banks.[56] True to form, the patriots in Wheatland County applauded attacks on the "treasonable" IWW for its opposition to the war.[57] The unanimous resolution passed by the Chamber of Commerce of Harlowton's northern neighbor, Lewistown, calling on the governor of Montana to "bring about the complete extermination of this copperhead organization within the state, no matter how drastic the step necessary to accomplish this end," met with the hearty approval of the *Harlowton Times*.[58] Any pretense of restraint was abandoned when the IWW labor organizer, Frank Little, was brutally lynched in Butte in 1918.[59]

In Livingston, superpatriots accosted a business owner (who was supposedly sympathetic to Germany), wrapped a rope around his neck, and forced him "to kneel in the wet snow and kiss the American flag." The vigilantes then ordered the frightened owner to empty his safe and "donate" all of the money to the Red Cross. A witness to the incident, who yelled at the perpetrators to leave the owner alone, received similar treatment.[60] The situation in Lewistown spun out of control in the spring of 1918. Not only was one man threatened with hanging when he refused to buy war bonds, but self-described patriots rounded up suspected slackers and "each one . . . was forced to kiss the American flag, to declare his loyalty to the United States and to carry the flag in a brief, impromptu parade on Main Street."[61] The mob, which quickly grew to five hundred citizens and had the full backing of the Lewistown Loyalty Committee, marched to the local high school and demanded that the principal, a suspected German sympathizer, relinquish every German book in the building, preempting the Montana Council of Defense's order to destroy a long list of German texts.[62] The mob besieged the school, "to make sure no one escaped," and several men crawled through a classroom window to seize the offending German literature. The confiscated books were then tossed into "a large bonfire." As the books crackled into flames, the crowd sang "America" and "The Star-Spangled Banner." The next day, in a self-congratulatory climax, Lewistown sponsored a huge parade in front of two thousand attendees.[63] One of the men who crawled through that high school classroom window was a well-respected medical doctor and "strong leader in the community" who would later become the Exalted Cyclops of Lewistown Klan No. 8.[64]

The Klan Rides Again

Shortly after the world war in Europe had begun, William J. Simmons, a self-proclaimed fraternal joiner, resurrected the Ku Klux Klan from the graveyard of Southern Reconstruction. Until he collaborated with publicity and fundraising experts Edward Y. Clark and Mrs. Elizabeth Taylor, however, the Klan remained a small, obscure secret fraternity that could claim perhaps three thousand members by 1920. Clark and Taylor deftly transformed it into a thriving money-making business of national scope that tapped the undercurrents of racism and nativism already present in American society. Fusing racial hatred, religious bigotry, and superpatriotism, Clark, Young, and Simmons launched a successful recruitment campaign that attracted over a hundred thousand new members within eighteen months. Soon, Kleagles ventured from the safety of their southern homes to establish Realms across the country. As the *Harlowton Times* gushed in 1922, the "remarkable" Imperial Wizard's physique resembled a "graceful Hercules," his demeanor "pleasing" and "gracious," and his "imposing and majestic presence" were suited for an earlier age when he could have "grac[ed] a throne."[65] Simmons's perceived qualities notwithstanding, a more effective recruiting tool nationwide was *The Birth of a Nation*, the landmark film that purported to justify the Klan as necessary and heroic.[66] Almost eight years later the *Great Falls Tribune* printed a large advertisement for the movie, taking up a third of the page, with its promise to inform the audience about the Klan's origins and purpose during Reconstruction.[67] Two months after that, an advertisement in the *Butte Miner* called the film "stupendous" and a "picture masterpiece."[68] Clearly, this was a film with staying power.[69]

As the Ku Klux Klan expanded its empire, internal tensions erupted in Imperial headquarters. Content with designing complex fraternal rituals and unwilling to participate aggressively in politics, Simmons lost the Imperial throne to the more ambitious Hiram Wesley Evans, a dentist from Dallas, Texas. By November 1922, Evans wore the purple hood and robe.[70] Two years later, Evans was speaking to the faithful in Billings, Montana, assuring Klansmen that they were indeed an important and welcome part of the Invisible Empire. Although the long distance to eastern Montana prevented many Klansmen from attending the lecture, approximately 1,300 enthusiastic Knights greeted the Imperial Wizard on November 14, 1924.[71] Evans first expressed his "satisfaction" with the election of Calvin Coolidge and then proceeded to reiterate the main principles of the Klan, with which the audience was undoubtedly familiar: the imperative of white supremacy, the menace of the Catholic church, and the threat immigration posed to the purity of native blood and to America's democratic institutions. Evans voiced confidence that these principles would continue to attract more Knights into the Empire's fold.[72] Larger membership numbers, as he knew full well, meant bigger profits and a more powerful voting bloc. While the Invisible Empire fell far short of the twenty million members Evans believed to have joined—roughly three to four million paid dues at the Klan's peak, in 1923–24—Evans could count on just over 5,160 Knights from Montana.[73]

Kluxing Montana

For the task of converting Montana into a potential source of revenue and political clout, Imperial Wizard Evans turned to Lewis Terwilliger. Terwilliger was a natural for the position of Grand Dragon. Evans, who appointed all of the Grand Dragons in the Empire, had likely heard of Terwilliger through business and fraternal circles. One of "the leading educators of Montana," as described in *Progressive Men of Montana*, Terwilliger had served as the principal of Park County High School in Livingston from 1903 to 1913.[74] "An excellent disciplinarian," the biography went on, who had "the somewhat rare power of imparting knowledge clearly and rapidly to others"—a tendency that could certainly be seen in his official circulars.[75] Some of his high school students, another biography added, referred to him as "Papa T," yet "it's uncertain if that was an affectionate nickname."[76] Terwilliger then left education for a quick stint in the banking business but cared little for it, according to his son Homer.[77] His next venture, however, proved far more successful as he moved on to operate and eventually own the Livingston Land and Abstract Co., which evolved into a very successful business in southern Montana. When he was not managing his business or his 640-acre ranch, just north of Livingston,

Terwilliger actively participated in business circles, especially the Chamber of Commerce and the Commercial Club. His civic responsibilities went hand in hand with his political aspirations, as Terwilliger, a Republican, went on to serve as mayor of Livingston from 1919 to 1922 (with a failed bid to capture the Republican nomination for state senator of Park County).[78] The final selling point for Imperial Wizard Evans would have been Terwilliger's impressive secret fraternal connections. Terwilliger, a thirty-third degree Mason, claimed membership not only in all of the important Masonic lodges—A.F. and A.M., Royal Arch Masons, Knights Templar, Order of the Eastern Star, and Scottish Rite—but also held leadership positions in those orders. In the local Elks lodge, he served as Exalted Ruler, and in the Knights of Pythias, he served as Grand Chancellor for the state of Montana.[79] Terwilliger's pedigree, therefore, infused with qualities of leadership and respectability, offered a perfect fit for command of the new Realm.

Terwilliger understood the vital role Kleagles played in establishing local Klans. A Klan populated with respected members of the community would bode well for the order's long-term prospects. In Montana, as across the Invisible Empire, the Kleagle's first order of business was to contact the leading men in the community and convince them to join. First, they had to learn to navigate the vast expanse of the state. If Kleagles were accustomed to good roads and short distances between towns in other parts of the country, they quickly discovered they had their work cut out for them in Montana. As the third largest state in the early 1920s, Montana was home to over 147 thousand square miles of terrain, ranging from the vast plains in the east to the Rocky Mountains in the west.[80] Travel then, and the mode of transportation, was an important consideration and a considerable investment. While the number of privately owned cars in the state more than doubled during the 1920s, the quality of roads did not keep up with the new traffic. (Most of the over 1,900 miles of roads built between 1923 and 1959 were graveled; others were graded and drained. Very few roads were hard surfaced).[81]

The condition of many of those Montana roads may have given Kleagles pause ("60 miles of mud" from Big Timber to Lewistown, grumbled one Klansman in 1923, and "mud up to the hubs" recalled another traveler, who ventured over St. Regis Pass in 1916).[82] In some areas, horses were still necessary to rescue stuck autos and their unfortunate passengers.[83] One seasoned traveler making his way across the state in 1928 observed "the roads of Montana are, I believe, the poorest of any state in the union."[84] During the winter months, the search for recruits was likely laid aside. Snow removal operations in Montana did not exist until 1927, and after that they were used only in emergency situations.[85] In 1930, the state owned just five snowplows.[86] "[Dirt] roads made winter travel by automobile almost impossible" in the 1910s, as one resident from Fergus County remembered.[87] Even the garages shut down for the winter.[88] Moreover, even in good weather, Kleagles had to know where to go. If they were unfamiliar with the area, they could wind up lost, since roads were inadequately marked. Signs, if they existed, were "maintained by local civic groups."[89] A more likely way to reach potential members was the railroad.

By the time the Klan arrived in Montana, thousands of miles of railroad tracks crisscrossed the state. The Northern Pacific completed its transcontinental journey in 1883; four years later, James Hill created the Great Northern Railroad, which hugged the Canadian border in the north. In 1909 the Milwaukee completed its road traversing much of the same path as the Northern Pacific.[90] All three major lines built northern and southern tributaries. Other railroads, such as the Utah and Northern; the Union Pacific (the first railroad to lay tracks in the state); and the Chicago, Burlington, and Quincy, found opportunities beckoning in Montana.[91] Most Montana Klans (those that have been identified) sat on one of these railroad routes, with the exception of those in the Flathead Valley. If Klansmen from Kalispell chose to journey around Flathead Lake to visit Lake City Klan (Polson) and Mission Valley Klan (Ronan), for instance, they would have traveled by car.[92]

The Ku Klux Klan's entry into Montana in 1921 occurred roughly at the same time as other western states.[93] One of the first signs of the Klan's arrival in the Big Sky appeared in June 1921 in the small town of Baker, located near the border of North Dakota. The low-key announcement in the *Fallon County Times* simply stated that representatives of the Klan were due to arrive in Baker to assist in setting up a local branch.[94] The *Harlowton Times* was more upfront as it declared "Ku Klux Klan Will be Organizing in Harlowton" that same month. The Klan's rapid success in recruiting members across the country made its march into Montana inevitable, the *Times* continued. "It is said that a number of well known citizens of this city have interested themselves in the organization and that the Klan representative . . . has come here to assist them."[95] Passive voice aside, many of the most prominent and powerful men in the county, including the editor, joined Wheatland Klan No. 29.[96]

The following month the *Great Falls Tribune* devoted almost a full page to the growing strength of the Klan in the Northwest and its plan to "fight

Un-Americanism." The reporter proceeded to describe what must have seemed a rather thrilling firsthand glimpse of the hooded order and the secrecy that enveloped it. At the very top of the page, for those native-born Montanans interested in learning more, the newspaper noted the ABCs of the order (Americanism, Benevolence, and Clannishness) and that Klan organizers were busily gathering support in Lewistown and Butte.[97] The county seat of Fergus would prove to be an easy sell, as the Kleagle went on to successfully create Lewistown Klan No. 8. Butte, fittingly, was a different matter. The first effort, in 1921, to create a local chapter sank as the Kleagle "became engaged in trouble with a woman," was promptly arrested, and left town quickly thereafter.[98] The warning from Sheriff Larry Duggan of Silver Bow County in August that Klansmen would be "shot down like wolves" if they resorted to violence (a "most commendable attitude" noted an approving *Butte Bulletin*), might have made other Kleagles hesitant about approaching the predominantly Catholic city.[99] It would be another year before the Klan quietly returned to Butte to establish Kontinental Klan No. 30.

Newspapers from other Montana cities and towns were soon reporting—some with skepticism, others with curiosity—on the Klan's arrival. In May 1922, the Klan touched down in Havre, Glasgow, and Missoula; the next month, it appeared in Roundup. By September the Klan had attracted attention, as well as 250 members, in Grand Dragon Lewis Terwilliger's hometown of Livingston. Klansmen made a dramatic appearance on horseback in Hamilton in October, and in December a Knight arrived in Belt and visited a Methodist minister's home, presenting him with "the most substantial personal gift he had ever received."[100] Throughout the next year, local Klans continued to form across the state. In Helena, Knights made a very public (and publicized) appearance at the Oak Street Methodist Church at the beginning of the New Year. In June 1923, they arrived in Ronan and initiated "200–300" new members into Mission Valley Klan No. 12.[101] By that fall, the Klan was solidly entrenched in the state—an indication, if nothing else, of the Imperial Palace's determination to establish a Realm in every state in the country.

"The growth of the Klan in [Montana]," declared the national Klan newsletter, the *Imperial Nighthawk*, in early October 1923, "has been rapid during the past few months. . . . The Grand Dragon is a well known business man of Livingston [and] the gathering was a most enthusiastic one." [102] The *Imperial Nighthawk*'s assessment of the first Klorero (state convention) was probably accurate. Fifty-nine representatives—hailing from diverse locations, ranging from Glendive and Thompson Falls to Havre and Red Lodge—had made their way to Livingston the previous month to create the Realm of Montana. Harlowton topped the list with six delegates, followed closely by Great Falls and Livingston with five each, while Missoula, Lewistown, and Bridger counted four respectively. After visiting officials from Imperial headquarters in Atlanta approved of Terwilliger's new position, the Grand Dragon set forth to organize his domain, adhering to the Klan constitution's explicit instructions and hierarchical chain of command. He first nominated nine Hydras to help him govern. The delegates then divided the Realm into four provinces, and Terwilliger, in turn, appointed four Great Titans to manage each one. Finally, the Great Titans each nominated nine Furies to help administer their respective provinces. After passing resolutions to enact a quarterly twenty-five cent Realm tax for each Klan and to appoint Frank Q. Linderman of the Havre Klan as a lecturer for the state (the latter's position receiving quick approval by the Imperial representative), the audience listened to "a very instructive and impressive talk" by a spokesman for the Imperial Klazik about building a successful Realm.[103]

Most of that success depended upon attracting a committed and loyal membership—a point Terwilliger stressed time and again. In 1924, he expressed pride that the Realm had welcomed "in the main only careful, conservative, level-headed men, with high principles and ideals."[104] While that assumption would be doused with a cold dose of reality two months later at the second Klorero, Montana newspapers had provided plenty of favorable advertising in those early months of organizing. The Klan could not have scripted its debut more effectively, as papers remarked on the number of prominent citizens interested in the hooded order. In Great Falls, Big Timber, and Livingston, the pattern stayed the same—local newspapers reported that Kleagles, often from adjoining towns, provided guidance to businessmen, doctors, attorneys, and other professionals in creating local chapters.[105]

The Klan, of course, capitalized on the coverage, letting the *Glasgow Courier* know, for instance, after the Klan had swept the town with posters announcing that it had arrived, that "among its members [were] some of the most influential citizens of the community."[106] "It will have a respected place in the community and it will be of real service in any emergency that may arise," remarked the newspaper.[107] "The Klan in Valley county," the article continued, quoting from the local chapter, "will grow in membership slowly because its members are carefully selected," while the Lewistown Klan boasted that only those who "inspire[d] complete confidence" could join."[108] In early 1922, the Klan arrived in the capital, Helena. While secrecy surrounded the proceedings, enough information was leaked to know that a national spokesman had played an advisory role in organizing the Helena Klan and had helped recruit "desirable" members, many of whom were particularly active in the local Chamber of Commerce and in the Kiwanis and Rotary clubs.[109] Not all newspapers reported with favor—some Big Timber residents, who wanted to note which of their neighbors attended a planned Klan gathering that included a visit from a "higher up" (most certainly Terwilliger) from Livingston, parked themselves outside the auditorium. The local paper declared that Klansmen who did not care to "face the music" used the "dark alleys and side streets leading to the Auditorium" to avoid detection. It did not work.[110]

The Klan also knocked on fraternal doors for prospects. While the Independent Order of Odd Fellows, the Benevolent and Protective Order of Elks, the Knights of Pythias, and Woodmen of the World found favor among Montana Klansmen, the Masonic orders were easily the most popular choice among secret fraternities. Not incidentally, the APA found willing recruits from Masonic lodges during the 1890s.[111] More Americans belonged to the Masons than any other secret fraternal order in the country, and Americans had been participating in its solemn and ritualistic ceremonies since the mid-1700s. In fact, the Masonic ritual and structure later served as the model for the hundreds of fraternal orders that materialized during the late nineteenth century.[112] The Masonic Lodge was not just a men's club, whose doings newspapers relegated to the back page. Newspapers devoted a great deal of space to Masonic activities, including the latest meetings, installation ceremonies, and picnics. Thus, a Klansman who was also a Mason had access to many possible candidates. He might already know colleagues within the order who would be apt to sample a new fraternity on a friend's recommendation. Certainly, the Klan depended more upon this loose association than did the Masons, who never officially sanctioned the relationship. In response to a claim that Masons constituted a large portion of the Klan and that the Klan enjoyed Masonic approval, the grand master of the Massachusetts Masonic grand lodges declared that the Klan "has no connection with and neither does it have the support of any masonic jurisdiction."[113] The *Butte Bulletin* reported, however, that a "prominent New York Mason" had alleged the close connection between the Klan and the Masons.[114]

Whatever the official position of the Masonic order, there was no doubt that the Masonic Lodge served as a pipeline for the Realm of Montana and Klans across the country. "Scottish Rite Masons and Orange Lodges were particularly rich hunting grounds," notes David Chalmers in his study of the Klan in the United States. Here, Terwilliger, by virtue of his prominence in the Masonic orders, could have easily sold the Klan to Masons across the state.[115] Judging from the obituaries in Butte, for example, of the 68 Klansmen who died in Butte, 58 were Masons; for Harlowton, 72 of 101 Klansmen who belonged to various secret fraternities and for whom data were found were Masons.[116] The number of men enjoying dual membership is very likely higher since background information for many Knights is missing.

Besides secret fraternities, Kleagles approached Protestant churches in hopes of convincing ministers to join. Since the Klan rarely passed up an opportunity to make money—it has been amply demonstrated that it was a money-making business—free membership to Protestant ministers indicated just how much the Klan sought to capture the aura of respect and legitimacy that the church pulpit offered.[117] Ministers often became officers in the local Klan—the office of Kludd (chaplain) was a natural. In Montana, judging from the limited data, at least eighteen reverends were Klansmen, although the actual number was certainly higher. If the calling was strong enough, ministers could try their luck on the national lecture circuit. Indeed, "almost all of the national Klan lecturers were ministers."[118] Perhaps hoping for a chance to tap into that profitable line of work, Wheatland Klan member Reverend A. C. Canole gave an address at the Methodist church frankly titled "Why I am a Klansman" in the spring of 1924. The *Harlowton Times* reprinted the speech in full on the front page. Canole, in explaining his antipathy to the Klan the previous year, maintained that he had been deceived by "the religious press." He had since launched his own "investigation" into "the truth." Plagiarizing almost word for word from the K-Uno, the first degree in the Klan's initiation ceremony, Canole extolled the virtues of the Klan of Reconstruction and assured listeners that the new Klan would stand for law and order, promote Protestantism and 100 percent Americanism, and adhere to the virtuous traditions of the "Gallant Knights of old."[119]

Reverend Canole's speech may or may not have convinced other residents to join or current members to remain—by the spring of 1924, anyone in Harlowton who was going to sign up probably already had.[120] Yet the appeal of belonging to a national movement made up of the "finest" citizens, who exerted power and influence in their communities, likely resonated with those curious about the order. It might have been especially attractive in towns such as Harlowton where threats to the status quo scarcely existed. In the absence of enemies, the Klan needed to convince residents that belonging to an organization with networking opportunities and a national purpose was reason enough to join.

When Kleagles made first contact with potential candidates, they often employed, as historian Thomas Pegram notes, "deception and subterfuge."[121] "Sell them the thing they want," as one successful Exalted Cyclops in Indiana advised. Kleagles could choose from a vast menu: the threat of Catholic power in politics and education, the specter of "negro rule" in the South, the promise of social and business networks, and a chance at political power. The trick was to find the right issue to exploit.[122] The *New Republic* recognized the tactic as well, adding to that menu anti-Asian sentiment on the West Coast and anti-Semitism in the East.[123]

Of course, Kleagles cared little why Montanans joined, just as long as they coughed up the required initiation fee. After creating the local chapter and stocking it with desirable members (or not, as was sometimes the case), the Kleagle would move on to the next assignment. It was a lucrative business. Most of the money from the Klectoken (initiation fee) percolated upward to enrich the coffers of Imperial headquarters, but four dollars of the ten-dollar fee went to the local Kleagle—a hefty sum and an incentive to pull in as many initiates as possible in a short amount of time. One did not even have to be a true believer to profit from the opportunity. A friend of Montana US District Court judge William J. Jameson's, for instance, "spent his summers soliciting memberships for the Klan to help finance his college education" at the University of Washington. Another friend told Jameson that he knew a Catholic who sold Klan memberships "for the same reason."[124]

The rank cynicism and opportunism of Kleagles in the rush to enlist members meant that local Klaverns were often left in disarray after the Kleagle left town. After a tour through the state in the summer of 1924, Grand Kludd Clarence Kopp, one of Terwilliger's Hydras, reported some disturbing news. His findings were the topic of intense discussion at the second annual Klorero, held in Billings in late August. "The house of many Klans should be cleaned of undesirable members," declared Terwilliger, who relayed Kopp's report. The Grand Dragon and the resolutions committee did not specify the nature of those "undesirable" characteristics, but some members' inability to follow Klan laws and procedures, especially the prohibition on sharing Klan secrets with "aliens," and their refusal to take the Klan's mission seriously likely topped his list. The resolutions committee agreed and demanded that a solution be found to "the deplorable condition in which some of the Klans of this Realm have been left by their organizers, in particular to the type of men naturalized." The committee concluded that more and better trained Kleagles would ensure a higher quality membership and recommended that a state lecturer be hired to devote his time to nurturing local Klans, and inspiring better Klankraft and Kloranic work.[125]

Whether or not Terwilliger was able to hire a state lecturer remains unknown, although he continued to exclaim through the 1920s, with increasing urgency, the necessity of attracting worthy members to the cause. But who was deemed worthy of wearing the hood and robe remained ultimately the purview of local Klans, and since they were scattered across the vast state, their relative isolation from Realm headquarters in Livingston made it difficult, if not nearly impossible, for Terwilliger to keep watch on them. Certainly, he continued to cite the instructions from the Klan constitution regarding eligibility and members' subsequent responsibilities to the order. But Terwilliger had more in his arsenal than his considerable knowledge of Klan law and his powers of persuasion. He could also tap into the power of secret fraternalism, which he firmly believed to be the essence of the Klan. With the Klan's principles of secret fraternalism to guide him—principles that evolved and were expanded, over the decade, by Imperial Wizards Simmons and Evans—Terwilliger hoped to create an army of Montana Klansmen ready and eager to defend America from her enemies.

CHAPTER 2

Secret Fraternalism and Klankraft

Klansman, Klansman of the Ku Klux Klan,
Protestant, gentile, native born man,
Hooded, knighted, robed and true,
Royal sons of the Red, White and Blue,
Owing no allegiance we are born free,
To God and Old Glory we bend our knee,
Sublime lineage written in history sands,
Weird, mysterious Ku Klux Klan.

"The Mystic City," 1925

"The Mystic City" (to be sung by a male quartet in B-flat) told the story of a "grand and noble wizard" who dreamed that a flood of immigrants was streaming into the United States determined to supplant the American flag with their own. Stunned out of his sleep, the wizard lit a fiery cross and united all Klansmen in a common purpose: defending America against her enemies. Inspired by the secret fraternal mysteries of the Mystic City—a reference to the Invisible Empire—and united by "bonds of Klansmenship" that were "stronger than bands of steel," Klansmen would willingly sacrifice themselves for their righteous cause. Grand Dragon Lewis Terwilliger fully embraced this vision. The Klan, to Terwilliger, represented a new and power-ful force in secret fraternalism that combined the traditional characteristics of secrecy and rituals with a distinct political and activist agenda. Interwoven through it all was Terwilliger's visceral hostility toward Catholics and the Catholic church.

A deep well of religious tensions had already rippled through Montana by the time Terwilliger assumed control of the Realm. The most powerful anti-Catholic organization of the late nineteenth century, the American Protective Association (APA), launched a crusade against the perceived Catholic threat in government and the public schools, warning Protestants that minions of the Pope were conspiring to control the country and hand it over to Rome.[1] While it is uncertain if Terwilliger was a member of the APA—he was born in 1869 and would have been eligible—as he searched for recruits, he certainly could have tapped into vestiges of the anti-Catholic sentiment the APA had aroused.

Joining the Klan

Potential Knights could be found in secret fraternities, many of which championed Protestantism and white supremacy. Americans were "the world's great joiners," stated Charles Merz in 1927; he estimated that thirty million Americans belonged to around eight hundred secret fraternal orders.[2] The number of lodges in Montana cities gives an indication of fraternalism's reach. Included among the thirty-one secret societies in Butte, for instance, besides five local chapters of several Catholic societies, were six lodges of the Independent Order of Odd Fellows, three lodges of the Knights of Pythias, and twelve lodges of the Masons.[3] The much smaller city of Livingston—7,000 residents in 1925—was home to the Benevolent and Protective Order of Elks, the Loyal Order of Moose, the Modern Woodmen of America, the Knights of Pythias, two IOOF lodges, and four Masonic lodges.[4] In 1927, Masonic membership reached 20,500, plus over 2,000 members who lived in Montana but belonged to lodges outside the state.[5] From Miles City to Missoula, towns and cities across the state could count on the presence of secret fraternities, and they, along with civic and business groups such as the Kiwanis and the Chamber of Commerce, provided a wide menu of social and service options from which to choose. Joining such organizations enabled members to expand professional contacts—doctors and lawyers could pass out business cards; politicians could hustle votes. Terwilliger understood how this worked. His extensive knowledge of and insight into these kinds of networks, especially his longtime involvement in secret fraternities, informed his tenure as Grand Dragon. To advance his agenda of creating a powerful and viable Realm, Terwilliger emphasized three main characteristics of secret fraternalism: the quality of membership, the opportunities that fellowship and community offered to Knights, and the importance of the ritual for imposing discipline and reminding members of the Klan's purpose. This ritualistic work reflected the larger set of beliefs inherent in Klankraft, and Terwilliger placed special importance on it.[6]

Secret fraternities insisted on rigid membership qualifications to keep most people out and to allow the select few in. Race, religion, and nationality comprised the main criteria for judging the suitability of potential candidates; the most common barrier to membership was race. "Racial exclusion," as Mary Ann Clawson states, "was a hallmark of mainstream American fraternalism."[7] The Masons, the Odd Fellows, the Knights of Pythias, and others included "whites only" clauses in their constitutions.[8] Any degree of Black, Asian, or Native American heritage, no matter how far removed, disqualified potential candidates. The Klan, of course, was the most overtly adamant in its quest to "exalt the Caucasian Race and teach the doctrine of White Supremacy," and the application for citizenship in the Invisible Empire reflected that sentiment.[9]

Yet, despite the clear directive of the application, Terwilliger needed to remind Montana Knights of its uncompromising meaning. In response to "many questions" about the suitability of "quarter breed Indians" for admission, for example, Terwilliger asserted that any amount of Native blood would void the applicant's bid, just as if he had "Negro or Chinese blood. I do not feel that we can overlook this strict provision in our Constitution," he declared.[10] Not everyone agreed. A Knight from a nearby Klan admitted frankly to the Butte Kligrapp, who had fielded such a question about eligibility to Terwilliger, "I think the character of the man would decide me."[11] To what extent these kinds of conversations in Klaverns took place across the state is unknown—only the minutes from Butte are available. But it seems reasonable to surmise that interpretations of who was qualified to join were not Butte's alone, and it indicates a discrepancy between Terwilliger's—and the Imperial Palace's—expectations of worthy membership and local chapters' need to work with what they had. There was some overlap, of course. The suitability of a Klansman's wife, for example, was fair game. Terwilliger expressed his approval of the Butte Klan's desire to ban any Knight who chose to marry a Catholic, Jew, or Black person. The list of undesirable mates, Terwilliger suggested, should also be extended to Chinese and Japanese women and, indeed, any woman "outside the Caucasian race," and he advised that the Butte Klan create a resolution to that effect.[12]

Much more important to Montana Klansmen than a few drops of undesirable blood was the candidate's religious affiliation. The application form for citizenship in the Invisible Empire specified that the candidate be Protestant, and while the initiation ceremony failed to mention the Catholic church by name, the oaths to which candidates had to swear forsaking any allegiance to or support of foreign governments or rulers made the Klan's intent clear.[13] The APA, the Klan's anti-Catholic predecessor, was not so circumspect. The APA offered joiners the usual package of rituals and secrecy; it also served, as founder Henry F. Bowers put it, as Masonry's more militant arm to protect American institutions from the grasp of Rome.[14] After being vetted for any connections with Catholicism, candidates took an oath "denounc[ing] the diabolical work of the Roman Catholic church" and promised to champion "the cause of Protestantism."[15] While anti-Catholicism was certainly present in Klan rituals and doctrine when Imperial Wizard Simmons was at the helm, the expectations that Knights, whether new recruits or longtime members, vigorously oppose the Catholic church took on a more prominent role under Imperial Wizard Evans. Grand Dragon Terwilliger, for the most part, kept his hostility toward Catholicism in check during the first few years of his tenure (at least within his official circulars), but it erupted during the Al Smith presidential campaign of 1928. Using frighteningly similar language to that of the APA, he emphasized to Knights that, although Smith had been soundly defeated, the destruction of "the Beast" was still paramount and that the Klan's hard work in revealing "its hideous, mediaeval and pagan nakedness" had saved America from a terrible fate.[16] Terwilliger expected Montana Klansmen and potential applicants for admission to share his attitude. Nevertheless, in his quest to increase membership in the Realm, Terwilliger reminded his men not to be "*too* careful" in recruiting drives. A man whose wife was Catholic was not a good bet since she might exert inappropriate influence over her husband or, more probable, because his marriage to a Catholic demonstrated a lukewarm commitment to Protestantism. An ex-Catholic who "has repudiated the Church," however, Terwilliger mused, "sometimes makes the best of Klansmen."[17]

Nationality was a third common criterion for membership in secret fraternities. The Klan's constitution stipulated that only native-born Americans could take the initiation rites, but Klans in Montana adopted a more relaxed view of eligibility. This deeply frustrated Terwilliger—always a stickler for rules and regulations—yet the requirement proved impossible to enforce. He warned in early January 1925 that it had "come to his attention" that some Klans had been "naturalizing foreign born aliens, especially those born in Canada." They would immediately lose their charters if they continued to welcome any foreign-born into their ranks. Promising non–native born recruits, if they championed Klan ideals, could find their fraternal home in the American Krusaders (formally the Royal Riders of the Red Robe, headed by a Supreme Ragon).[18] Either Montana Klans simply ignored Terwilliger's order or, more likely, candidates lied on their application forms. The Klan in Butte, for example, naturalized at least two Englishmen, perhaps reasoning that, in the mining city—which drew many Catholic immigrants who were seeking work—committed anti-Catholic recruits who were willing to join the Klan were hard to come by. If the decision to accept or deny an applicant came down to place of birth or hostility toward Catholics, Montana Klans chose the latter. Obviously Terwilliger did not realize that one of his state officers—chosen by him, at Montana's first Klorero, to serve as the Grand Kligrapp—was born in Ontario, Canada. But the vast majority of Montana Knights were native-born, at least those for whom records were found. Thus, Terwilliger's threat to disband local Klans must have seemed ludicrous to some, considering that Canadian-born Klansmen, especially in Harlowton, were no slouches when it came to promoting patriotism and civic duty. Some Knights must have thought that Terwilliger—and, by extension, Imperial Wizard Evans—was not only overreacting to what in their eyes was a nonexistent problem but also interfering in what was essentially a local matter.

Moreover, candidates born outside the United States would have had a tough time finding fraternal brotherhood in the Krusaders since the organization was not as successful as Terwilliger and Imperial headquarters would have liked. A chapter in Roundup formed (Supreme Ragon Stephen Tighe, at the time, lived in the town), but the response in Butte indicated wariness. The Butte Kligrapp noted, in a letter to Terwilliger in 1924, that Tighe's request for a list of "25 prospective candidates" and funds for travel to Butte to organize them into a local chapter was neither financially feasible nor prudent. "We do not think it advisable . . . for him to come here because in all probability some of the legal fraternity might see him and begin to surmise the object of his visit. Things here," added the Kligrapp, "as you know, are very tender."[19] Whether or not the Kontinental Klan ever created a chapter of the Krusaders is unknown (the Kligrapp had suggested to Terwilliger that if Tighe sent instructions, Butte could take care of it). But it is unlikely since the 1927 Klorero urged a "campaign among the Klans of the State" to organize local chapters and start enrolling eligible foreign-born. The attendees, after listening to a paper on the Krusaders by the Grand Dragon of Massachusetts (a guest of Terwilliger's) and discussing the matter, reiterated Klan policy: only native-born Americans could join the Invisible Empire, and those states "which have been admitting Krusaders to the Klan must cease this practice at once."[20]

Clearly, the Klans in Montana had not paid any attention to Terwilliger's demand two years earlier. Nationality, to many Klansmen in the state and outside it, was of little importance and not an impediment to membership. Perhaps this reflected the growing assimilation of foreign-born into American culture. One's worldview did not depend on "the accident of birth."[21] By the summer of 1928, the Klorero had not given up. Attendees recognized the difficulties facing the Krusaders "due to the great distances" in the state as well as the "small numbers of desirable foreign born men" and suggested that local Klans assist in "foster[ing] the Krusader spirit" whenever possible.[22]

Terwilliger understood that determining a candidate's religion, race, and nationality were vital requirements as demanded by the *Kloran*. But loyalty, he believed, provided the glue that held it all together. Loyalty was key. With an eye toward electoral victories, Terwilliger emphasized time and again the need to induct "faithful and dependable" men into the order—men who would disregard political party in favor of Klan ideals and Klan-backed candidates. The APA, too, had scoffed at political parties; only loyalty to America and APA principles mattered.[23] Echoing sentiment from the *Examiner*, Terwilliger proclaimed that the best way to strengthen the Klan in the Realm was by "sifting and cleansing and perfecting our membership" and admitting only those Knights who could demonstrate steely resolve in the face of adversity and steadfast loyalty to the cause.[24] That loyalty included the Klan's vow of secrecy, pledged by Knights in the initiation and degree ceremonies.

In the summer of 1924, a breach in Klan secrecy in the Realm—what it was about and who was responsible is unclear—incurred Terwilliger's wrath. He devoted an entire official circular to the question, dictating that it be "read at four consecutive Klonklaves," a rather excessive but telling demand. The "unklannish and unmanly" action deserved swift retribution. "A loose tongue in a Klansman's head is one of the worst enemies of our Order," Terwilliger added.[25] Aliens, he grimly reminded Montana Klansmen, desired to learn everything they could of "the inner secrets and working plans of the order."[26] The fact that most outsiders probably cared little about the Klan's fraternal secrets was beside the point. Stressing that the Klan's secrets were valuable commodities assured Klansmen of the exclusiveness of their order. It also heightened the sense of their own self-importance, for if enemies wanted to uncover the Klan's fraternal secrets for preserving and championing Americanism, surely it indicated that, for the good of the country, the Klan needed to expose those enemies.

At the Klorero held two months later, that earlier breach of secrecy had not been forgotten. A report from the Grand Kludd (chaplain), who toured the state that summer visiting Klans, and the subsequent resolution offered by the resolutions committee concluded that Knights needed to do a better job guarding the order's secrets and protecting members' identities.[27] The next year's Klorero revealed that some Klansmen in the Realm were still being indiscreet. The convention once again reminded Knights that disclosing a fellow member's identity violated his oath; it also "jeopardize[d] the interests of the organization."[28]

Loyalty involved more than keeping the order's secrets; it also meant unquestioning obedience to the Klan. Klansmen were expected to obey their superiors without question—"It is NOT FOR THE INDIVIDUAL KLANSMAN to judge WHAT IS IMPORTANT AND WHAT IS UNIMPORTANT," Terwilliger lectured. in what would be a recurring theme of his leadership.[29] Some Montana Knights may have chafed at this reprimand. Realm and Imperial headquarters, after all, were far away and divorced from local realities. Others may have taken comfort in allowing authorities to dictate to local Klans what they could and could not do, an attitude Terwilliger encouraged. As he repeated in his official circulars, the Klan's hierarchical structure was created with wisdom and purpose, and with the expectation that the Klan, as a national force and America's army, could spring into action at a moment's notice. Members, therefore, were expected to fall into line.

Permeating Terwilliger's demand for loyalty and obedience was his expectation that only "real men" would have the courage to stand for what was right and face the challenges with a "steady conscience."[30] Only those with manhood enough to take an oath were fit to join, Imperial Wizard Simmons declared in 1922, while the Imperial Klazik's opening speech to the Grand Dragons in North Carolina applauded the "untold thousands of big, manly

men" who, inspired by the Klan's 100 percent Americanism, were eagerly joining the cause.[31] The *Imperial Nighthawk* avowed that the Klan needed "men
who will not lie, shirk, or dodge, men who are not too lazy to work nor too
proud to be poor."[32] The Klan's attempt to paint itself as an organization in
which poor people would be welcome is hardly persuasive, considering the
hefty financial toll membership demanded. More significantly, these slogans
implied that membership brought with it tremendous responsibility. Working
for America's best interests, as the Klan defined them, was both an honorable
path and a heroic obligation.[33] "We wish no drones or sluggards in our ranks,"
Evans added in 1929.[34] Grave responsibilities rested upon these men, and those
who acted otherwise, stated Terwilliger, proved themselves unworthy to wear
the hood and robe.[35]

The Klan's predecessor, the APA, also wore its masculinity with pride,
claiming that the organization stood "for manhood that dares to be true to its
highest convictions."[36] Catholics, on the other hand, forced to "wear the chains
of slavery," would always cower in unmanly subservience to the church.[37] Like
the Klan, the APA showed scant patience with members who spent more time
posturing than embodying the characteristics of manhood. Members who
exuded bravery and proper patriotic spirit within the protected walls of the
lodge but failed to demonstrate that spirit after the meeting concluded were
scornfully dismissed. "If you are ashamed of defending American rights, well,
go to Mexico or Cork. You don't belong here, and this country would be better
without your cowardly, traitorous presence," spat a contemptuous *Examiner*
in November 1895.[38] While Terwilliger showed a little more restraint in his
writing, he too aimed special contempt at those Knights who wavered in their
vows and failed to dedicate themselves 100 percent to the order, calling them
"too weak-kneed to stand for the greatest movement of modern times."[39]

Secret Fraternal Socializing

Controlling the quality of membership kept Terwilliger busy, as did ensur-
ing that Knights participated in communal and social activities. This component of secret fraternalism Terwilliger deemed particularly vital in the
wide expanse of Montana, where the long distances and terrible roads often
prevented Klansmen from frequent visiting and engendered a sense of isolation from the Realm and the Invisible Empire. Terwilliger's challenge was to
keep members enthusiastic and committed. Thus he suggested that Klans
conduct open-air ceremonies in times of good weather, hold joint meetings

with neighboring Klans, and attend the talks of national lecturers sent out occasionally by the Imperial Palace. Klansmen should travel to other Klaverns to relish the camaraderie of fellow Knights and appreciate the beauty of Montana. "It will pay you to see this section of the State," Terwilliger said of an upcoming meeting in Harlowton, located in central Montana, "with its wonderful grain fields, this year." In the same official circular, Terwilliger shared the Columbus Klan's invitation to all members in the Realm to attend an open-air ceremonial and to sample "600 miles of the best fishing streams in Montana." "Plan a fishing trip and go," encouraged Terwilliger.[40] Fishing trips aside, however, the Grand Dragon worried that Klan gatherings would devolve into purely social affairs. Communal gatherings should be centered on the Klan's broader agenda, including recruiting more members, achieving power in the community and state, and eliminating Catholic influence wherever it may lurk.

That is where public demonstrations played a role. Public demonstrations reflected the Klan's secret fraternal program in that they not only exhibited the Klan's power in the community but also enticed those who might be watching with promises of excitement and mystery. On the eve of the Realm's official entry into the Invisible Empire, for example, a giant crowd in Lewistown enjoyed an evening complete with fireworks, two burning crosses, a picnic lunch, and a speech by a national lecturer from St. Paul, Minnesota.[41] Around the same time, the Billings Klan held an initiation ceremony one night on the Rimrocks, a spectacular site overlooking the city, which would have been visible throughout the Billings area. An estimated two thousand attended and were treated to a fifty-foot burning cross, buglers, "aerial bombs," and Knights singing "Onward Christian Soldiers" and "America."[42] Such displays of the Klan's version of patriotism reminded onlookers that membership afforded entry into an exclusive secret fraternal community—those watching could admire and wonder at the sights, but only those who "made the honorable decision to forsake the world of selfishness and fraternal alienation and emigrate to the delectable bounds of the Invisible Empire" could truly participate.[43]

Those men who made that "honorable decision" to join soon understood that fraternal brotherhood in the Klan meant serious dedication to learning the deep mysteries of Klankraft: the principles and values embedded in the ritualistic work and educational programs. Klankraft to Terwilliger was like a spiritual calling, a chance to learn, discuss, and contemplate the wisdom inherent in the Klan's mission. Embracing the spirit of Klankraft was a privilege; it was also a necessity to move the Klan's agenda for America forward.

Klankraft: Rituals and Degrees

For all secret fraternities, rituals played a vital role in establishing esprit de corps, providing a common experience and purpose, and revealing to the worthy the mysteries of the order.[44] The Klan was no different. Rituals, as Imperial Wizards Simmons and Evans recognized, provided the means to impart the power and knowledge of Klankraft. While the Klan and other secret fraternities created and dramatized various rituals, including opening, closing, installation, reception, and funeral ceremonies, the initiation rite proved the most important and the most elaborate. It marked the magical transformation of an alien outsider into a trusted brother. It also was the candidate's first impression of the order—and favorable impressions could lead to continued financial support and recruitment of new members. Imperial Wizard Simmons created the Klan's initiation, or "naturalization," ceremony (which granted the candidate the K-Uno degree). His successor, Imperial Wizard Evans, forged the final three degrees: K-Duo (Knights Kamellia), K-Trio (Knights of the Great Forest—named after Nathan Bedford Forrest, founder of the first Klan), and K-Quatro (the House of Mirth—the "fun" degree, which was not implemented, at least in Montana).[45]

The candidate's journey into the Invisible Empire began by proving his worthiness to the Klokann, an investigatory committee of three that scrutinized the applicant for appropriate qualifications and hints of suspicious activities in his past. Once past this initial test and, importantly, after paying the Klecktoken (anywhere between $10 and $15), he was initiated into K-Uno, or the Order of Citizenship. After the designated Terror prepared the altar and lit the fiery cross, Klansmen sang the opening Klode, and the Kludd delivered the leading prayer to attentive Klansmen, who stood "steady with heads reverently bowed." The Exalted Cyclops then officially opened the Klonklave and proceeded with the naturalization ceremony.[46]

This rite of passage was designed to impress upon the candidate the great secrecy, seriousness, and exclusiveness of the Invisible Empire. After the Exalted Cyclops and his Terrors considered the candidate's "manly petition" for membership, they asked the candidate a series of binding questions to make sure that he was fully committed to the principles of the Klan. More grave speeches and reminders of the seriousness of the candidate's commitment

("Mortal man cannot assume a more binding oath") ensued, then Klansmen sang a short stanza asking God to give "grace" to remain true to the
pledge. This last prayer should be sung, it was suggested, "in a low, soft, but
distinct tone, preferably by a quartette."[47] If the candidate betrayed the trust
of the order (by revealing members' identities, for example), he would face
the ultimate punishment of banishment, while his "conscience would tena-
ciously torment him, remorse would repeatedly revile him, and direful things
would befall him."[48] At the end of the ceremony, the Exalted Cyclops recited
the lecture on K-Uno, a memorial to the "valiant, chivalric Ku Klux" of Reconstruction, which rescued wives and daughters from the "licentious longings
of lust-crazed beasts in human form." The blatantly racist script of the Klan's
origins was followed by a list of the Knight's obligations to the order and, by
extension, to America.[49] His symbolic journey complete, the newly naturalized citizen of the Invisible Empire could look forward to further instruction
in Klankraft.[50]

The candidate would have also noticed the symbolic artifacts that adorned
the Klavern, which secret fraternities often incorporated into their rituals.
Members could identify with these objects and recognize them as part of a
culture they were trying to defend. During the opening ceremony, the American flag was draped over the altar, upon which the designated Terrors placed
a sword (which represented Klansmen's willingness to defend Christianity), a
bottle of dedication fluid (water), and a Bible. Typical of Protestant orders, the
Klokard opened the Bible to a specific passage, in this case, to Romans XII,
that depicted a good Christian life.[51] In K-Trio, the Klan added the US Constitution. Most secret fraternities did not include the cross in their rituals,
but the Klan made the fiery cross their calling card. The order declared that
it symbolized the "sincere, unselfish devotedness of members to the order's
principals," but more accurately and more aggressively, it marked the Klan's
presence in the community.[52]

As the new Knight began to learn the meaning of the fiery cross and of his
obligations to the Klan, he could look forward to earning more degrees, on
which much of secret fraternalism's appeal rested. According to fraternal tradition, this social stratification developed fellowship and motivated members
to earn more honor and responsibilities. A gradual process, it also ensured
stability and allowed the most diligent members to advance.[53] Only those dedicated Klansmen who proved themselves worthy, claimed Imperial officials,
could advance their knowledge of the philosophy of Klankraft.[54] Degrees

further presented an opportunity to introduce new dramatic elements into the ritual and rekindle sagging interest.[55] The entertainment value of the rituals, secret fraternities recognized, often provided a competitive edge in soliciting applicants. Grand Dragon Terwilliger believed that if the ritualistic work were conducted properly, newly initiated Klansmen would remain intrigued and former members would automatically rejoin. He insisted that "many fine orders thrive on RITUAL ALONE," and to obtain the maximum benefits, local Klans should train their degree teams to perfection.[56] These teams, which primarily consisted of the Exalted Cyclops and his Terrors, studied the ritualistic dialogue and diagrams for K-Uno, K-Duo, and K-Trio, each covering 30–50 pages. The offering of three to five degrees was typical of most orders.[57]

Yet the Klan's commitment to the traditions of fraternalism was another matter. One former Knight contended in 1928 that the Klan "utterly despoil[ed] fraternalism" by its greed for money and its superficial overtures to fraternal benevolence.[58] He had a point, since the Klan's intake of millions of dollars offered profitable opportunities for the few and empty pocketbooks for the rest.[59] Moreover, the Klan's inconsistent policies regarding the attainment of degrees ignored fraternal practice and instead reflected Evans's political ambitions.[60] Granting K-Duo and K-Trio free of charge to brand new members and members in good standing, as the Imperial Klonvocation did, for instance, was a shameless solicitation of support with no attempt to determine, as traditional fraternal lore demanded, a member's worthiness.[61]

The Klan's purpose in conferring these degrees in haste were the 1924 and 1928 presidential elections. By enticing Klansmen with an extra degree, Imperial headquarters hoped to keep interest level high enough to reap rewards at the polling booth. This was the work of Imperial Wizard Evans. When Evans assumed command of the Invisible Empire in late 1922, he guided the rituals in a more political (although no less bigoted) direction. On the eve of the general election in 1924, Evans commanded the Imperial Klonvocation to approve of a new degree, Knights Kamellia, or K-Duo, which would be given to all members in good standing free of charge. Since the Klan was always trying to find ways to enrich its treasury, Evans clearly hoped that the excitement of a new degree would convince those members teetering between leaving and staying, to remain. As an extra incentive to stay and as a reminder of the seriousness of the Klan's mission, Imperial headquarters and Realms sent specific recommendations to local Klans about the slate of candidates and which of them deserved the Klan vote. A robust membership and favorable results at the polls were more important than any financial gain from granting a new degree.

The hooded order had already scored victories in 1924 with the passage of the Immigration Act, signed into law in May, and the defeat of Al Smith's bid for the presidential nomination at the Democratic National Convention later that summer. Evans wanted to continue that momentum. Thus, K-Duo, the second degree, reminded Knights that their mission to keep America safe from foreign and Catholic designs remained an ongoing struggle. Reflecting Evans's ambitions for political influence, K-Duo demanded that Knights take an additional oath that expressed their loyalty to the Klan (the "great militant body of American Protestants") and to America, "where is spoken that language in which the chosen of your heart, blushing, whispered the first word of love."[62] "With greater honor comes greater responsibilities," added the ritual, and Knights must fulfill this pledge, wielding the Sword of Knights Kamellia if necessary.[63] The concluding lecture of the new ritual stressed those individual obligations and directed Knights to weed out unworthy and corrupt colleagues who sought to destroy the Klan from within via "the lure of gold, the lust of flesh, the passion of hatred, or the whisperings of personal ambition" (perhaps foretelling the downfall of the powerful David C. Stephenson, the Grand Dragon of Indiana, the following year).[64]

Contending with the disgrace of Stephenson as well as other upheavals across the Invisible Empire kept Imperial Wizard Evans thinking of new ways to revitalize interest and stop hemorrhaging members.[65] The massive parade at the nation's capital in August 1925, the Klan's first, made headlines and demonstrated considerable enthusiasm and not much else among the forty thousand participants who marched with disciplined precision. The next year, Montana Knights participated in the second and much smaller national parade.[66] In late 1927, however, the momentum shifted once again when Al Smith sought the Democratic presidential nomination for a second time. To battle this perceived new danger, Evans announced the launching of a new degree, K-Trio, Knights of the Great Forest. As with K-Duo, the third degree was given without charge in the early months of 1928. The Imperial Wizard addressed two grave concerns in the ritual—declining membership in the Klan (which had been spiraling downward, especially since the Stephenson fiasco in Indiana) and the specter of a Catholic in the White House. Anti-Catholicism drove the third degree—the imperative of maintaining white supremacy, while mentioned, was added almost as an afterthought. The tone of the third degree was more urgent and more political than the previous two degrees and warned of the consequences if Klansmen neglected their sworn duties.

In all of the Klan's rituals, but especially the third degree, militaristic rhetoric transformed the ceremony from a simple directive to champion Protestantism and Americanism to a demand for physical sacrifice. The ritual of K-Trio drew comparisons between the Klan's war against the Catholic Church and America's struggle for independence from Great Britain. A portrait of Nathan Hale ("I only regret that I have but one life to give to my country") even held an honored place in the northeastern corner of the Klavern, with a light timed to shine on his portrait at a key moment in the ceremony.[67] Evans also reached back to Arthurian legend, comparing the "search for the Holy Grail" with Klansmen's quest to create a perfect Protestant America.[68] The Knights of the Great Forest, like their knightly predecessors, were "soldiers of destiny." If Klansmen doubted the seriousness of this mission, the Exalted Cyclops' scripted query set them straight—"Have you made a will?" And if not, "will you make such a will at the earliest consistent date?"[69]

Training soldiers, fighting enemies, and winning battles were not only essential phrases in the third degree; they were also woven throughout Terwilliger's official circulars. How could any true Klansman refuse Terwilliger's call to save America from the scourge of the Catholic Church? In January 1928 Terwilliger sent an official circular to the Klans in the Realm:

> It is impossible for me to find words sufficiently strong to tell you how important for our God, our country and our Realm will be the meeting to be called upon a certain night in every Klanton throughout the bounds of the Invisible Empire . . .
>
> When the call comes, let nothing except serious illness or unavoidable accident keep you from your Klavern. At a single moment, throughout the Invisible Empire, further knowledge of Klankraft will be given you.[70]

Terwilliger understood the importance of fraternal mysticism as he sought to elicit support for K-Trio; he cleverly intertwined fraternal appeal—more insight into the Klan's deeper mysteries—and Americanism. That "knowledge of Klankraft" generously shared by the Imperial Wizard was none other than "the force of fraternalism" seeking "righteousness" throughout the ages. For the first time in history, instructed the Klokard, the three branches that had defined the nature of secret fraternities—the "contemplative," "philosophical," and "operative" orders—were now combined into one unique organization, the Ku Klux Klan, which remained America's best and only chance to defend her interests.[71]

For Terwilliger, here at last was a secret fraternal organization that combined the comforts of mystery and ritual with a hardcore commitment to militant Protestantism and white supremacy and a path to political power and influence. No other organization to which Terwilliger belonged—the Masonic orders, the Knights of Pythias, local business organizations, or political parties—offered such an attractive package. But Terwilliger recognized that it would require more than fraternal rituals and degrees to make the Klan's program work. It demanded an education, one specific to the Klan's worldview and one that Knights could take with them into the alien world.

Klankraft: Educating Klansmen

In 1918, before the Ku Klux Klan became a national force, Imperial Wizard William Joseph Simmons published a convoluted and pedantic lecture on the "First Lesson in the Science and Art of Klankraft," in which he gave detailed instructions on how Klansmen should comport themselves at all times. From moral Klannishness ("No Klansman will throw aside his qualities of a gentleman and give himself over to debauchery") and vocational Klannishness (buy from Klansmen) to racial, patriotic, and imperial Klannishness (honor the Imperial Wizard and commit "both personal and financial" resources to the cause), Simmons outlined the essence of Klankraft—a way of living, thinking, and understanding.[72] While Imperial Wizard Evans did not entirely reject Simmons's version of Klankraft—a Klansman's character remained vital to the Klan's success—his conception of Klankraft embraced a more pragmatic edge; he cared less about the need for slavish devotion than about acquiring power.

Evans admitted in 1928 that, over time, his own thinking had evolved about the Klan's philosophy. The "three manifestations of Klankraft," as he called them before the Imperial Klonvocation, involved the physical (train an army of Knights to champion America), the mental (convince Americans to abide by the Klan's principles), and the spiritual (incorporate an inspirational component supporting the other two). All three components merged to inspire Knights to step out from the safe harbor of the Klonklave to actively "spread our evangelism" and to "make our principles instinctive in the American mind." Secret fraternal rituals and the attainment of degrees played a critical part in Klankraft, Evans recognized, but were insufficient to transform

Klansmen into "soldiers of Americanism and Protestantism."[73] Grand Dragon Terwilliger agreed. Montana Klansmen must commit "to a study of the principles and practical work of our organization. All of us need training in this great movement, if we are to work together for the good of our Country and humanity."[74] Educating Klansmen, then, became a top priority for the Imperial Palace and for the Realm so Knights could parry detractors and convince skeptics as well as dues-paying members that the Klan's vision was America's vision. Understanding current topics through publications, educational programs, and lectures would also inspire Knights—Montana Knights in particular needed that inspiration—and remind them of their obligations to the order and to America.

One of the first points of contact for Klannish wisdom was the Ku Klux Klan press. Officials pushed subscriptions to monthly publications such as the *Imperial Nighthawk* and the *Kourier*, while pamphlets from Imperial headquarters helped round out a Klansman's education. There were many to choose from. Evans was, if nothing else, a prolific writer—"Ideals of the Ku Klux Klan," "The Klan Today," and "The Klan Answers" provided insight into the order's principles and agenda, while others discussed topics such as "The Negro Situation," "The Menace of Modern Immigration," and "The Obligation of American Citizens to Free Public Schools." These pamphlets were often available either free of charge (first come, first serve, stated Terwilliger) or for a price (if you were too late).[75] Essays about Soviets' insidious plans to conquer the United States and Communists' attempts to install "Black Supremacy" reassured Montana Klansmen that the national organization was looking out for America's safety and security. Meanwhile, news about other Realms— including, perhaps to Montana Klansmen's surprise, two new Klans in the Canal Zone: Pacific No. 1 and Atlantic No. 2—reminded Montana Knights that they were part of a larger movement.[76] Sample copies of other publications, such as the viciously anti-Catholic *Fellowship Forum*, a Klan-backed publication that touted itself as "A National Voice for Protestant Fraternal America," were sometimes distributed to local Klans free of charge.[77] The *Fellowship Forum*, declared Terwilliger, provided "the unvarnished truth about all current matters, civic and political," while the *Kourier* was "dignified, conservative ... [and] filled with the essence of Klankraft."[78] Both were available for a mere $2.00 per year, with fifty cents going to the local Klan, just in time to get informed for the upcoming political battles in 1928.[79] Terwilliger urged Montana Klansmen to subscribe to both.

While the *Fellowship Forum* promised to "smash Rome" in the 1928 presidential election, more anti-Catholic propaganda was available through the Rail
Splitter Press, self-proclaimed as the largest anti-papal publishing house in
the country and whose founder, William Lloyd Clark, had been active in the
APA.[80] Klansmen would have to wait until 1932 to read Clark's reminiscences
about "tam[ing] many a vicious papal mob" in *The Story of My Battle with
the Scarlet Beast*, but, in the meantime, eager Knights could pick up the latest
literature from the *Rail Splitter Catalogue*, such as the "Dastardly Deeds of
Irish Sinn Feiners," "God's World Against Romanism," or "The Anti-Catholic
Joke Book."[81] With these, combined with other magazines and pamphlets, the
devout Knight was well armed for any political election or conversation.

National news and instruction about Klankraft were one thing—newsletters
and pamphlets were readily available—the local equivalent was something
else. To meet this need, Terwilliger vigorously supported a Klan newspaper for
the Realm. Efforts to secure some financial assistance from the national Klan's
Bureau of Publication and Education failed, even when Terwilliger traveled
back east and "conferred at length" with officials from the Imperial Palace and
the Publicity Committee. A disappointed Terwilliger was told that money was
not available for such a venture. (The funds were surely there, but earmark-
ing them for a sparsely populated state would not have been a priority.) "This
was indeed sad news for us," admitted W. W. Casper and Shelton Hampton of
Belgrade, who nevertheless decided to launch a newspaper on their own. "We
felt we just couldn't stand by and see the project fail," they stated and appealed
to Montana Klansmen for their support.[82]

The Klorero enthusiastically gave their unanimous consent and voted
to assess each member in good standing fifty cents to help with the initial
financing.[83] The remaining costs of publishing the Realm's official newspaper
would be covered by subscriptions at two dollars per year and advertising. It
was a small price, declared Terwilliger, to "assist the whole Realm in its mor-
als and education in Klancraft, [and] help the deserving brothers who have
assumed the responsibility of the paper."[84] It would also provide opportunities
for Knights to practice vocational Klannishness, as informed Knights could
support Klan businesses with a clear conscience knowing that their dollars
were going to the right people. The newspaper sought to publish all newswor-
thy items, especially those that impacted "the moral, civic or religious life" of
members' respective communities. For those concerned about confidential-
ity, which likely included most everyone, Terwilliger assured Knights that the

editors deeply valued discretion and would keep membership lists safe. Moreover, each issue of the *Montana Klansman* would be "securely wrapped" so as not to arouse the suspicions of prying mailmen.[85]

To the dismay of Terwilliger and the two enterprising editors, Montana Knights failed to back the effort. There were only sixty subscribers after Casper made his plea for support that summer, and the situation had not improved several months later, when Casper admitted that "the response has been somewhat slower than we anticipated."[86] Members chose not to subscribe or advertise their businesses; they also neglected to submit their required assessments.[87] Even Terwilliger's reminder that Klans could not disobey Klorero law fell on deaf ears.[88] Finally, in March 1925, a frustrated Terwilliger disclosed that the Realm finance committee had decided to discontinue the *Montana Klansman* after a seven-month run and fill the remaining subscriptions with the *Kourier.* "Very little local news of the Montana Klans could be published without uncovering the Klans in the State," Terwilliger explained with obvious disappointment, "and many subscribers were fearful of being disclosed by receiving the paper through the mails."[89] In what was surely a losing cause, Terwilliger reminded local Klans that they were still obligated to cover the costs of the publication and should send in the money owed immediately.[90]

Although a Realm newspaper remained out of reach, there were other opportunities for disseminating Klankraft. The *Imperial Nighthawk* suggested in 1923, for example, that Klans follow the lead of a Great Titan from Texas who created an educational program in which select Klansmen would give lectures on such topics as the Declaration of Independence and the Constitution, the Roman Catholic Church, "Oriental" religions, radicalism in America, and the causes of the Civil War.[91] Two years later, the Imperial Palace created such an educational program for Klans across the Invisible Empire. Planned "by the leaders of our movement," Terwilliger stated with enthusiasm, a ready-made batch of lectures was being distributed to every Klan in the Realm so that all Montana Knights would "catch the spirit and get the true vision of Klancraft."[92] True to form, Terwilliger ordered each Exalted Cyclops to follow the exact instructions accompanying the lectures. "No excuse for failure to have these lectures given will be accepted," warned Terwilliger when the second series of lectures arrived in March.[93]

Besides wanting to show the Imperial Palace that Montana was a ready and worthy partner in the Klan's cause, Terwilliger recognized that the lectures carried more than just the lessons of Klankraft; they had the potential to connect Montana Knights in a Realm where Klans existed in isolation. "We need these Educational programs in Montana especially," Terwilliger pleaded, "since the distances are too great to allow us to visit each other and gain the inspiration and new ideas that we all need."[94] As autumn transitioned to winter, Terwilliger again urged that the national lectures provided by Imperial headquarters demanded the full attention of every Montana Knight. "The evenings are now getting longer, the attendance at the Klan meetings should increase. . . . we should all deem it a privilege to get the fund of information and inspiration contained in these excellent lectures."[95] Yet not all Klans were as committed to the "inspiring and enlightening" lectures as Terwilliger hoped, since a note of frustration started to creep into his official circulars about the slow rate of compliance.[96] He should not have had to work so hard. The lectures were already written; all that was required was for "some competent member"—and Terwilliger must have started to wonder about the level of competence in his Klans—to present them. After Knights engaged in what presumably would be a lively conversation about the chosen topic, all the Exalted Cyclops needed to do was to submit a detailed report about the evening's discussion to the Grand Dragon's office.[97] This was not happening to Terwilliger's satisfaction.

He had better luck in the Kloreros, which were, by their nature, more self-selective than the local Klaverns. Those who attended had already demonstrated their commitment to Klankraft by carving out the time necessary to participate in the annual state conventions as well as assuming the costs of travel and lodging. Sometimes the Imperial Palace sent guests, as at the first Klorero when the Imperial Klazik gave an "instructive and impressive talk" about how to grow the Realm. One of the best guest speakers, according to the minutes in 1927, was Grand Dragon Arthur H. Bell of New Jersey. Bell's "powerful address" about "the menace of the Jew" and Jewish control over every aspect of American lives found a captive audience. Other enemies were not forgotten as Bell's almost two hour address included the "menace of Catholicism" and the "atheistic societies." Montana Knights loved it. "This address was considered to be one of the best ever heard in Montana" added the minutes, and it rejuvenated the spirit of Montana Klankraft.[98] That may well have rung true in the comforting halls of the Klorero, where participants could revel in the togetherness of the moment, but it is doubtful whether that sentiment filtered down to the local level, especially in 1927 as Realm membership was slipping. It would take the new and all-encompassing threat of an Al Smith presidency to revive that commitment to Klankraft, assisted as ever by the vitriol of Imperial Wizard Evans's and Grand Dragon Terwilliger's political calculations.

If members preferred to receive lessons in Klankraft during open-air meetings rather than in lecture halls, there were plenty of options across the state and in other Realms. Emphasizing the social and fraternal pleasures of such meetings, Terwilliger encouraged Knights to travel to Glendive in the summer of 1929 to hear an address on "Religious Liberty." "You will have a jolly good time and hear an instructive and entertaining address," encouraged Terwilliger.[99] Still, it was a forty-mile journey from the nearest Klan, in Terry, and seventy-six miles from Miles City on the Northern Pacific line. Attending these gatherings meant an all-day commitment. If Klansmen could afford the time and the money to travel out of state, Terwilliger suggested attending the St. Paul, Minnesota, Klan picnic, a huge annual affair where representatives from different Realms were always present. "The program is out," remarked Terwilliger at the 1929 gathering, "and it is a good one. You will be sure to get a lot of inspiration by planning to attend."[100]

Closer to home was the annual Tri State Roundup in Belle Fourche, South Dakota. Terwilliger announced with pleasure that thousands of Klansmen from the Dakotas, Wyoming, and Montana would descend on the town, located just over the Montana and Wyoming borders, in July 1925. Knights would be treated to speeches, music ("we hope to have two Montana bands among the list," Terwilliger revealed), parades, fireworks, and a huge naturalization ceremony to cap off the three-day affair. Accessible by rail at a reduced rate or automobile via the Custer Battlefield Highway, the Roundup was sure to be "one of the greatest meetings ever held" near Montana. Terwilliger planned to attend and hoped to see a good showing of Montana Knights.[101] While the actual number of Knights attending fell well below the 65–80 thousand predicted by Imperial officials, the *Belle Fourche Bee* reported that Klansmen came "by the thousands" to watch the parade, admire the floats portraying "The Little Red Schoolhouse, the Home, and other scenes dear to the heart of every true American," and listen to a lengthy address by an Imperial official.[102]

Terwilliger hoped that as Klansmen were learning the essentials of Klankraft—the lessons contained within the rituals and degrees, pamphlets, articles, and lectures—they would also realize that Klankraft was not simply an academic exercise. It required purposeful commitment and unwavering loyalty to work for the greater good as the Klan defined it. It came back to individual responsibility—just how committed were individual Klansmen to the Realm, to the Klan, and to America? Terwilliger's dedication was second to none—he was ready to make sacrifices for the cause. Could Montana Knights do any less? Terwilliger did not think so. The next step was to transform the lessons of Klankraft into action.

CHAPTER 3

Fighting Enemies

There's a mighty organization
Of an empire that's unseen,
Sweeping steadily o'er the nation
'Neath the fiery cross beam.
With a pure and noble purpose,
They are bound to make men free,
As they go marching on. . . .

They have sounded forth a trumpet
With a blast that's loud and long;
Calling Protestants together
Whose hearts are brave and strong
Oh! Be swift dear souls to answer,
Join this great and happy throng,
As they go marching on.

"The Battle Hymn of Klandom," circa 1923

Grand Dragon Lewis Terwilliger gladly answered the Battle Hymn's call to those "brave and strong" Protestant hearts. Klansmen, he believed, were engaged in a mighty battle that spelled either the tragic death of an America they loved or a righteous victory over the forces of evil. Only Montana Knights' dedication to the lessons of Klankraft and their embrace of the order's "pure

and noble purpose" could achieve that final triumph. Fighting enemies—
enemies of the Klan and thus enemies of America—consumed Terwilliger's
tenure in the state. His efforts to showcase Montana's grit and commitment
to the cause would, he believed, prove to Imperial Wizard Hiram W. Evans
and to everyone else in the Invisible Empire that Montana was a 100 percent
Realm of which the Imperial Palace could be proud. For that to happen, Montana Knights needed to not only comprehend the ways of Klankraft but also
understand that, at its core, the Klan was a military organization that required
its soldiers to carry out their leaders' orders with unquestioning obedience.
That meant, above all else, recruiting more eligible white Protestant men
into the Invisible Empire, wielding political influence at the local, state, and
national levels, and defeating the Klan's enemies. To take meaningful action
against those enemies, however, Terwilliger first had to identify who they were
and what dangers they posed.

Enemies

At the top of Terwilliger's list of enemies was the Roman Catholic Church, the
source, he believed, of almost every threat facing the United States.[1] The Church's
reach was long. It commanded, the Klan argued, the obedience of legions of
immigrants rushing to American shores. It corrupted the intent of Prohibition.
Most of all, Terwilliger and the Klan charged that the Catholic Church hungered
for political power and would do everything it could to crush America's constitutional form of government. It was not the Catholic religion the Klan opposed,
insisted Terwilliger and Imperial Wizard Hiram W. Evans, only the Church's
supposed political ambitions. "The schemes of the Roman political Heirarchy
[sic]," argued Terwilliger, justified the Klan's fears since it assumed American
Catholics' first allegiance was to the Vatican and not to the United States.[2] The
implication, of course. was that the church dictated the lives and choices of Catholics who, devoid of free will, only served to do the Pope's bidding.

The irony was lost on Terwilliger and other Klan leaders. The Klan made
no apologies for its authoritarian and hierarchical structure, where absolute
and unquestioning obedience to the Imperial Wizard and his orders was
expected. Evans may not have had the same need as his predecessor, William Joseph Simmons, for Klansmen's personal devotion, but he and Terwilliger did demand utter commitment to and sacrifice for the cause.[3] That tough
independence of the iconic Protestant settler whom Evans was so fond of mentioning disappeared if it ran contrary to the Klan's wishes.[4]

The Klan's demand for loyalty among its members made sense to Terwilliger. How could the Klan effectively fight the Catholic Church and champion patriotic Protestantism without it? Yet the organization's self-appointed role as the only true defender of Protestantism could reach absurd heights. The Grand Dragon of Mississippi, for example, tapping into a deep well of hubris, claimed that "since the time of Martin Luther never was there such a Reformation" as the Ku Klux Klan. America was witnessing its first "spiritual renaissance" as the Klan shone its light upon a "sin-racked, despairing world."[5] His speech was among many that were published from the annual meeting of Grand Dragons held in North Carolina in the summer of 1923, and it was hardly alone in declaring the Klan the champion America urgently needed. While Terwilliger likely did not participate in this particular meeting—the Realm of Montana would not be officially recognized as part of the Invisible Empire until September of that year—he would have agreed with the sentiments expressed: the Klan was on a righteous holy crusade to save America from Jews, Mormons, Blacks, Japanese, and most of all, Catholics, who posed the most frightening menace to the white Protestant order.

The thought that there existed in the West white Protestant men who failed to grasp the eminent dangers facing America was especially hard to bear for both the Klan and its predecessor, the APA. The West, after all, was perceived as a place where masculinity and rugged individualism had combined with perseverance, hard work, and hope to create a special breed of men. Carving out a life in the West was supposed to be a transformative experience.[6] As the Montana State Department of Agriculture and Publicity stated, "ambitious" and "virile" settlers could find plenty of opportunities in the West, provided they put in the effort.[7] The Grand Dragon of Wyoming argued that manhood's true essence had been forged in the wilderness of the West and, in fact, that tough frontier mentality would give a real boost to the Klan's agenda if only officials would relocate Atlanta's Imperial Palace out to "the real west."[8] It was an exceptional place, Montana Klansmen believed, where faithful Knights burned giant crosses on the rimrocks overlooking Billings, Prospect Hill in Great Falls, and Square Butte in Laurel; where Harlowton Klansmen helped create the Rifle and Pistol Club, the Wheatland County Sportsmen's Club, and the Three-Pound Trout Club; where Klansmen could gather at the gate of Yellowstone National Park for a photo-op; and where Terwilliger and his Knights could ponder whether or not to buy property at Flathead Lake.[9] The West, and Montana in particular, comprised part of the Realm's "cognitive map," a desire to create "idealized geographic spaces" available only to Knights and those who supported their objectives.[10]

Recent immigrants did not fit into that map. One of the Klan's most immediate concerns was the renewed wave of immigration in the wake of World War I. If Terwilliger needed an unlikely refresher about that alleged danger, he had only to review Imperial Wizard Evans's speech on "The Menace of Modern Immigration" given at the Texas State Fair on "Klan Day" in October 1923. Evans's vitriolic twenty-eight-page lecture, published by the Klan press, offered "indisputable facts and figures" to paint a terrifying picture of America's certain collapse if "hordes of inferior immigrants," who brought with them illiteracy, disease, and criminal behavior, continued to flood American shores.[11] Of special concern were the Irish and their "proclivity to insanity," but "mercenary minded, money mad" Jews, Blacks with "low mentality," and Catholics, whose allegiance to the Pope was "the deadliest, most menacing, of national dangers," also threatened the Klan's version of American identity.[12] They could never assimilate into American society, Evans added, nor would the Klan want them to.[13]

Drawing from two well-known contemporary works, Madison Grant's *The Passing of the Great Race* (1916) and Lothrop Stoddard's *The Rising Tide of Color* (1921), Evans declared that the Klan's fight for restriction and 100 percent Americanism was a just one.[14] He encouraged Klansmen to believe that science, most notably biology and anthropology, supported his eugenic arguments for immigration restriction. The speech also revealed that Evans and other nativists had categorized the recent surge of European immigration into degrees of whiteness, creating what Matthew Fry Jacobson has called "a hierarchy of plural and scientifically determined white races."[15] Certain kinds of white people, in other words, were deemed more capable, intelligent, and independent than others. Immigrants from southeastern Europe did not make the grade, neither did the Irish. The *Imperial Night Hawk* explained the Klan's position: "Contact and crossing with the negro was bad enough, but the intermingling with the mongrel hordes threatens the wholesale ruin of the white race in America and the destruction of the republic of our forefathers."[16] South America was already ruled by "mongrel half-breeds," and the same fate awaited America if strict measures limiting immigration were not immediately passed.[17] Yet Evans continued to insist that there was "no hatred in my heart" and that he "love[d] all humanity."[18] Terwilliger echoed the sentiment that the Klan did not dictate "a gospel of hate." Both leaders, of course, attacked anyone who questioned the white Protestant order.[19]

Evans's assault on immigration in the Dallas speech did not go unnoticed in Montana. Bishop John P. Carroll of Helena declared that Evans had finally admitted the Klan's intention all along was to "ostracize Negroes, Jews, and Catholics, and to bar entry to America to all foreigners except 'Anglo-Saxon.'"[20] Montana newspapers also passed judgment. Predictably, the *Anaconda Standard* reported that the Klan had always lied about its true purpose, but at Dallas, "the hood slipped from the Ku Klux face, and from all over the country come howls of derision and contempt."[21] The *Missoulian* mocked the speech and suggested that the Klan knew little of immigrants' positive impact on important historical events.[22] At times, however, the anti-immigrant rhetoric in Montana took a vicious turn. Shortly before the Emergency Immigration Act of 1921 was passed into law, the *Harlowton Times* remarked that "Immigrants hereafter are to be combed, washed, and defleed [sic] before starting for America. It is said that some of them will lose all the pleasure of the trip,"[23] while three years later the *Billings Gazette* urged Congress to "ladle off the scum" of immigrants seeking entry.[24] The 1924 Immigration Act's quota system, which favored northern European immigrants, met with Livingston's *Park County News*"s approval. "The native stocks," praised the editor, "are given consideration that is decidedly refreshing."[25]

While Evans celebrated the Immigration Act as a victory (giving the Klan far too much credit for its passage), Terwilliger failed to mention it in his official documents.[26] Certainly, he favored such restrictions, but perhaps he assumed that any dangers posed by continued immigration, especially from southeastern Europe, were negligible. In Montana, people on the Klan's targeted list of undesirable immigrants settled mainly in Butte, which would prove troublesome for the Kontinental Klan but not for other chapters. According to the 1920 Census, the top six countries identified as places of birth for immigrants who moved to Montana included Canada, followed by Norway, England, Germany, Ireland, and Sweden. These were hardly places the Klan identified as threats, except for Ireland, and just under half of the Irish had settled in Silver Bow County.[27] The small number of southeastern Europeans were scattered throughout the state or had joined the Irish in Butte.

Canada may have contributed the most immigrants to Montana, but the state's northern neighbor offered much more than thousands of people

searching for a new life in the United States. The 545-mile-long border between
Canada and Montana served as a sieve during Prohibition. This was aggra-
vated, according to the federal Prohibition director for Montana, Addison K.
Lusk, by Canadian officials who cared little about stopping the flow of alcohol
into the United States.[28] "Montana does more liquor running by automobile
than any other state in the United States," he stated in despair,[29] and with
"whiskey roads" and farmers' fields edging the border, Prohibition agents
faced an impossible task. One resident in Lewistown recalled that bootleggers drove freely across northern Montana with their haul of Canadian whiskey, got stuck in the muddy roads, and then hired homesteaders to haul them
out with teams of horses.[30] Other residents in Lewistown remembered the
"many prominent citizens" who participated in smuggling, the enormous
amount of drinking behind closed doors, and the rum-runners, who drove
the fastest and most powerful cars.[31] Havre, close to the Canadian border
and a division point for the Great Northern Railroad, was a bootlegging
paradise.[32] Even as the Havre Klan praised the mayor in the spring of 1922
for attempting a "moral clean-up," bootleggers operated with impunity
and "made Havre a hub for a network of illegal liquor routes running from
Canada into nearly every state in the union."[33] Clearly there was enough
business to keep twenty-eight bars open in a county with less than fourteen
thousand inhabitants, as well as three distilleries and a brewery located in
underground tunnels.[34] Bootlegging was also common in the northeastern
section of the state and often served as a major source of revenue for struggling farmers.[35]

It was in Butte where Prohibition met some of the greatest resistance. The
almost daily appearance of arrests and destruction of distilleries in the city
papers prompted the *Kalispell Times* to label Silver Bow as "probably the most
open county in the state."[36] As in other parts of Montana, Prohibition opened
the doors for more entrepreneurial-minded citizens who did not mind skirt-
ing the law.[37] Saloons were quickly rebranded as soft drink parlors, which
joined newly established businesses with the same names.[38] One resident
of Butte recalled that some of the "big outfits . . . would turn out hundreds of
gallons a day," while consumers could purchase wine with ease in Meader-
ville.[39] A few months before the Kontinental Klan received its charter, federal
agents blew up a three-thousand-gallon distillery just south of Butte, the largest discovered in Montana.[40] Butte was not alone in its well-deserved status
as a wide-open town. "Confidentially I may say," Lusk admitted to Governor

Joseph Dixon in 1923, "that in [Great Falls, Helena, and Butte] the police authorities do absolutely nothing to prevent the sale of liquor."[41]

Bootlegging did not capture much attention in the minutes of the Kontinental Klan, a surprising omission considering the rampant flaunting of the law. Perhaps members had more or less accepted the fact that they could do very little about it. If Klansmen had decided to crack down on violators, however, they would have had their work cut out for them. Any attempt to dismantle a distillery would incur the wrath of an irate bootlegger, who could probably round up more support in a hurry than could a small contingent of Klansmen. Still, in one instance, a committee of two Klansmen set out to investigate a "moonshine joint" in the back of the First National Bank.[42] In another case, the Exalted Cyclops ordered a Klansman to make inquiries about a fellow member who had been arrested for handling liquor, an indication, if nothing else, of the attractions of earning some cash marketing alcohol.[43] The Kligrapp was silent about the results of these investigations and what, if anything, they yielded.

In other parts of Montana, local Klans announced their support of city officials who fought the growing tide of liquor traffic. Missoula's sheriff and mayor received the University City Klan's praises for successfully stopping whiskey running, while in Harlowton, the sheriff and his men (including several Klansmen) pursued distillers of "Harlowton Hooch."[44] Wheatland County's district attorney, who also served as the Grand Kligrapp of Montana, obliged by filing criminal charges. But even in Harlowton, a respected doctor and Klansman enjoyed his spiked eggnog during the holiday season, suggesting that whatever the official Klan line was regarding Prohibition, individual Klansmen made their own choices.[45] In Big Horn County, the sheriff's department hunted moonshiners, who distilled "good wholesome products into liquid headaches and slow death," but the sheriff, who was also a member of the Hardin Klan, was still unable to shut down Hardin's five saloons.[46] As was the case in other parts of the state, if Klansmen were involved in enforcing Prohibition, they did so as individual Klansmen or in their capacity as city or county officials, not as part of an organized Klan raid.

The "booze problem" at local dances remained a challenge. In response to Harlowton residents' complaints, the Grand Kligrapp, this time serving as city district attorney, drew up an ordinance to reign in "minors frequenting pool and billiard halls" that passed unanimously, creating a curfew, establishing penalties, and "declaring an emergency."[47] In Helena, hundreds of residents flocked to a meeting called by the parent teacher association and city churches to discuss the worrisome prevalence of students drinking alcohol at high school dances and other venues. Providing some political heft to their concerns, former governor Sam V. Stewart oversaw the proceedings. At the meeting's end, participants concluded that, although the students (primarily male) may have purchased liquor from bootleggers, the most common source was likely "grandmother's wine" and "Demon Rum" from "father's private stock."[48] Parents, in other words, were the responsible parties and needed to use a firmer hand.

Rather than leave the fate of Prohibition entirely in the hands of ordinary citizens, Terwilliger decided in 1925 to team up with the state Republican committee chairman, the head of the Anti-Saloon League, and two politicians from Idaho to try to force the resignation of Montana district attorney John L. Slattery and replace him with a former county attorney out of Great Falls. The group justified their attack by claiming that Slattery failed to support Prohibition with appropriate prosecutorial vigor, a charge at least one newspaper contested.[49] That Slattery was Catholic added fuel to the group's attacks.[50] The *Helena Independent* quipped that Slattery did "not own a clean nightshirt or a fool's cap with peek-holes in it" and so had naturally incurred the Klan's ire, while other newspapers began to benignly suggest that Slattery "was meeting some local opposition in Montana."[51] The reasons for the decision to not reappoint Slattery in late 1925 remain murky—neither the White House nor the Department of Justice was forthcoming—but President Coolidge nominated Republican Wellington D. Rankin, without protest from Senators Burton Wheeler and Thomas J. Walsh, to succeed Slattery in late December 1925.

Terwilliger may have claimed victory for the Klan in this particular battle, but he and the Klan were losing the bigger war. More Montanans began to recognize by mid-decade the futility of trying to regulate private behavior. A series of initiatives to repeal state prohibition laws began to appear on ballots across the country, including Montana.[52] Prohibition still had its supporters, however, and much of the central and eastern part of the state opposed the 1926 initiative, as did the Klan and the Republican Party. The Republicans condemned the initiative to repeal state prohibition laws in convention, and the *Spokane Review* noted that the Klan, despite "gossip" to the contrary, was still "a powerful organization especially in the eastern half of the state." It would throw its support behind the party that opposed repeal, declared the paper, and that meant the Republicans.[53] In Harlowton, for example, local

branches of the Woman's Christian Temperance Union (populated by Klansmen's wives), the Anti-Saloon League (headed by the Exalted Cyclops), and
Harlowton churches convinced the majority of Wheatland County residents
to vote against the measure, but most of the state had had enough.[54] Silver
Bow County led the way with over 73 percent voting for repeal, followed by
Glacier and Deer Lodge Counties.[55] With the state officially out of the enforcement business, federal agents—Governor John Erickson estimated eight to
ten at best—were expected to patrol the immense interior of Montana and the
long border with Canada.[56] Surely Terwilliger sharply criticized the state initiative to repeal in his official circulars; unfortunately, documents from 1926
are missing. Beyond his assurance to a Butte resident in 1928 that the Klan still
favored the enforcement of Prohibition, little more was said.[57]

Montana Politics

"Prohibition failed all across the country," Michael Malone affirmed, "and
nowhere more spectacularly than in Montana."[58] But Prohibition was never
on Terwilliger's list of priorities. Neither was immigration. Any difficulties
involving those issues were symptoms of a larger problem—the political ambitions, as he saw it, of the Roman Catholic Church. Shaping the political future
of Montana, therefore, presented by far the most critical task for the Klan. A
true believer, Terwilliger genuinely desired political success; he also wanted to
impress Imperial headquarters. Favorable results at the polls were the litmus
test of the Realm's strength and vitality as well as the Grand Dragon's ability
to lead and inspire. "The eyes of the Klan world are on Montana,"[59] Terwilliger
urged in the August before the 1924 general election. Knights needed to "go
about this the real Montana way and show the Imperial Headquarters that the
Klansmen of Montana can always be depended on."[60]

Terwilliger emphasized one point time and again: those Knights who
knew the true meaning of loyalty—loyalty to Klan principles and not to a
particular political party—would make victory possible. To guide members
in these important state and national contests, the Realm's political committee gathered intelligence on candidates "without fear or favor" so Klansmen
would make an informed decision at the polls.[61] The committee, Terwilliger
admonished, "had information at their command that is not available to you,"
thus Knights must trust and abide by its endorsements.[62] The election guides
consisted of a list of candidates' names followed by a series of letters and,
mailed in a separate envelope one or two days later to avoid possible leaks to

the alien world, the code to decipher what those letters meant. There were no great revelations—the guide with the accompanying code revealed fairly tame and accessible information such as political party, religion, fraternal affiliations, and stance on Prohibition, but even so Terwilliger instructed Klansmen to destroy the code after memorizing it.[63] What Terwilliger really wanted to conceal was the asterisk by candidates' names that indicated if they were present or former members of the Klan. Four candidates, all Republicans, were identified as such in the 1928 primary election for state offices. Two won their primaries and would go on to win easily in November—the secretary of state and the clerk of the supreme court in Montana.[64] Such a clarification was not present in the 1924 guides, and those from 1926 are missing. By the time the 1930 elections rolled around, the Realm's political committee had disbanded, and in place of its recommendations, Terwilliger cryptically wrote, "it will be easy for any one desirous of knowing something about the candidates to remember the names of the worthy ones, and also the unworthy candidates."[65]

One of those unworthy candidates in the 1924 election had been on the Klan hit list since 1921, when he declared that the Ku Klux Klan was "a public enemy and should be treated as such."[66] Montana Democrat Senator Thomas J. Walsh, who rose to national prominence during the Teapot Dome Scandal of the Warren G. Harding administration, was running for a third term.[67] The Realm's political committee noted Walsh's Catholicism and membership in the Knights of Columbus, while his Republican opponent for the senate seat, Frank B. Linderman, offered the more favorable pedigree as a Protestant and thirty-third degree Mason.[68] The *New York Times* identified the Klan as the instigator of religious tensions in the battle between Walsh and Linderman and the "dominant issue" in the campaign. Plenty of rumors circulated around Linderman's past and present affiliations. The *New York Times* reported that the Montana Klan was aligned with the Republican Party—and most Klansmen for whom information was found were Republicans—but also that Linderman was "said to be closely affiliated with the Klan." "The Republican organization does not deny Mr. Linderman's Klan affiliations," the paper went on to say in mid-October 1924; neither did the party deny "that he was a power in the old A.P.A."[69] State Democratic chairman Tom Stout argued that the Democrats were "morally certain" that Linderman was a Klansman (no evidence has been uncovered regarding Linderman's status) and that he had certainly belonged to the APA.[70]

As the rumors about the Montana Klan's influence in the senate race continued to percolate, the national Klan made headlines across the country when
the contentious Democratic National Convention opened in New York City.
For a record sixteen days fist fights, tears, and prayers permeated the delegates'
warm discussions about the party platform and whether it would condemn
the Klan by name (it would not) and who would be the standard bearer for
the Democrats in November—William McAdoo from Tennessee or Al Smith
from New York. After 103 ballots, the exhausted delegates compromised by
nominating John W. Davis, who would be soundly defeated by the Republican
nominee, Calvin Coolidge, in November.[71] At the State Democratic Convention held in Lewistown, the presence of the Klan in Montana was enough of a
concern that former mayor of Butte W. H. Maloney introduced an anti-Klan
resolution. After a heated debate, the state convention, unlike the national,
endorsed the resolution, which "denounc[ed] the alleged political activities
of the Klan" and condemned the hooded order and any other organization
that used "racial and religious beliefs as a test of fitness for public office."[72] The
Democrats need not have worried. While parts of eastern and south-central
Montana favored Linderman, Walsh easily won the rest of the state.[73] Walsh,
in fact, declared that his reelection to the senate demonstrated that Montana
voters had wisely rejected "that evanescent uprising proclaiming its exclusive
and superior Americanism."[74]

The Klan also failed in its bid to return Republican Joseph M. Dixon to
the governor's mansion. Although the political committee acknowledged
the Protestant and Masonic credentials of both Dixon and his opponent,
Democrat John E. Erickson, it questioned Erickson's commitment to public
education. A potentially bigger problem was the Anaconda Copper Mining
Company's support of the Democrat. The ACMC had its own reasons for
attacking Dixon—mainly the governor's advocacy of a graduated mine tax,
but also his agenda for championing other progressive reforms. Association with the Company would become a flash point for Montana Klansmen,
as future guides noted if the office seeker was "considered as the candidate
of the A.C.M. Company,"[75] an obvious signal to vote for his opponent. The
committee's designation likely held multiple meanings for the Montana Klan.
As the most powerful company in the state—the "Land of the Copper Collar," as discussed by the Nation in the fall of 1923—the ACMC's reach was
enormous. Any candidate who enjoyed the support of the Company might be
expected to return the favor once in office, a charge refuted by the Democrats

in the convention.[76] Perhaps Klansmen were wary of corporate power and the vast accumulation of wealth, as was their predecessor, the APA.[77] The Realm's committee may have also recalled the origins of the Company and Marcus Daley's hiring of Irish Catholics in the Butte mines.[78]

Whatever the reasons, the ACMC's endorsement of Erickson sealed the Klan's decision. As Grand Dragon Terwilliger told the Butte Kligrapp, "We want to elect these two [Dixon and Linderman] without fail."[79] Wheatland Knights were on board, especially since their Knights in the state legislature backed Dixon, while the Klansman editor of the *Harlowton Times* charged that the ACMC, the Montana press, and other unnamed companies had obstructed Dixon's agenda throughout his tenure in office.[80] As with the senate race, the Klan found itself the subject of rumors. In 1924, the *Big Timber Pioneer* suggested that both Governor Dixon and Attorney General Wellington D. Rankin sympathized with the Klan; indeed, "rumor has it that the governor has asked for the Klan's support."[81] The *Helena Independent*, one of many newspapers owned by the ACMC, charged that Dixon had created and was overseeing "his newly formed Ku Klux" and that he was "determined" to form his own political party made up of old members of the Non-Partisan League, the Montana Labor League, the Klan, and the Bull Moose Party.[82] That strange mixture aside—at the very least it is hard to imagine Terwilliger and Montana Knights having too much in common with the socialists who joined the NPL—Dixon never stood a chance.[83] Moreover, the *Helena Independent's* claim that both Rankin and Dixon harbored sympathies toward the Klan and that Dixon actively solicited Klan support were false, and the paper printed a retraction the next day.[84] The power of the Company, which included "a growing chain of newspapers, [and] most of the state's major dailies" ensured Erickson's victory with well over 54 percent of the vote, although eastern and central Montana, with a few exceptions, voted for Dixon.[85] As Michael Malone stated, Erickson's victory signaled the end of progressive reform and cemented the "awesome might" of Anaconda Copper in the state.[86]

A disappointed Terwilliger admitted that the Klan was "only partially successful" in its efforts to seat its preferred candidates. Montana Knights could celebrate knowing that the Klan "made a remarkable showing" and had successfully put state politicians on notice, but the real work of transforming Montana into a 100 percent Realm still had a long way to go.[87] In fact, Terwilliger wasted no time in analyzing the electoral failures of 1924. The fault rested in part, accused the Grand Dragon, with Montana Klansmen themselves. "Those who are not willing to go with us with their whole heart and soul and vote should be asked to withdraw, and let us know that they are with our enemies," he declared.[88] Yet Terwilliger could hardly blame Knights for Senator Walsh's victory—with just over 4,000 Klansmen in the Realm at the time and around a 17,500-vote spread between the two senate candidates, the outcome was well beyond the Klan's control, as was the governor's race, with a narrower, yet still substantial spread between Erickson and Dixon.[89]

Erickson went on to win the governorship again in 1928 and 1932 as Terwilliger warned that Anaconda Copper was "doing everything possible to re-elect" the governor.[90] In the meantime, Erickson likely had few worries about Klansmen giving him trouble in the state legislature. Just how many Knights served in the legislature remains uncertain, but the available records show that the Wheatland Klan sent representatives and senators to Helena, and they were joined by Klansmen from Big Horn, Gallatin, Roosevelt, and Musselshell counties. Surely there were more, but even as Terwilliger claimed in the spring of 1925 that "all adverse legislation was carefully watched and killed" (he never mentioned what that legislation was), he admitted the small numbers of Klansmen in the legislature forced the Realm to take a "defensive" posture.[91] The situation remained unchanged in 1928 as Terwilliger brushed aside the Butte Kligrapp's proposal that legislators pass a law mandating all teachers be native-born and educated in public schools, because such legislation had next to no chance of passing.[92] The Grand Dragon hoped that the next election cycle would usher in a wave of Klansmen in both houses to ensure passage of "real American legislation," but Terwilliger's misplaced optimism continued to be tested as members drifted away, leaving less than a thousand in the Realm by 1930.[93]

Other Battles

Local efforts in fighting Catholic influence were also important, Terwilliger reminded his troops. Most of the time such work involved clear-cut cases of supporting Protestants over Catholics in contests such as school board elections, but at other times the path to defeating the enemy took a more circuitous route. The Indian Citizenship Act of 1924, for example, did not immediately signal a troublesome development regarding Catholic perfidy. The Act may have granted Native Americans citizenship, but voting rights were left up to the individual states. In Montana, the state legislature "systematically denied voting rights to Indian people," a trend that began in the late nineteenth century

and continued well into the twentieth.[94] Right in the middle of the fray was Big
Horn County, home to the Crow reservation and the county seat of Hardin.
Keeping a close eye on the impact of the Indian Citizenship Act was the *Hardin
Tribune*, which warned that anywhere between five thousand and nine thou-
sand Native peoples in Montana would be able to cast ballots in 1924.

In response, the Hardin Klan passed a resolution claiming that giving
"illiterate Indians" the vote would guarantee political corruption throughout
the county, the state, and the nation. They reasoned that Native peoples could
be easily "exploited" to vote for the Klan's enemies—perhaps thinking of the
historical presence of Jesuits on reservations. Conceding that illiterate whites
could present similar problems, the Hardin Klan suggested that the next log-
ical step was to pressure their legislators to pass laws requiring a minimal
amount of education to vote and prohibiting outright illiterates from voting.[95]
While the state legislature failed to consider those particular measures, it was
remarkably effective in shutting down Native peoples' political influence in
the late 1920s and 1930s.[96] Regardless of the minuscule threat of Native peoples
exercising their right to vote, as the Klan viewed it, Terwilliger approved of
the Hardin Klan's resolution, noting that it was "worthy" of Montana Knights'
attention.[97]

In local contests, the Klan ran or supported candidates with mixed results.
As with other Klans across the country, education seemed to be an easy and
accessible path to victory. At least two Butte Klansmen ran on the so-called
Citizens Ticket for election to the school board in 1924. The Ticket, acknowledging the religious tension that simmered in Butte and preempting possible
questions about the Klan's influence, stated that religion should not be a factor
in hiring schoolteachers, although the three candidates admitted they were
"on the Protestant side of the fence." All three were soundly defeated in the
election.[98] After the loss, most of the Butte Klan's efforts concerning education
focused on investigatory committees such as the one that claimed in alarm
that 85 percent of local schoolteachers were Catholic.[99]

Klansmen also ran into some trouble in an election in Roundup in
April 1924, which witnessed "the largest vote ever cast in a Roundup city
election." The incumbent mayor defeated the Klan-supported challenger
by only an 81-vote margin with a total of 963 votes cast, while the "antis,"
as the *Roundup Tribune* labeled opponents of the Klan, elected two alder-
men.[100] Fifty miles south of Roundup, the Billings Klan enjoyed more success in "the most hotly contested school election ever held in the history of

the city."[101] The anti-Klan ticket, known as the Citizens Non-factional Ticket, targeted the Klan by running an ad in the *Billings Gazette* that asked voters to choose between a "Visible or Invisible Government" and to reject the taint of "religious or racial prejudice."[102] Another ad appeared the following day, this time suggesting that "many good men" had joined the Klan, in an obvious attempt to separate the character of the members from the true nature of the organization. William J. Jameson, who had been in private law practice in Billings during the 1920s, recalled that one of his partners had run on that anti-Klan ticket and he, and the others, failed to sway the voters.[103]

Other matters concerning education occupied Terwilliger and the Klan. Advocates for parochial schools, according to the Grand Dragon, were intimidating local school boards and demanding tax dollars to fund their schools and textbooks.[104] Whether or not this was actually the case, state legislators discussed a proposal in 1927 where the state would provide free textbooks to parochial schools.[105] Jameson, who had been elected in 1926 to the state legislature, stated that this proposal was "one of the most controversial issues" in that legislative session. "Fortunately, the proposal was withdrawn or tabled by the action of two of its sponsors," he remembered, "without coming to a vote in the legislature."[106] Terwilliger announced the legislature's rejection of the proposal as a victory for the Klan, but it was only one battle in a larger war against the troubling influence of Catholics in Montana.

Another concern of Terwilliger's was to protect girls from the supposed abuse of the Catholic Church, and that meant keeping a watchful eye on the House of Good Shepherd. The House of Good Shepherd, founded in 1889 in Helena by Father Charles G. Follet and the Sisters of the Good Shepherd, was one of two correctional schools in Montana for "incorrigible girls"; the other was the state vocational school.[107] The Klan chose a different line of attack than the APA, which "conducted salacious campaigns across the country against the Houses of the Good Shepherd" by claiming lecherous priests seduced innocent girls.[108] Terwilliger and the Realm believed that girls were being held at the House of Good Shepherd against their will; moreover, the school's commercial laundry was exploiting and profiting by the girls' labor. Finally, the school undermined privately owned laundries by offering its services at lower rates to businesses such as the Northern Pacific Railway and area hotels.[109] This "slavery," as the Grand Dragon termed it, simply enriched the treasury of the already vastly wealthy Roman Catholic Church. How, Terwilliger asked his Knights, can we "remedy this evil?"[110]

In response to Terwilliger's challenge, the Klorero in 1927 passed a resolution demanding that delinquent girls be sent only to nonsectarian institutions and promised to ensure passage of such a law at the next legislative session. Terwilliger sent the resolution with an explanatory letter to the judge of the district court J. J. Lynch from Butte, who oversaw juvenile court hearings. Lynch, clearly annoyed with the Klan's attempt to interfere with the legal process governing juvenile delinquency, retorted that Montana law allowed the girls' religion to be a factor and that the parents or guardians chose the school for their troubled daughters. In fact, some non-Catholic parents preferred the House of Good Shepherd because of the "spiritual guidance" it offered. He praised the institution's instruction and pronounced that the girls were in much better shape by the time they departed. Predictably, Terwilliger and the Klorero forged ahead with a plan for Klan sympathizers to introduce a bill in the state legislature in early 1929. By a wide margin, the Montana House passed H.B. No. 295, which would require wayward girls to be sent to a state institution, but the bill met with defeat in the state senate. Those who voted against the bill, stated Terwilliger, said that it would have the undesirable effect of prohibiting pregnant girls from being sent to the privately owned Florence Crittenton Home in Helena, a home for unwed mothers.[111] A disappointed Terwilliger also informed his Knights that critics of the bill considered the State Vocational School for Girls, also located in Helena, unstable and poorly managed. Once the legislators' concerns were addressed, however, Terwilliger stated with confidence, the legislature would reintroduce the bill and it would pass, with Protestants voting for it and Catholics opposing it. Predictably, Terwilliger insinuated that Montanans would then owe the Klan a debt of gratitude for its work in smoothing the way for such a law.[112]

Just as predictably, Terwilliger displayed not a glimmer of self-reflection in his desire to shut down the House of Good Shepherd as he and the Klan failed to consider what the best situation was for girls in need. The State Vocational School for Girls did indeed have problems. Opening its doors in 1920 for girls ages ten through twenty who had run away from home or who had behavioral problems, the school quickly became overcrowded. The girls took classes on hygiene and agriculture but spent most of their time working on a farm that helped sustain the school, since the matrons in charge contended that "Satan finds some mischief still for idle hands to do."[113] Punitive measures for misbehaving were severe, including corporal punishment, deprivation of food, and solitary confinement. Often, the matrons "made girls stand for long periods of time, sometimes with a piece of soap in their mouths."[114] Terwilliger and the Klan were oblivious to these issues. Their hostility toward the House of Good Shepherd prevented them from examining the situation at the state school. It also punctured their argument that they objected to the Catholic Church solely because of its supposed political ambitions.

1928

The penultimate battle between the forces of good and evil, as Terwilliger and the Klan defined them, consumed the entirety of 1928. Even as Terwilliger and the Montana Klan labored to make a difference in local and state matters, the national Klan began to unleash its considerable anti-Catholic venom toward Governor Al Smith from New York, the eventual Democratic nominee for the presidency. As January 1928 ushered in a new election year, Imperial Wizard Evans declared that if elected to the White House, Smith would destroy the country in multiple and nefarious ways. Knights needed to don their "armor of patriotism," he commanded, and "go forth to battle for God and country."[115] This was war. Ratcheting up the sense of urgency, Terwilliger exhorted Montana Knights "to plan your winter's work." "Upon your activity may depend the saving of America. . . . Get your forces in readiness."[116]

As it had in 1924, the Klan launched an ambitious, and even more intensive, membership drive in 1928. To bring delinquent members back into the fold, Terwilliger outlined a complicated plan where local Klan officials had to create a card (which the Realm office provided for a fee) for every delinquent member and calculate the money each member owed. Klansmen then had to visit every lapsed member and, in a no-nonsense tone, "explain the matter, secure his $3.00, leave him his dues card, or secure his resignation from the Klan." Terwilliger expected Kligrapps to send him a report promptly upon completion.[117] One wonders how many Klan officials were willing to devote energy to this time-consuming task. This assignment, along with a new requirement to send Terwilliger carbon copies of the minutes from the Klavern's twice-monthly meetings, demonstrated to Knights not only the Grand Dragon's seriousness about following Evans's directives to enlist more members but also his tendency to keep a watchful, if not judgmental, eye on local Klans.[118]

Al Smith, "the candidate of Rum and Romanism," elicited the worst fears and prejudices of Montana Klansmen. The Bozeman Kligrapp predicted "in a few years we and our families will be slaves" if Smith took office, while Terwilliger called Smith's candidacy "the greatest crisis in the history of our nation."[119] Worried about the integrity of the polls, the Butte Kligrapp asked Terwilliger to seek support from the U.S. Marshals by deputizing fifty men from areas outside of Butte to oversee the election in November, obviously thinking that Terwilliger and the Klan pulled more clout than they actually did.[120] Supporters of Smith drew jeers from Knights—the Klansman editor of the *Harlowton Times*, for instance, attacked the Democrats in Butte for holding a gathering for Smith in mid-January 1928. "The clarion note was sounded for the assemblage of the great unwashed," he declared, "the gushing over him [is coming from] the political fodder scenters and the crowd that wants its booze."[121] No doubt existed about the Kontinental Klan's point of view. Irate members wrote a scathing three-and-one-half page response to the *Butte Miner*'s defense of the Democratic candidate. The Klan blasted the editorial and the Democratic Party for backing Smith, "a Tammanyite of small education, who has no knowledge of world affairs and longs for the return of the day when he can put his foot on the rail and blow the froth off." Only editors who were Catholic or were Protestants "of the luke warm variety" could support Smith and the Catholic Church. Miffed Klansmen also objected to the "decidedly insanitary condition of affairs in the kissing of the [Bishop's] ring by so many different lips"; surely medical health officers were derelict in preventing this practice.[122] The *Butte Miner* elected not to print the response.

Montana Klansmen could count on a steady stream of warnings and outright vitriol from their Grand Dragon and from the Imperial Palace. Terwilliger kept up the drumbeat of imminent doom if Smith won, interspersed with demands to reinstate old members and recruit new ones as well as declarations meant to appeal to Knights' patriotic duty and service. "When you joined the Klan you said you could be depended upon," stated Terwilliger at the beginning of 1928. "Your Grand Dragon is depending on you."[123] "DO NOT FAIL US," Terwilliger warned the next month.[124] "The call of the Klan has come," he asserted in late April 1928. "The hour has arrived for action. The responsibility is yours. What will be your answer?"[125] At the end of almost every circular letter, his pleas for Knights to take action became more insistent. "THIS IS OUR BATTLE," he cried in mid-July 1928.[126]

Terwilliger's fears were echoed by the usual suspects in the network of Protestant newsletters, especially the *Fellowship Forum*. The manager of the newsletter informed the Butte Kligrapp, Albert Jones, that if he wanted "a Protestant American newspaper that will bore down under the hide of alienism, boozeism and Romanism," Jones must immediately submit his order for the November 3rd issue. "This number will actually sizzle with facts" about the Catholic conspiracy to destroy America's system of government "with Al. Smith as the head of the serpent."[127] Jones asked the *Fellowship Forum* to rush his order: "We are so far away and this town needs to be woke [*sic*] up."[128] Other Protestant publications sought to take advantage of the charged political climate: the Society of Protestant Americans, the Rail Splitter Press, the American Publicity League, and the International Protestant Foundation offered more anti-Catholic propaganda, the latter claiming that "Rome is now driving desperately for the White House" and, with no sense of irony, that "intolerance is no part of Protestantism."[129]

While Jones was pondering whether or not to pay the $25 for a life membership to the International Protestant Foundation, his colleagues in Butte could count on at least one resident who despised Smith as much as they did—seventy-one-year-old Mrs. D. Cohn, who had been a writer for the APA's *Examiner* in the 1890s and was a frequent correspondent with Terwilliger. Addressing her letters to the "Brothers of America," Mrs. D. Cohn kept him posted on local conditions, complained about the number of Catholics in Butte, and decried the "Protestants [who] are going to sleep at the switch." Often, she would send Terwilliger gifts. On one occasion, she gave him a miniature replica of a little red schoolhouse, and, after the 1928 election, she sent him a small statue of Al Smith in a coffin ("where he belongs," applauded Terwilliger). The Grand Dragon assured Cohn that the Klan was present in Butte "to give Protestants and real Americans a fair deal"—a sentiment that may have given her some comfort, but not much else.[130] Terwilliger mentioned to Jones that he believed her heart was "in the right place" and suggested that "some of the boys" visit her now and then to let her know the Klan cared.[131]

As election day drew nearer, the Grand Dragon urged Montana Knights to organize committees to make certain all Protestants voted (how this was to be accomplished was left unsaid) and to observe the polls to ensure a fair count.[132] Just how many Knights answered Terwilliger's call is unclear, but they need not have worried since Republican Herbert Hoover swept to victory nationwide. Smith even lost the Democratic stronghold of the South—five southern states chose Hoover over the Catholic governor of New York. In Montana, Hoover took all but three counties by a healthy margin, and Senator Burton Wheeler suspected that the Montana Klan's campaign against Smith played a significant role in some Democrats' dissatisfaction with the nominee.[133]

What Next?

An ecstatic Terwilliger congratulated his Knights for their "excellent work during the campaign" and said Smith's defeat proved that the Klan was responsible for "shaping and moulding [sic] the national mind" toward 100 percent Americanism.[134] Hardly allowing time for Knights to savor their victory, Terwilliger posed a question to them immediately after the election: What next? He already knew the answer. The Klan may have won this particular battle against Smith, but the larger war still raged. Enemies of the Klan and the United States still existed and were plotting "perhaps a more insidious and dangerous attack upon our ideals and our institutions."[135] Montana Klansmen, Terwilliger reminded them, were still obligated to fulfill their oaths to fight those enemies—the fate of the country rested on their shoulders. But Klansmen had heard this story before. For those hoping for a period of calm after the frenzy of the Smith campaign and a break from the added degree requirements, membership drives, and other demands of the Realm and Imperial headquarters, Terwilliger's command to gird themselves for the next assault must have sounded exhausting.

Not to Terwilliger, who continued to take aim at the Catholic Church. One can sense his desperation to revive the Realm from its slow downhill spiral as he grasped for ways to motivate Klansmen. "Does anyone doubt that every Catholic in America was COMMANDED to vote for Smith?" "Will [the church] declare that the will of the pope [sic] is superior to the constitution and laws of the United States?" Will the church demand "that none but a Roman Priest can perform a valid marriage ceremony?" Will the church assert that it has an exclusive "right to control education of the children?" The Catholic Church, Terwilliger cried in late December 1928, "is attempting to kill the Klan through Romanized legislatures and through the Courts." "Men, this challenge of the Beast is hurled in the face of every true man and woman. We must rally to all points on the front lines."[136]

It did not work. A month into the new year, Terwilliger tried to stoke anti-Catholic hostilities with a proposed series of lectures by Reverend W. M. Pysher, an expert on conditions in Mexico, according to the Grand Dragon of Nebraska. Pysher had embarked on a speaking tour of western states and was eager to give several lectures in each Montana town about Mexico and the church's grip on the Mexican government and people.[137] All that Pysher required was a venue for the talk and proper advertising. Over two months later, to the dismay of Terwilliger, no Montana Klans had yet expressed any interest. "He can do your community and your Klan an immense amount of good," pleaded the Grand Dragon. "Please discuss this matter."[138] Another two months passed, but Montana Knights remained indifferent.[139] Terwilliger attempted again to generate some interest, adding that, as extra incentive, Pysher would bring with him "some Mexican musicians" to attract an audience. The effort fell flat, in part because Pysher kept changing the terms from assuming all of the costs of the lecture tour himself to demanding lecture fees plus daily expenses. Terwilliger's growing irritation with Pysher aside, Montana Klansmen could not have cared less, with the possible exception of Butte's Kligrapp, Albert Jones, who decried any effort to "reduce Mexico to priestly slavery and industrial feudalism."[140] Mexico was too far away to generate any enthusiasm; besides, anti-Catholic agitation, especially on the heels of the 1928 election, had likely reached its saturation point with most Montana Knights.

Yet the memories of the Al Smith campaign and the Klan's battle against Catholicism lingered after 1928, with a new white supremacist twist. Imperial Wizard Evans, who claimed that unscrupulous "negro-loving" Republicans and even some Democrats in the South, who should have known better, had sought to "use negro votes" to try to elect the governor of New York to the presidency. Until the Klan expelled those traitors, thundered Evans, white supremacy in the South would remain imperiled.[141] The concern, if not outrage, that African Americans supported Smith, instead of realizing that "the negro has had no better friend" than the Ku Klux Klan, also captured the Butte Kligrapp's attention.[142] He shared with Terwilliger just before the election a story he had heard in the local Republican headquarters about a "straw vote" for president that took place on a train. An anonymous traveler had witnessed the event and told the Republicans in Butte that the observers—it was not clear who conducted the election or who counted the votes—"watched the colored vote very close." Twelve out of fourteen African Americans had cast their lot for Smith; the other two chose Hoover. The reason given, relayed the Kligrapp, was "on account of the Klan."[143] No further explanation was given.

Terwilliger was already on board. In the same official circular in which Terwilliger attacked the Catholic "Beast," he also made his most blatant comments about upholding white supremacy. "The Klan must train, educate, improve and enlist the white people of America . . . White civilization SHALL be maintained," he bellowed.[144] Yet Terwilliger's remarks seemed almost scripted as he was trying to inspire Klansmen to choose anything from the Klan menu of bigotry for their next course. He likely did not care what they chose, as long as they became excited about something and that excitement would translate into increased membership numbers. That Klansmen were racist was hardly surprising—"inter-racial marriages," declared one Montana Klansman in the national Klan's primary newsletter, the *Kourier*, bred criminality and immorality, which was why "God demanded a pure race"—but they may have already believed that maintaining white civilization was not a convincing rallying cry in a state that was over 96 percent white.[145]

Whether or not the United States should join the Permanent Court of International Justice, or the World Court as it was commonly called, was another topic Terwilliger occasionally broached in his official circulars, and Imperial Wizard Evans made it the highlight of his lecture tour in 1930. Speaking to audiences of around three hundred in Great Falls and five hundred in Kalispell, Evans bemoaned the fact that both Montana senators were Catholic. He said that Walsh, running for another term, was the most problematic because of his support for the World Court. Joining could drag America into another European war, claimed Evans, while Terwilliger wondered out loud if membership would jeopardize American independence.[146] On the eve of the general election of 1930, Terwilliger expressed his regret that the Republican Party seemed solely focused on "the wet and dry issue" for the US Senate race between Democrat Thomas J. Walsh, running for his fourth term, and Republican Albert J. Galen. Both were Catholics, but Walsh was clearly the bigger danger because of his support for the World Court and his advocacy of "Roman Catholic views." In such a situation, Terwilliger reminded his Knights, it was their duty to vote for the best candidates possible, even if they must "choose the lesser of two evils."[147] But even Klansmen nationwide expressed little interest in the subject.[148]

And this was Terwilliger's dilemma: when enemies failed to materialize, he created new ones; when the presumed threat dissipated, he moved on to the next battle. For Montana Klansmen, however, Terwilliger's concerns were academic—the World Court was a distant issue argued over by faceless politicians in the nation's capital, hardly relevant in Montanans' daily lives, and white supremacy was never in question in Montana communities. Immigration and Prohibition were non-issues for most by this point—the Immigration Act of 1924 had tightened the valve controlling the intake of Europeans, and the repeal of the state's Prohibition law signaled the eventual acceptance of distilling, marketing, and drinking alcohol. Finally, an Al Smith presidency had been thwarted and the White House saved from the menace of the Catholic Church. Through the 1920s, as Terwilliger talked politics and membership numbers, local Klansmen listened but also forged their own paths. Klansmen in three of those communities, Butte, Roundup, and Harlowton, are the subject of the next chapter.

CHAPTER 4

Three Communities—Butte, Roundup, and Harlowton

Let us cheer for home and country,
As the Klansmen pass along;
Let them know our hearts are with them
As we sing this cheery song.

They are gathered from the hillside,
They are gathered from the glen
And our Country finds them ready
At the stirring call for men.

"Keep the Crosses Burning," c. 1924

A mong the over 5,100 Montana Knights gathering from hillside and glen were those who lived in Butte, Roundup, and Harlowton. There was no special reason why Kleagles entered these particular communities in the early 1920s other than the command from Imperial headquarters to establish Klans everywhere they could, beginning in the county seats. The availability of a membership list in each of these three communities, however, allows for a better understanding of who Montana Knights were, and, for Butte, a rich trove of archival materials, such as minutes from meetings and letters, adds greater depth to its story. These Knights' experiences and activities varied because of the unique economic, social, and cultural context of the communities in which they lived.[1] Ultimately, those experiences would determine the life span of the local chapters in unexpected ways.

Butte: Kontinental Klan No. 30

Klan officials must have felt some apprehension entering Butte even after the trouble between a Kleagle and a local woman in 1921 had dissipated. After all, Sheriff Larry Duggan had made no secret of his attitude toward the Klan that year and again in 1923: "Our men have orders to shoot any Ku Kluxer who appears in Butte."[2] Regardless, the second attempt to usher Butte into the Realm fared better. The Kleagle, presumably a different one, approached Butte more quietly and convinced leading members of the community to become charter members. This list included a lawyer, two managers of large department stores, the president of Montana Motors, an accountant, and the manager of Western Fuel.[3] After receiving its charter a few months after the Realm officially organized, the Kontinental Klan welcomed another 195 residents who joined between 1923 and 1929.

Yet attendance records never came close to reflecting that number, as men joined at various times and drifted in and out of the order, perhaps participating in the naturalization ceremony and then losing interest. The Kligrapp's records reveal that the highest numbers of members in good standing—those who paid their dues on time—were in 1924 and 1925, with 93 and 83 members respectively. Attendance records tell a different story, as just over a quarter of those members showed up to the twice-monthly meetings.[4] The number of members in good standing took a precipitous dive in 1926 and 1927, dropping by almost half. It is unclear why membership dropped so dramatically, although the reality of the unfavorable situation in Butte may have convinced some members that joining was a futile effort. The year 1926 might have spelled the end of the Kontinental Klan. Attendance was so low in February (7 attended) and early March (8 attended) that one member suggested that meetings be held once, instead of twice, a month. In July, the Kligrapp noted that there were "not enough members to hold [a] meeting."[5] Strikingly, even the specter of Al Smith in the White House failed to regain those lost members as the average number of Knights in good standing through 1928 held at just over 48, although the Kontinental Klan was able to reinstate 15 members in the fourth quarter, just before the general election, the highest number of reinstatements recorded.[6]

Butte Knights hailed from a variety of socioeconomic backgrounds, but the most interesting revelation is that Klansmen were vastly underrepresented in mining, Butte's dominant industry. Moreover, of the twenty-six Knights who worked in the mines, less than half worked for the Anaconda Copper Mining Company, founded by Marcus Daly, while the others worked in the Elm Orlu, a William A. Clark–owned mine. The so-called War of the Copper Kings, the explosive feud between Daly and Clark in the late nineteenth century, had as much to do with religious tensions (Daly "wore his Irish Catholicism like a badge," while Clark was a Protestant and an Orangeman) as with seeking and maintaining power over the vastly profitable mining industry. The Protestant-Catholic split played out in the Butte mines, including controversy over Daly's and Clark's hiring practices. Irish Catholics arriving in town could count on finding employment in one of Daly's mines, which spurred even more immigration to Butte and undoubtedly contributed to Irish loyalty to Daly. Clark, on the other hand, preferred to hire Cornishmen, who had no love for the Irish. These practices continued through the 1920s, long after Daley's death and Clark's effective retirement from the mining business.[7]

Two explanations could account for the relatively few Klansmen working in the mines. One was that Daly's mines still employed immigrants and the sons of immigrants. The Irish in particular constituted a large portion of the working force in Butte, along with other European-born laborers. Catholicism was the religion of choice and, certainly, this was true of the Irish. The 1926 census notes that 70 percent of church members in Silver Bow County, which was essentially Butte, identified as Catholic.[8] By sheer numerical odds, then, the majority of miners, particularly in the Anaconda Copper mines, were foreign and Catholic, which would make the mines unlikely places for recruiting members and spreading Klan doctrine. Another possibility, although not as easily substantiated, was that Klansmen simply chose not to work underground because they refused to work alongside immigrant Catholics. More to the point, a Klansman would find himself in a precarious position if Irish Catholic miners discovered his affiliation thousands of feet underground. In the hazardous depths, it would take only one "accident" to send a miner to the hospital with a serious injury or to the morgue. Realizing that membership in the Klan begged for trouble, sympathetic miners may have chosen not to join.

Of the Klansmen miners who worked for one of the Anaconda Mining Company's twenty-five mines in the Butte area, most were engineers, shop foremen, and electricians, which indicates that Klansmen who worked for the

Company enjoyed a more elevated job status and would not run as great a personal risk as ordinary miners if their identities were exposed. A different pattern emerged at Elm Orlu, where most Klansmen labored in lesser-skilled jobs. Moreover, 65 percent of the Klansmen employed at Elm Orlu joined the order in 1927, which suggests a massive recruitment effort on the part of the Klan in anticipation of the Al Smith nomination and indicates some consistency with the Protestant-Catholic split drawn decades earlier. Those Klansmen not in the mines worked in clerical positions, over double the norm in Butte. About a quarter of the men working in transportation or communication jobs drove for the Butte Electric Railway, another of Clark's businesses.

Only one Klansman from Butte, a master mechanic at Elm Orlu, acted as one of Terwilliger's officers for the Realm for one term. Even at the provincial level—Montana was divided into four provinces—only two Butte Knights served as officers, and one of them disappeared with no notice, according to a frustrated Terwilliger.[9] A glance at the slate of Hydras recommended by the nominations committee and appointed by the Grand Dragon throughout the decade suggests that the Grand Dragon and other Realm leaders may have looked to white-collar workers to assist in Realm responsibilities. It could also indicate that Butte Klansmen rarely participated in governance other than in the local Klavern. The latter may well have been the case. Salesclerks, machinists, and carpenters (anywhere in the Realm, not just in Butte), would have found it difficult to secure the money and time off work to attend the two-day state conventions or to travel to Livingston to consult with Terwilliger for Klan business. Moreover, any activities sponsored by the Klan, whether conventions or outdoor meetings, increased the chance of being discovered. Butte Klansmen chose not to risk it.

Their desire for secrecy became an obsession. Keeping the order hidden from the outside world while, at the same time, trying to nudge the community toward accepting the Klan's agenda proved to be an impossible task. The most basic requirement, a room in which to meet, created more headaches than anyone had anticipated. Kontinental Klansmen spent much of their time skipping from one fraternal home to another, adopting a new public name with each move. Members enthusiastically called themselves the "Protestant Men's Community Club," the "Protestant Men's Welfare Council," and the "Magian Society" (reserved for special ritualistic work) during the first year and paid rent to both the Scandinavian Brotherhood and the Odd Fellows. During the spring of 1924, members held meetings in the Moose Hall, but in July, the Exalted Cyclops announced that the hall was "indeed insecure," too costly, and too small. As Klansmen moved to the Knights of Pythias Hall, "considerable discussion" concerning the new public name took place. It required a committee of seven to conclude that "The Butte Men's Literary Club" would be appropriate, and they promptly ordered matching stationery for business transactions. For reasons that are unclear, Klansmen once again packed up their robes and Klorans and transferred to the Masonic Hall in Walkerville the next year. The public name changed accordingly, this time to the unlikely "Krishna Improvement Association." Their paranoia continued off and on for at least a year with occasional meetings at the Odd Fellows Hall under the alias of the "Monarch Club" or at a Klansman's home.[10]

The frequent hopscotching about town and changing names demonstrates that the Kontinental Klan hoped to escape the scrutiny of other fraternities and the community at large. In one case, members cited expensive rental rates and inadequate space in which to conduct the ritualistic work (the naturalization ceremony required three rooms), but these concerns played a secondary role. Whether or not the more established fraternities even cared about the much smaller Klan is not as important as the fact that the Klan believed they cared. Always watchful and feeling besieged, the Kontinental Klan posed no real threat to other orders—the Knights of Columbus in Butte failed to remark on the Klan, and the same held true for the Ancient Order of Hibernians.[11] Some fraternalists, however, especially those who kept up with the notices in the *Butte Miner* about the Klan's terrorist activities in other parts of the country, may have ascribed the same patterns of violence to the Klan in Butte.

The secrecy Klansmen held so dear did not fool the mailmen of Butte. Letters would show up months late; batches of pamphlets and membership cards failed to arrive.[12] The APA encountered similar difficulties in the 1890s, as editors of the *Examiner* offered a reward for the arrest of those responsible for stealing the newspapers.[13] In late 1924, Kligrapp Floyd Johnson asked Terwilliger to relay a message to the Imperial Palace recommending that it not leave a "mark of any kind that will even suggest Atlanta or the Imperial Palace or the KKK."[14]

Frustrated, Johnson ran for postmaster in Butte in 1924 to, as he put it, "stop the mysterious straying of mail" in the community.[15] He even assumed an alias to ensure that packages from Terwilliger and the Imperial Palace were delivered safely. In one instance, he informed Terwilliger, not without a hint of pride, that he would use "Knute Karl Knuteson, a real genuine Nordic name" for his next order of robes. In another case, he requested that the Imperial Palace mail a box of supplies to the post office and address the package to "August Wilhelm" so that Johnson could pick up the package without causing suspicion.[16] After Johnson was banished in 1925 "for conspiracy to upset the harmony within the Klan . . . and for marked insubordination," his successor, Kligrapp Albert W. Jones, also experienced his share of problems.[17] He remarked to Terwilliger in 1928, "I dont [sic] think it is necessary to mark my mail personal. The last number of letters you sent, the envelope was torn on the end."[18] An anxious Jones even began to wait for the mailman each day to make sure that no one else would tamper with his mail. The situation deteriorated so much that Terwilliger finally secured a post office box for the Kontinental Klan under the name of his son. Jones could use the post office box as the return address to ensure that the mail would "come back to the right hands."[19] Terwilliger even assumed responsibility for public-facing activities in Butte, such as pleading with the Butte Chamber of Commerce for permission to march in the July 4, 1928, parade ("several thousand ready to parade in full regalia").[20] The Chamber of Commerce declined the request.

Since Butte Knights remained "rather alarmed at the danger" of taking any measures that might expose the order to unwanted attention, members spent much of their time in fraternal pursuits.[21] Klansmen organized "sick committees" to report on ill members and provide appropriate gifts.[22] One committee, for instance, gave an ailing "brother Parker" four dozen donuts, some assorted fruit, and a box of cigars over a period of time.[23] Parker especially appreciated the cigars and expressed his gratitude by asking Kligrapp Albert Jones to "give my best regards to all the Boys."[24] Klansmen also sent flowers to sick mothers or wives on more than a few occasions. Jones's mother described the Klansmen who remembered her on her seventy-seventh birthday as "good thoughtful friends."[25]

Klansmen went beyond purchasing cigars and flowers for sick members. In early 1924, they attempted to establish a relief fund, separate from the Klan treasury, to provide financial assistance for needy members or for deceased Klansmen's families.[26] This was a worthy endeavor, reminded the committee. Klansmen could raise funds by giving "dances, card parties, smokers, or any other of numerous social activities." In addition, a relief box could be placed "in a conspicuous place" in each Klonklave for direct donations. Although a steadily declining membership doomed the Fraternal Assistance

Fund, unofficially, Kontinental Klansmen attended to their own. One example was the case of Klansman #10, who fell ill in late 1923 and died the following year. As soon as a committee reported that he was suffering from financial difficulties, the Exalted Cyclops instructed it to start soliciting funds. Collection efforts quickly netted $100.[27] Besides debating the merits of fraternal assistance for members, Kontinental Klansmen spent a good deal of time discussing rules and regulations and proposing new in-house rules, and they occasionally listened to guest lecturers from other cities: "Brother Terwilliger took up most of the evening in giving a very interesting talk which was heartily enjoyed," the Kligrapp enthusiastically remarked in the fall of 1925.[28] Often, an appointed member read from the national Klan's lecture series on subjects such as Christ as the Klan's role model or the Klan's obligations in the community. At other times, the desecration of the American flag, the oath of the Knights of Columbus, or the decoration of the graves of Klansmen captured their attention. Racism permeated the minutes as members jumped into lively discussions about the supremacy of the Nordic race, intermarriage between Black and white people, or "the evils existing in this community." Almost as an afterthought, one Kligrapp dutifully noted that during a meeting "a motion [was] made and carried" for the Exalted Cyclops to tell "six nigger stories."[29]

That Klansmen in Butte were racist is not a surprising discovery—it was a requirement for joining. More revealing in the minutes, however, were the Kontinental Klan's deliberations on the esoteric details of the ritualistic work, including the shortened versions of the opening, closing and naturalization ceremonies. Just what the shorter versions omitted remains unclear, but probably much of the ritualistic dialogue was excluded. Occasionally, Klansmen objected to paring down the rituals, such as the time in 1924 when the Klan naturalized two candidates in the short form. After the meeting, the Kligrapp, a bit perturbed, "commented on the manner in which the work was put on" and urged the Exalted Cyclops to reopen the meeting for comment.[30] Terwilliger, who believed in the sanctity of the rituals, would have approved. During another meeting, in 1927, a Klansman made a motion to give a candidate the initiation ceremony in short form, but the other members voted against it.[31] In yet another instance, Klansmen repeated the initiation ceremony for one Klansman who had previously received the shortened version at Walkerville, "which was very unsatisfactory."[32] Debate over the long and short versions of the rituals indicate that some Klansmen were struggling to retain the traditional elements of the order just as secret fraternities everywhere were trying to cope with slipping membership and growing apathy. Obviously, the rituals imparted some significance to Kontinental Klansmen, not only the specific ritual itself and the message it contained but also the ceremonial aspects of secret fraternalism—the solemnness, the responsibility, the secrecy, and the exclusiveness.

Despite the constraints facing Butte Knights, many remained committed to advancing the cause. Perhaps not everyone expressed the same kind of enthusiasm as Kligrapp Floyd Johnson, who wrote a letter to Imperial Wizard Evans in 1925 assuring him that "our soul [sic] and only aim is to try for perfection," but members took their obligations seriously enough to craft four amendments to their by-laws in 1924 and eight more in 1929 and to ask Grand Dragon Terwilliger for advice on each, which he was only too happy to dispense.[33] Indicating that some discord, or at least annoyance, had crept into the Butte Klavern, one proposed amendment limited a member's discussion on a topic to five minutes and stipulated that "no member will be allowed to talk more than twice on the same subject."[34] Another proposed amendment stated that charges against any Klansman must be in writing and the accused "shall have a fair trial before the Klan."[35] Terwilliger noted that the former should be a "rule of order" instead of an amendment, while the latter was already provided for in the Constitution. Much like the conversation about the long and short versions of the rituals, discussions over the amendments may have given the Kontinental Klan some sense of control over their situation. In the safety of the Klavern, they felt free enough to invest their time in the minutiae of rules and regulations, as well as to discuss broader questions of what belonging to the Klan meant and the responsibilities it entailed.

As membership dwindled by the mid- to late 1920s, meetings assumed a more relaxed air. Members may have conducted the initiation ceremony in the long form, but they tended to use the short form of the closing ceremony. Often, a banquet followed the meeting, and the Kontinental Klan and the Jefferson Klan at Whitehall held joint gatherings with greater regularity, so long as there was no conflict with Masonic meeting nights.[36] Refreshment committees began to replace political ones, as the two Kligrapps discussed the cost of hot dogs, pickles, and cigars. The appeal of belonging did not diminish for Kligrapp Albert Jones. In 1931, two years after the Kontinental Klan had disbanded, he wrote a letter to Terwilliger hoping for a bit of fraternal benevolence in finding Jones's brother a job. He also wanted to purchase the January *Kourier*. Ever cautious, Jones requested that the Imperial Palace send the magazine "under a plain cover" and without the "letter K 30" after his name.[37] Butte may have forgotten about the Ku Klux Klan, but the former Kligrapp still yearned for the camaraderie belonging had provided.

Roundup: Roundup Klan No. 18

Created in 1911, Musselshell County evolved in much the same way as their eastern and central neighbors, with cattlemen settling in the region followed by "an insane stream" of homesteaders, among whom were at least nineteen Klansmen.[38] While raising stock and farming remained vital sources of employment after the turn of the century, coal mining soon dominated the economy. This began when scouts from the Chicago, Milwaukee, and St. Paul Railway discovered a rich vein of coal in the Bull Mountains near the town of Roundup. The Milwaukee quickly organized the Republic Coal Company, and two years later its Number Two mine, operating a few miles south of Roundup in Klein, was "producing between 2,000 and 3,000 tons of coal a day."[39] Republic was soon joined by the Roundup Coal Company, which opened the Number Three mine just west of the town and was considered to be "the largest commercial mine in Montana" by the end of the decade.[40] While smaller mines cropped up in the region, one of them owned by a Klansman, the two largest remained Republic's Number Two and Roundup's Number Three mines. Recently discovered oil fields added to the belief (and hope) that Roundup was the "Miracle City of the Musselshell."[41]

By 1920, around three thousand residents called Roundup home.[42] Immigrant workers, attracted to the promise of jobs and the creation of communities, settled in Camp Three, close to the Roundup Company's mine, and in Klein, near the Republic's Number Two mine.[43] The largest ethnic group came from Yugoslavia (Croatians and Slovenians), although plenty of other foreign-born made their home in the area—almost one-fifth of the white population in Musselshell was born outside of the United States.[44] Anna Zellick, a daughter of Croatian immigrants who settled near Lewistown but whose family often visited Roundup, remembered that South Slavs were seen "as social inferiors" by Anglo-American whites, and those who lived in "uptown Roundup regarded themselves as superior to those living in Camp Three and other South Slav settlements."[45] The geographic division between the immigrant community that lived near the mining camps and the native-born whites who resided in Roundup proper may have contributed to the greater visibility of the Ku Klux Klan once it arrived, as compared to Butte. Roundup

Klan No. 18 likely did not worry about stolen mail or repercussions for burning crosses. Yet that confidence in their status as a secret organization would take a hit by mid-decade.

The Ku Klux Klan arrived in Roundup to organize a local branch in the summer of 1922.[46] Editor Alfred W. Eiselein of the *Roundup Record* frankly hoped that the effort would fail, but he admitted that some men "of high character and good reputation" might be attracted to the Klan's program.[47] Paying no heed to Eiselein's plea, a number of prominent men, including some "big politicians and doctors," were among the over 280 Knights to take the oath.[48] "Most of those," claimed one resident, only joined "for the business thing [and] most of them dropped out."[49] Although that claim cannot be verified, an impressive number of Roundup's leading citizens donned the hood and robe, including attorneys (one of whom became the county attorney in 1924 and served as an officer of the Realm under Terwilliger), a district judge who also owned the Independent Mining Company, the local mortician (an assistant recalled finding Klan robes in the basement), a manager of a drug store, several doctors, the owner of one of the largest clothing stores in Roundup, and the "Boss" of the Number Three Mine.[50]

Of the Knights who lived in the Roundup area, at least forty-three worked for mining companies, around half indicating their place of work on the census. No pattern emerged, unlike in Butte, where many Knights were employed by the Protestant-friendly Elm Orlu. About one-third who worked for mining companies identified themselves as superintendents, clerks (two as chief), bookkeepers, electricians, and master mechanics. The largest number of Roundup Klansmen were employed in the trades, such as sales, dry goods, retail, real estate, and banking, including the president of the Roundup National Bank and the vice president of Citizens Bank. A greater percentage of Roundup Knights favored working as white-collar professionals, such as attorneys, ministers, doctors, and dentists, than in either Harlowton or Butte.[51] Many Klansmen were civic leaders and enthusiastic boosters of Roundup, and most were married with children. The 1930 census revealed that thirty-eight Knights served in World War I and were joined by the South Slavs, who "were among the first to join" the US military when war began.[52] Two Knights fought in the Spanish American war.

Like other Klansmen who held multiple memberships in secret fraternities, Roundup Knights preferred the Masonic orders above all others. At least seventy-five attended Masonic meeting nights; others participated in the Independent Order of Odd Fellows, followed by the Knights of Pythias, Benevolent and Protective Order of Elks, and Loyal Order of Moose. Knights served as top officers in both the IOOF and the Knights of Pythias. Yet it was the Masonic connection that captured the attention and the imagination of Roundup residents. Chat Oliver, who grew up in Roundup, recalled overhearing a conversation between two women in which one confided to her friend that "all Masons were Klansmen." Oliver ran home, rummaged through the house, and searched the closets for evidence of Klan membership (which he did not find) since his father was a Mason.[53] Louise Rasmussen said that her father, Alfred W. Eiselein, thought that the Masonic Lodge was behind the Klan. He had a point. Over one-third of the Master Masons of United Lodge No. 71 paid dues to Roundup Klan No. 18.[54] A few Klan members paid Eiselein a visit and threatened to boycott the *Roundup Record* to the point of financial collapse if he refused to join the order. Eiselein, a Master Mason himself, refused. "He was never an active Mason after that," his daughter remembered.[55]

Rasmussen also observed that religious tensions were already simmering in Roundup when the Klan appeared, fueled in part by the influx of South Slav coal miners and other workers who brought with them a deep sense of community as well as a devotion to the Catholic faith. Antagonism emerged even between the children who attended the public and parochial schools, Joe Vicars recalled, while Rasmussen stated, "They didn't even play baseball together."[56] Religious differences melded with parental concerns. Oliver remembered that he and his friends had to be "careful of who they associated with," since they were not allowed to play with the miners' kids. Suspicion and "bad feelings" filtered through the town as residents recalled the hostility between Protestants and Catholics and even, in one instance, an attempt to "burn the Catholic church down."[57] These overlapping memories and others suggest not only the intensity of the religious split in Roundup but also that residents recognized that the Ku Klux Klan exacerbated those divisions.

Religious tensions were far more visible than racial issues, because African Americans were deliberately kept out of Roundup after dark.[58] A sundown town, Roundup forced Black porters who worked on the Milwaukee Railway to lodge in nearby Lavina and return the next morning to work.[59] A married couple who had grown up in Roundup affirmed the town's racial bigotry as they remembered a sign posted outside of town that declared, "Nigger, don't let the sun set on you in Roundup."[60] Although they could not recall if the

Klan was responsible for erecting the sign, it hardly mattered. Even those who opposed the Klan accepted the racial prejudices of the larger culture. Referring to Lothrop Stoddard's *The Rising Tide of Color*, editor Eiselein of the *Roundup Record* agreed with Stoddard's basic premise—that the laws of nature gifted whites with superior intellect and physical capabilities, while "yellow" and Black people were forever doomed to live a subservient existence. "Triumphant" whites, added Eiselein matter-of-factly, would always dominate the world.[61] The census reflected the grim racial reality of Roundup—out of a population of just over twelve thousand in Musselshell County, the only Black residents listed in 1920 were two women, who likely worked as domestic servants and, in 1930, one Black man and no women.[62] Three Japanese people were the only Asians present in 1920, and they had left by 1930.

The divisions in Roundup were exploited not only by the Klan but also by "that other outfit," remarked Joe Vicars, the Royal Riders of the Red Robe, the secret fraternal home for white Protestants born outside of the United States. Organizing for the Riders depended upon local Klansmen to assist in identifying worthy members, as Supreme Ragon and local attorney Stephen Tighe relayed to a Klansman who had requested more information about creating a chapter in Butte in the spring of 1924. Tighe was pleased to report that the Riders had "gotten a fair start" in the community. "It will be only a matter of a short while before their influence will be felt throughout the state," he assured the Knight from Butte.[63] While that prediction fell short, the activities of the Riders and the Klan in Roundup provided a combination of excitement and terror for at least two boys.

One late night, Chat Oliver, who admitted that he was grateful for the Klan because of the thrills and mystery its presence provided, decided to investigate a Riders' outdoor meeting with a friend. The boys crawled to the edge of the meeting site on their bellies and saw a huge burning cross emitting a reddish glow. (Oliver attributed this to the oil the Riders used on the cross instead of gasoline.) Around the cross, the Riders were "doing ritualistic things." Eager to explore some more, the boys started to creep closer, but the Riders spotted the intruders and, "waving their swords," chased Oliver and his friend away.[64] Another time, away from the watchful eyes of his parents and out with friends, Oliver furtively lit a cigarette and his friends warned him that "the Klansmen will kill you" if they found out he was smoking. Such a minor infraction would have hardly stirred Knights' ire, but there was no denying

that the Klan's violent potential had filtered into the larger culture and distilled into a single potent lesson for these boys—stepping out of line could
have consequences, real or imagined.

In any case, the Klan in Roundup was more interested in staging dramatic
appearances than in policing the antics of local children. In February 1923,
for instance, Roundup Knights silently slipped into the concluding ceremony
of Dr. L. H. Thurston's funeral, performed a short ritual, left flowers, and
then departed while surprised onlookers watched. Up to that point, reported
the *Roundup Record*, only rumors of the Klan's presence existed.[65] Honor-
ing Dr. Thurston again on Memorial Day, eighteen Knights wearing "flowing white robes and hoods" appeared at the city cemetery, laid a cross of red
flowers by his gravesite, and held a brief ceremony.[66] Just over a month later,
several hundred Klansmen celebrated July 4, as did other Klans across the
Realm, since it was a perfect opportunity to showcase their patriotism to a
wide audience, by lighting a "huge fiery cross on the cliffs" near town as well
as providing plenty of fireworks and bonfires.[67]

The July 4 spectacle, especially since it included the initiation of close to
one hundred new members, offered the perfect antidote to the other big event
scheduled on that day—the boxing match between reigning world heavy-
weight champion Jack Dempsey and challenger Tommy Gibbons in Shelby,
Montana. Roundup Klansmen expressed moral outrage at the proposed match
and sent letters to other Klans in the Realm urging them not to attend. What
they objected to was not the sport itself—Montana had recently legalized
boxing—but the participants.[68] As reported by the national Klan's *Imperial
Nighthawk*, the Roundup Klan accused Dempsey of being a "slacker" who
had not fought in World War I, and Gibbons was a member of the Knights of
Columbus. Which character lapse was worse was unclear. The *Imperial Nighthawk* quipped that Montana did not need this kind of advertising and that
Roundup Klansmen cared little about "which of the scrappers gets killed."[69]
Montana Klansmen may or may not have attended—this was a prize fight after
all, and Shelby financiers had built a forty-thousand-seat arena in anticipation
of making 1–1.4 million dollars. But "the Shame of Shelby," as the Roundup
Klan put it, proved to be a financial fiasco with promoters losing hundreds of
thousands of dollars and contributing to several bank failures.[70]

In the meantime, the Roundup Klan continued to plan their activities for
the remainder of 1923. At the end of the summer, Klansmen hoped to reserve
a special train to Lewistown for what Lewistown Klan No. 8 promised would

be a spectacular naturalization ceremony. Knights needed only to purchase in advance 125 round-trip tickets, and they could travel in style. As an added incentive, the musically minded among them could bring their instruments and entertain the Roundup party with a "musical session to and from Lewistown."[71] Forced to drive instead, Knights climbed into fifty cars to make the seventy-six-mile journey to Lewistown, assisted by "lights along the road . . . to mark the way to the field."[72] Klan officials claimed that eight-thousand people attended the naturalization ceremony, where three hundred were initiated, but, as the *Lewistown Democratic News* wryly noted, there were so many people coming and going it was hard to get an accurate count. "Practically everyone who had a car" drove out "to witness the spectacle, which was what the Klan desired."[73] The last demonstration of the Klan that year occurred just before Christmas. Roundup Knights, perhaps joined by the Riders and out-of-town guests, although that is unclear, held a magnificent dance (by invitation only), as reported in the *Roundup Record* and the *Billings Gazette.* "One of the largest dancing crowds assembled since the benefit dances of the late war period," gushed the Billings paper, where over six hundred attendees marveled at the display of fiery crosses decorating the dance hall. The centerpiece, a giant cross "illuminated with crimson electric globes," complemented the smaller crosses that "were suspended from the rafters."[74]

What is notable about these two incidents was Klansmen's sheer confidence in their standing in Roundup. They may not have been able to secure that special train to Lewistown, but they did feel free to publicly issue the call in the first place. When it failed, they were still able to muster enough support to send fifty cars full of Klansmen, presumably without the bulky musical instruments, to the naturalization ceremony. The organizers of the Christmas party and the attendees, who made up considerably more than one-fifth of the adult population of Roundup, enjoyed a pleasurable evening that included a lunch served at midnight and no hostile interference from their opponents.

That situation changed by mid-decade, in part due to the Knights of Columbus. Perhaps in reaction to the Klan's arrival in 1922, the Knights of Columbus organized its first council in Roundup in the spring of the following year.[75] While the exact date is unknown, Catholic Knights broke into the Masonic meeting hall and stole partially filled Klan membership lists. Louise Rasmussen remembered the break-in, and both she and Joe Vicars noted that multiple copies of "The Klan Unmasked," which listed the members of the Roundup Klan, had been made. Montana US District Court judge William J. Jameson added that the stolen membership list "did obtain rather wide circulation."[76] Grand Dragon Lewis Terwilliger never mentioned the break-in in the available official circulars, but one can imagine his consternation about the security lapses and exposure of the Roundup Klavern.

Klansmen and Riders had more serious concerns to worry about as the 1920s wore on. The coal industry had begun to suffer by mid-decade, Anna Zellick has explained, as "competition from other sources of fuel were affecting the industry's vitality as well as the local economies of communities like Roundup and Klein."[77] Bank failures racked the town in 1922 and 1923 as all Roundup banks closed their doors—joining the over half of all Montana banks that failed between 1920 and 1926.[78] It was little wonder that miners in Roundup insisted on being paid in cash.[79] Homesteading, as in other parts of Montana, became increasingly untenable as drought swept through central Montana in the postwar years, and if any homesteaders made it to the early 1930s, they had to battle infestations of grasshoppers and army worms, which decimated everything in their path.[80] Altogether, Musselshell County lost around 35 percent of its population between 1920 and 1930, joining the other counties as "Montana was the only state . . . to lose population" during the decade.[81] As Alfred Eiselein admitted to his daughter, "the depression in the '30s wasn't so bad, Roundup had already hit bottom during the 20's after the bank failures."[82]

Harlowton: Wheatland Klan No. 29

The story of the Wheatland Klan begins with the creation of Harlowton in 1900 in what was then Meagher County. The crucial factor in Harlowton's growth, as was the case in so many Montana communities, was the railroad. Its arrival paved the way for the homesteading boom in central Montana, in which future Harlowton Knights were eager participants. As immigration into central Montana and Meagher County surged, civic boosters in Harlowton, including many who would later join the Klan, began vigorously advocating for the creation of a new county with Harlowton, naturally, as the county seat.[83] An intense competition with other towns ensued, but as the editor of the *Meagher County Democrat* recognized in February 1915: "Harlowton is now rolling up its sleeves and will fight this thing through to the finish."[84]

Harlowton's chances, which were already favorable because of the rise in the number of homesteaders, an increase in railroad mileage, and the recent construction of the only grain terminal in the state, were enhanced considerably when future Klansman W. E. Jones, who would become known as "the Father of Wheatland County," won the election for state senator of Meagher County in 1916.[85] Armed with a list of county commissioners who were ready to serve Wheatland, almost half of whom would join the Klan, Jones made his case before the state legislature. He met with a receptive audience. In early 1917 Wheatland was carved out of Meagher and the northern tip of Sweet Grass.[86]

The celebratory atmosphere surrounding the victory quickly gave way to wartime patriotism. Wheatland County residents enthusiastically supported America's effort in World War I. Besides approving of the school board's directives to burn German textbooks and to prohibit the teaching of the German language in the schools, Harlowton residents listened to Four-Minute Men's speeches, sponsored by the Committee on Public Information, such as "Danger to Democracy"; viewed "The Kaiser: The Beast of Berlin" at the local theater; and participated in Liberty Loan drives. The *Harlowton Times* proudly announced that Wheatland stood as the top county in the state for its part in war work.[87] Patriots, including seven future Klansmen, created a Wheatland County Home Guard for local protection when the National Guard was called into service in summer 1917, as did many other states across the country.[88] Of the fifty-eight Wheatland Klansmen found in the Fifteenth Census, twenty-six listed their military service in World War I. Three more were veterans of the Spanish American War, one of them a Rough Rider with Theodore Roosevelt in Cuba. After the Armistice, the patriotic fervor of the war years funneled back into local concerns as Harlowton boosters renewed their quest to promote their community as a center of civic pride and economic opportunity. It would be a common theme throughout the 1920s, championed in particular by the *Harlowton Times* and the Chamber of Commerce. But front and center in the effort to put Harlowton on the map were individual members of Wheatland Klan No. 29.

The first resident in the area to join the Klan was Ward Beley, a Ford automobile dealer and a two-time state representative. Beley was likely responsible for convincing other prominent members of the community to join, an easy enough task since he knew almost everyone. In the spring of 1923, in the first and what would be the largest initiation ceremony in the county, thirty-four residents became naturalized citizens of the Wheatland Klan. By the time the Realm of Montana officially entered the Invisible Empire, in September of that year, the Harlowton chapter boasted seventy-five members.[89] Among the first to pay the $10.00 Klectoken were the chief of police, the county clerk and recorder, the county treasurer, five managers of local businesses, a notable attorney, a minister, a dentist, and a yardmaster for the Chicago, Milwaukee, and St. Paul Railway. Other county employees—the county surveyor, assessor, and commissioner—would join in August, along with the sheriff, the under-sheriff, a pharmacist, and the editor of the *Harlowton Times* (who doubled as Harlowton's postmaster).[90] All members of the Wheatland Klan except three joined in 1923 and 1924, which could indicate that in this town of less than two thousand the pool of likely candidates had been tapped dry.

Wheatland Klansmen could be found in a variety of jobs—many were managers of small businesses or worked for the county, and others were farmers and ranchers. Most of the Klansmen who identified as skilled workers such as electricians, yardmasters, and boilermakers were employed by the railroads, probably the Milwaukee, although another likely employer was the Great Northern, which rolled through Judith Gap just north of Harlowton. While the percentage of skilled workers was far higher than in other western cities, Wheatland's numbers make sense.[91] The number of railroad workers—at least forty-seven and most of them skilled—reflects Harlowton's status as a major link on the Milwaukee.[92]

Like other Klansmen across Montana and the country, Wheatland Knights proved to be eager joiners. Records for individual Klansmen are incomplete, but the data suggest that at least 101 out of 191 Klansmen found time for extra lodge nights. Of those the vast majority were Masons, an unsurprising finding. They dominated the top echelon of both the Harlowton and Musselshell Lodges, as well as the Palestine Commandery in the Knights Templar. Their travels to Billings, Missoula, and Helena to participate in degree work and enjoy picnics enabled them to connect with other Klansmen (all three cities had active Klans).[93]

The Independent Order of Odd Fellows was the next fraternity of choice with twenty-six Klansmen as members, many with dual membership in the Masons, and, as with the Masonic orders, Klansmen controlled the upper tier of Carbonate Lodge No. 39. Ritualistic work was obviously important to those Klansmen in the IOOF—they often competed in degree contests, one of which culminated in a state victory in 1923. (Eight of eleven members of the degree team were Klansmen.) At least eight Klansmen belonged to the Knights of Pythias. They made an impression on Grand Chancellor Lewis Terwilliger, who remarked in admiration at the Knights of Pythias's statewide convention in 1921, hosted by Harlowton, "All our doubts were immediately dispelled. No other town of its size in the state could do as well as Harlowton did. . . . It was a splendid convention and everyone left with a warm feeling for Harlowton."[94] It also provided Terwilliger with an opening to sound out potential Knights. Klan literature had arrived in Harlowton earlier that year; fraternal joiners most certainly would have heard of it even if they did not live in the county seat.

Knights in Wheatland seemed to be the most eager of Montana Klansmen, at least at the outset. Wheatland not only sent more representatives to the first Klorero in Livingston in September 1923 than any other Klan in the Realm; it also provided the convention with the temporary chair, County Attorney W. C. Husband, who had obviously established a name for himself in fraternal and business circles to gain the confidence of those who elected him. He continued to impress the newly appointed Grand Dragon, Lewis Terwilliger, who awarded him the office of Grand Kligrapp.[95]

Inspired by the success of the Realm's first statewide meeting, Wheatland Klan No. 29 wasted little time in making its presence known in the community. Recruiting continued into the fall, as the *Harlowton Press* reported that a significant number of residents attended lectures about the principles and goals of the secret fraternity offered over a late September weekend at the Masonic Hall.[96] The enthusiasm carried over through November, when the Klan made its first and only recorded visits to Harlowton Methodist and Presbyterian churches. "While these visitors came in robes and did not tarry long," noted the Methodist Church approvingly, "they were welcome just the same," especially, it is presumed, after leaving sizable donations.[97] Finally, as an exclamation point to end 1923, Klansmen ignited a fiery cross on Good Hill, near Harlowton, a week after their appearance at the churches. The display gave Harlowton residents further notice, as if they needed any more reminders, that the Klan had arrived.[98]

There was always some ambivalence, however, about the Klan's presence in Harlowton. One resident recalled that someone, probably a member of the Knights of Columbus, had infiltrated a Klan meeting—it was unclear how— and discovered that the town's leading businessmen had joined. They did not steal the Klan's membership list as did their brethren in Roundup; they chose a different response: "The Knights of Columbus decided they would boycott all the businesses in town. They started ordering their groceries by mail through Sears and Roebuck. The local postmaster wondered what was going on since there was so much more merchandise coming through the post office than before."[99]

Howard Squires, editor and publisher of the *Harlowton Times*, vacillated between admiration and reproach. The front page article about an initiation ceremony in Alabama in 1921, for example, reveled in the veiled mysteries and secret rituals that welcomed the five hundred new Birmingham Knights into "the mystic cave . . . where they [could] sit among the gods of the Invisible Empire."[100] Yet that same year an amused Squires shared a letter to the editor that declared the Klan was "going to rule the country just as they wiped out the carpetbaggers." "This is not a warning," claimed the writer, "but good advice from a wel [*sic*] wisher. Heed ye! Heed ye!" Squires noted wryly that he was not sure if the letter was sent in jest, but "we feel sorry for the perpetrator."[101] The next week—this time the letter made the front page—the author asserted that "the Klan is coming and is going to be in power for good in Montana and in Harlowton and don't forget it. Your publishing of my personal letter and your remarks on it was uncalled for." To which Squires scoffed, "Why don't you sign your name? Take off your pillow case headgear and let's see who you are."[102]

At least in this exchange, Squires's disdain and impatience rested not only with the writer but also with the Klan's culture of secrecy. Perhaps the anonymous letters were too abrasive and coarse for Squires to digest, or perhaps he had been keeping up with the New York *World*'s exposé of Klan violence in the fall of that year. One year later, Squires kept insisting that there was no Klan in Harlowton. It was doubtful, Squires claimed, "if Sheriff Clark would allow any Kus to Klux if they were here."[103] Both Squires and Clark would set aside any apprehensions and pay the Klectoken less than a year later. It is puzzling why Squires changed his mind about the Klan (although he did decline to purchase the required "pillow case headgear.") Maybe he bowed to pressure from his colleagues and friends, or he might have believed that joining would procure more fraternal and business opportunities. It could be the case that he always believed in the Klan's mission but deemed it more prudent to publicly dismiss the order—especially given the crudeness of the anonymous letters and the murderous activities of the southern Klans.

This brief flurry of activity essentially ended the Klan's public presence in Harlowton, apart from one speech by the only Klansman who openly expressed his membership, at least as noted in the *Harlowton Times*. After heaping praise upon the Klan of Reconstruction, Reverend A.C. Canole homed in on more local matters. Canole claimed that "many of the very best citizens of the community" believed as he did. He declined to disclose how many of those citizens actually belonged to the Harlowton Klan, but he smoothly indicated that, if necessary, he could purchase nearly every item for sale in the city from a Klansman. He may have been close to the mark, considering that Knights owned or managed at least nine businesses, including three garages, a lumber store, a pharmacy, a butcher shop, a laundry, and a grocery store. Canole further conveyed in no uncertain terms that the Klan enjoyed enough power and prestige to "carry out any program" it wished in the county.[104]

Yet the program the Wheatland Knights wanted to pursue was simply the promotion of Harlowton.[105] "This is your town, my town and our town," president of the Chamber of Commerce and Klansman Grover C. Perkins implored, "let's make this town great."[106] The Chamber of Commerce operated as the primary vehicle for Klansmen to advocate for Harlowton, and it was a common one for Klansmen nationwide.[107] Knights rotated in and out of top positions in the Harlowton Chamber throughout the decade, serving as president, vice president, secretary, treasurer, and members of the executive committee. They also dominated the Chamber's working committees, such as those concerning irrigation, publicity, and better roads. In 1923, for example, over half of the businessmen who served on the committees were Klansmen.[108] Similarly, the Kiwanis Club, in which Klansmen were active participants, assisted the Chamber in championing the interests of Harlowton.[109] Squires continued to boast about the town's virtues, in the pages of the *Harlowton Times*, such as its "splendid system of schools" and railway facilities, and showed little patience with those who thought otherwise.[110] Residents were living in "God's country," declared Squires, and if folks did not like it, the solution was simple: "Move to Russia."[111]

"God's country," however, lacked decent roads. W. C. Husband and others noted that Montana "was receiving unfavorable criticism" about its highways, which would surely impact tourism and commerce. Sending delegates to the Annual Good Roads Congress and proposing new routes, such as Harlowton to Helena, occupied the Chamber of Commerce and the county commissioners (and the Klansmen who served in that capacity) throughout the 1920s, but most of their time was spent debating the wisdom of federal assistance in building and maintaining roads.[112] Reflecting Wheatland's and eastern Montana's distrust of and dissatisfaction with the state highway commission and general interference (as they saw it) with county affairs, a federal aid project to build good roads in the state was soundly rejected by the county commissioners.[113]

The battle with the state highway commission demonstrated exactly the kind of local civic pride that Squires approved of, and he urged Harlowton residents to elect "the best men available" to help the town realize its destiny.[114] Heeding Squires's call, Klansmen were only too willing to serve.[115] They ran for and were elected to city, county, and state offices. Sometimes they challenged each other in the primaries, other times in the general election. While a few notable Democrats joined the Wheatland Klan (Dr. S. K. Campbell, for instance, became known as "one of the party leaders in this section of the state"), twenty of the twenty-five members for whom political affiliations were discovered belonged to the Republican Party, a not unusual choice for Klansmen in Montana and elsewhere outside of the South.[116]

Klansmen in Harlowton not only collaborated to promote the best interests of their community but also socialized with each other at dinner parties, bridge and chess tournaments, baseball games, and secret fraternal gatherings.[117] They created and eagerly participated in the Wheatland County Sportsmen's Club and the Three-Pound Trout Club.[118] The Rifle and Pistol Club, a local chapter of the National Rifle Association in which Klansmen held top offices, competed in matches against Ryegate and Roundup, whose club had elected Stephen Tighe as president.[119] "Come out to the range and join a real crowd of Americans," urged Wheatland Knight W. L. Dysart.[120] The club also competed with "the boys"— the Harlowton National Guard unit, half of which were Klansmen.[121] If Knights wanted to contemplate civic and moral issues, they could become involved in the Harlowton Brotherhood. Formed in the Methodist Church in January 1921 by several Klansmen, the Harlowton Brotherhood sought "to inspire higher ideals and promote good citizenship" among men through dinners and lectures. W. C. Husband, for example, gave an address of "exceptional merit" that provided young men with advice on how to forge a successful life. The *Harlowton Times* printed the speech in its entirety for the benefit of those who missed the lecture.[122] Although one of the functions of the Klan nationwide was to promote bonding between like-minded members in order to champion the Klan's agenda, it was clear that a good part of that mission in Harlowton was already being fulfilled outside of the hooded order.

Klansmen were firmly in control of the most important political and civic offices in the area, and they enjoyed plenty of other fraternal and social options. The evidence indicates that the Klan in Harlowton was concerned not with stamping out Catholic influence or African American ambitions (the number of Catholics in Wheatland County was negligible; the number of Black people was even smaller), but with creating a prosperous and thriving community. This does not mean that Klansmen in Harlowton were any less virulently racist or anti-Catholic than Klansmen elsewhere, but it does suggest that in this homogeneous community, leading citizens considered such attitudes as normal and self-evident. In the context of the 1920s, when nativist sentiment collided with an expanding urban and modern culture nationwide, such views probably did not change throughout the decade.

With the exception of those last few months of 1923, the Wheatland Klan did not appear in public again. Large-scale community celebrations, such as Independence Day and Days of 49—a huge three-day festival (over six thousand in attendance in the fall of 1927)—presented perfect opportunities for the Klan to show its strength, but members evidently believed otherwise.[123] While individual Klansmen actively (and merrily) participated in the festivities— serving on planning committees and competing in the "whiskers" contest (where men vowed to refrain from shaving for about two months), obvious displays of power were considered unnecessary.[124] There was no need to impress. There was also no need, ultimately, to retain membership in the Klan. Even as the Invisible Empire waned in power and influence in the late 1920s, Harlowton Knights were hanging up their robes. By March 1927, only twenty-four Klansmen were current on their dues; the following year, that number had been whittled down to one. Once eager to be involved in the Realm, Harlowton Klansmen did not participate in the Kloreros in 1927 and 1928.

□   □   □

The Ku Klux Klan created local chapters in Butte, Roundup, and Harlowton, and each of them enjoyed a promising start, even in Butte, if just judging by individual Klansmen's enthusiasm. But their paths sharply diverged. The Klan in Butte was a Klan under siege. As Grand Dragon Terwilliger admitted to Mrs. Cohn in 1929, "We realize that Butte is the worst place in the State of Montana, so far as alienism and Catholicism are concerned."[125] The Kontinental Klan constantly believed it was under attack, and each suspiciously torn envelope only intensified that paranoia. That was not the case in Roundup and Harlowton, where the Klan could act with impunity. Yet it was the Klan in Butte that lasted the longest, with the largest number of dues-paying

members still present—fifty-five by 1927. Butte's massive membership drive
in 1927—absent in Harlowton and likely not present in Roundup—indicates
that there was enough interest among white Protestants, at least through the
1928 presidential election.[126] Perhaps the different rate of the Klan's collapse
had something to do with the level of control Klansmen felt they had over
their respective situations. In both Roundup and Harlowton, Klansmen were
recognized leaders, free to direct and guide their respective towns the way
they wished. They were in charge. Why continue to pay dues to a secret fraternity, since other secret fraternities demanded their own financial commit-
ments, not to mention multiple meeting nights? Moreover, Klansmen could
likely enjoy similar conversations at the Masonic Lodge, or the Chamber of
Commerce, or any number of clubs and organizations to which Klansmen in
Roundup and Harlowton belonged.

The role of the Knights of Columbus is also noteworthy, in that Catholic
Knights had little patience with the Klan in Roundup and Harlowton, choos-
ing two different ways of striking back at the largest anti-Catholic organization
in the country, shame and exposure in Roundup and economic boycotts in
Harlowton. The Knights of Columbus may or may not have been involved
in some of the pranks that plagued Kontinental Klansmen, such as stealing
mail, but it did not matter in the end, since the Klan in Butte was clearly in the
minority and not a threat.

Moreover, both Roundup and Harlowton were young towns, created in the
early 1900s. The men involved in boosting each town and championing civic
pride were the leaders of those towns and very often members of their local
Klans. Butte had charted a different course, with its founding as a small mining camp in the 1860s and evolving into a major industrial city by the end of
the nineteenth century. By the early 1920s, the *Butte Bulletin* felt free enough
to call Klansmen "organized assassins," and it published an illustration of a
target with a Klansman in the center.[127] This was an established immigrant
mining city that had not forgotten the deadly confrontation between the APA
and immigrant Catholics in 1894. Mrs. Cohn kept that antipathy toward the
Catholic church alive as she claimed to Terwilliger that Catholics "have dyna-
mited homes that didn't agree with followers of their darkened ages religion,"
while Kontinental Klansmen established a special committee to ensure that
Knights joined shooting clubs and learned how to use guns. The next chapter explores the theme of violence, which continued to be associated with the
Montana Klan throughout the decade.

CHAPTER 5

Kluxing Montana: From Violence to Victimhood

When the Kluxers we shall gather
In our klavern over there,
And the fiery cross is burning bright and fair;
When our foes in this land have vanished
And the Pope is in despair,
When the Kluxers Klux over yonder I'll be there.
"When the Kluxers Klux Up Yonder," c. 1923

On the night of July 4, 1923, Musselshell county attorney Charles F. Huppe, acting on a tip that Roundup "Kluxers" were holding a public demonstration a mile from town, arrived at the site to find the remains of a giant still-smoldering cross that had been "left in the dry weeds and brush to burn."[1] What happened next generated some controversy, reported the *Roundup Record*, but the most consequential impact was that one week later Huppe found himself under arrest for second-degree assault on a Klansman.[2]

The drama that played out in the *Roundup Record* and the *Roundup Tribune* over the next several months reflected the fraught relationship between Montana Klans and the communities in which they gathered. For his part, Grand Dragon Lewis Terwilliger sincerely believed the Klan worked for the common good by championing the interests of white Protestants against the "foes in this land"; therefore, Montana communities should be grateful for the Klan's efforts and recognize that it represented a force for good. But desiring that respect was one thing; receiving it was something else. Residents of those communities, including Huppe, understood all too well the Klan's national record of instigating violence and terror. So did Montana Knights. Some Knights played the victim, insisting that the Klan upheld the law and that it was being unfairly targeted. Others seemed genuinely puzzled as to why the community failed to embrace them. A few Montanans, who may not have been members, capitalized on that reputation to intimidate their neighbors. They also knew enough about the Klan's methods and secret fraternal foundation to use the hooded order for their own purposes. In the end, no amount of charitable giving or supportive letters to law enforcement by local Klans would erase the persistent stain of violence.

Law, Order, and the Huppe Case

After Charles Huppe discovered the burning cross on the site where the Roundup Klan had conducted its naturalization ceremony, a "brilliant spectacle" with "unusually magnificent fireworks" according to the *Roundup Record*, the county attorney hurried to reproach the departing Klansmen about the potential fire damage to nearby property.[3] He managed to wave down the last car, containing four Klansmen, all of whom would later testify that Huppe threatened them with a gun. Huppe, aware of the Klan's brutality in other states, asserted he only wanted to give the *impression* he had a gun. (It was revealed at the trial that Huppe carried a "wrist pin" or "piston pin" from a car engine that resembled the barrel of a gun.)[4] Huppe recalled that one of the Klansmen advanced toward him "in a threatening manner" and told Huppe to "go to Hell."[5] If he had not pointed the wrist pin in the Klansman's direction, Huppe felt certain that the Klansman would have attacked him.[6]

Three days after the incident, Huppe wrote a letter to Stephen Tighe, organizer of the Royal Riders of the Red Robe and Huppe's former law partner.[7] Addressing it to "My dear Mr. Tighe," Huppe immediately threw down the gauntlet. Huppe confronted Tighe about his membership in the Klan and his participation in the July 4 demonstration. All subsequent public activities of the Klan, warned Huppe, would be attended by representatives of the sheriff and the county attorney to "suppress any unlawful act upon the part of the organization." If a Klansman committed a crime, Huppe would consider all members of the Roundup Klan accessories to that crime. He informed Tighe that he had "absolutely no fear of your organization or any of its members," even though Klansmen had recently told him that Tighe planned to accost Huppe on what would presumably be a lonely stretch of highway, injure him, and wreck his car. Finally, Huppe requested that Tighe, for whom Huppe still had the "highest personal regards," read his letter in full at the next Klan meeting and let him know that he had done so. If Tighe refused this task, Huppe said he would have no choice but to submit the letter to the local newspapers for publication.[8]

Tighe probably read Huppe's letter to Knights gathered in the Klavern and, just as likely, chose not to personally reply to him, since both the *Roundup Record* and the *Roundup Tribune* eventually printed the letter. The *Record* also published the Roundup Klan's response to Huppe, which accused the county attorney of harboring "a very wrong idea of the nature and purposes of the Order."[9] In the meantime, Huppe had more serious concerns. A week after the confrontation, one of the four Klansmen from the July 4 demonstration filed an official complaint accusing Huppe of assault. In turn, Huppe accused the Klansman of retaliating against him and alleged that the only reason for the complaint was to intimidate those who spoke out against the Klan. Certain that the justice of the peace who issued Huppe's arrest warrant for second-degree assault on July 12 was either a member of the Klan or a sympathizer, Huppe contacted State Attorney General Wellington D. Rankin and asked him to step in (as did the Fergus county attorney, who had been keeping up with the news in Roundup and would have been all too familiar with the "very active" Lewistown Klan).[10]

The tension surrounding the incident continued to escalate. After Huppe had posted a $2,000 bond, an anonymous letter warned him that something "startling" would occur on the evening of July 27 and to "watch his step." Sure enough, when Huppe returned to his residence late that night after dining out, neighbors told him that someone had fired three shots near his home, an event Roundup resident Joe Vicars remembered.[11] Asking the district court judge for permission to carry a gun for protection on August 1, Huppe argued that the gunshots, along with the clear antipathy of the complainant from July 4 and the hostility of those he prosecuted for violating liquor laws, justified his application. Huppe may have told Tighe that he did not fear the Klan, but he was obviously concerned enough to make the request, which the judge granted. More to the point, especially given the newspapers' coverage of Huppe's desire to carry a gun, the county attorney wanted to publicly announce to the Roundup Klan that he was ready to defend himself.[12]

In the end, the state's case against Huppe fell apart. It not only failed to prove that he carried "a weapon likely to produce grievous bodily harm"; it also revealed that the county sheriff had deputized Huppe just before the July 4 demonstration; therefore, Huppe "had the right to lawfully use such force as was necessary" to ensure compliance.[13] Led by Rankin's detailed instructions about what evidence to consider and how to consider it, the jury took less than twenty minutes to acquit.[14] Huppe, no stranger to tough fights as he had also served as the Montana attorney for the United Mine Workers and affiliated labor unions, had publicly confronted one of the more visible Klans in the state and won.[15]

In the weeks following the July 4 confrontation, Huppe often mentioned the Ku Klux Klan's penchant for violence and disregard for the law. Montanans would have also known this since newspapers across the state reported on the Klan's brutality nationwide—such as the Mer Rouge massacre in Louisiana and the Klan's whipping squads' attacks in Oklahoma, not to mention the New York *World's* investigation of Klan violence in 1921. The Klan, naturally, thought differently. The Roundup Kligrapp, who had publicly responded to Huppe's letter to Tighe in August before the trial, proclaimed that only "honorable and upright men of a respectable vocation" joined the Klan and readers of the *Roundup Record* could be assured that such men obeyed the law.[16] So severe was the punishment for criminal activity (banishment from the Klan), it was inconceivable that any Klansman would engage in such behavior.

Such sweeping assumptions about Klansmen's devotion to the order (and to the law) probably raised some eyebrows. More predictable was the Kligrapp's charge that the newspapers that attributed violent incidents to the Ku Klux Klan were misinformed as well as complicit in spreading false allegations about the order. Reverend A. C. Canole of the Harlowton Klan, for example, had conducted his own "investigation" of the press's supposed bias and echoed the refrain that misdeeds had been mistakenly or purposefully attributed to the Klan.[17] Whenever "hooded bands" committed illegal acts, it "always" turned out that the Klan was innocent, claimed a lecturer from the Imperial Palace who addressed Missoula Klansmen in 1924.[18] Grand Dragon Lewis Terwilliger contended that newspapers blamed the Klan for "alleged floggings, whippings, and other unlawful activities," yet unscrupulous outsiders and even individual members could be using the Klan as a convenient shield to cover up their own crimes.[19] The most probable explanation, however, concluded Terwilliger as the Realm accelerated its preparations for the

1928 election, was that the Al Smith campaign hired troublemakers to discredit and vilify the Klan in the eyes of the public.[20]

This was nonsense, of course. Terwilliger's obsession with Smith aside, violence, whether in the form of floggings, tarring and featherings, or general beatings, occurred throughout the Invisible Empire, especially in the South and Southwest, and Klansmen, whether as part of an organized effort by the Klavern or acting outside of the Exalted Cyclops's authority, were eager and willing participants. That kind of brutality puzzled the editor of the *Harlowton Times*, who remarked in the spring of 1921:

> The Ku Klux Klan of the South is a direct action organization and while they say some sensible things they also burn down cotton and tobacco warehouses and act like bandits generally. They say they are 100 percent American; that suffragettes and women's movements are causing us to lose sight of exalted womanhood, and that insidious attack[s] upon the home [have] been made by modernists. Maybe it has, but burning and murdering is not the remedy.[21]

One wonders what "sensible things" the editor had in mind besides his concern about the impact of modernity on women and the family, but the reasons must have been convincing enough for him to join Wheatland Klan No. 29 two years later. Presumably, the Montana Klan would set a better example than its counterparts in the South.

Threats, Intimidation, and Violence

Not all Realms in the Invisible Empire engaged in vigilantism, and Klan leaders such as Terwilliger frowned upon extralegal measures. Some Realms, even the powerful Klan state of Indiana, "were generally devoid of violence."[22] But there was no escaping the fact that violence or at least the threat of violence—whether it was aimed at African Americans, bootleggers, whites who had transgressed the Klan's moral code, or anti-Klan agitators—permeated the Klan's veneer of patriotism and lawfulness throughout the 1920s.[23] Indeed, the numerous accounts of Klansmen assaulting whites who violated unspoken moral codes speak to the willingness of the Klan to use extralegal methods to secure compliance with their worldview.[24] As the editor of the *Helena Independent* mused, while praising the Exalted Cyclops of the Helena Klan as "an upstanding protestant churchman [and] a friend of the common people": "If he can keep his hooded Knights under control, and not let them indulge in any rough stuff, kidnapings [sic], whipping women, branding men or carrying people out into the woods and giving them warnings, we may be able to get along and people who do not belong nor agree with the Knights, permitted to live in peace in the same community."[25] The casual way in which the *Helena Independent* characterized the Klan's "rough stuff" not only suggested that the very specific types of brutal acts committed by the Klan were common knowledge but also implied that Klansmen could easily succumb to the base instincts for violence that had attracted them to the order in the first place. Stating that Klansmen needed strict oversight, as if they were not responsible adults, gave lie to Grand Dragon Terwilliger's and the Roundup Kligrapp's insistence that only somber, level-headed, conservative men in the community joined.

Realm officials did not dispense whipping squads, sanction break-ins to homes in the middle of the night, or order tarring and feathering of wrongdoers, yet the threat of violence in the state continued to manifest in multiple ways. The deliberate use of intimidating language, the sudden blaze of crosses on a hillside, the thundering hooves of horses carrying white robed figures, and the unexpected knocks on the door late at night had a chilling effect on anyone who already felt threatened, or at least uneasy about the Klan's presence in their community. The hooded and robed Klansmen who suddenly "stepped out of the bushes" at Greenough Park in Missoula to hail a taxi counted on shocking the driver into stopping. "I thought it was a hold-up," admitted the driver, and when one of the Knights demanded, "Have you nerve enough to take us to the Salvation Army meeting?" he obliged. Upon exiting the vehicle, they warned him to "keep right on driving and don't look back."[26] Safely alone in the car, the driver sped off, while the Klansmen quickly entered the building, handed the uneasy Salvation Army captain an envelope, and, just as quickly, "were spirited away before the spectators had time to realize what had happened." The end result for the University City Klan, besides giving a gift of $50 and a lengthy note declaring that "several hundred . . . red-blooded men" were at the organization's service, was the local Klan's successful melding of mystery and fear wrapped up in a charitable gift to generate publicity in Montana newspapers.

The Missoula taxi in which the Klansmen rode ("with the shades drawn") and other automobiles provided a modern method of transporting Klansmen quickly to their destinations, but for sheer spectacle with an added dose of terror, nothing surpassed Klansmen in full regalia on horseback. Harkening back to frightening visions of nightriders conducting unrestrained campaigns of murder and torture during Reconstruction, Klansmen who saddled their horses—as some did in Hamilton, to drop off a note at the newspaper's office announcing their arrival in the Bitterroot Valley—knew exactly what they were doing and what impact it would have.[27] They remounted their horses to visit a church in Corvallis, where they commanded the pastor to read a message warning "certain elements to 'beware.'" As the three Knights silently exited the church and galloped away, the congregation "sat spellbound," likely wondering who or what those "certain elements" were.[28]

Sometimes Klansmen favored a more direct approach, as when they intruded on the workplace of Yellowstone National Park superintendent Horace Marden Albright and not only insisted that he join the order and relay their offer to his employees (both of which he refused to do) but also demanded that he fire Catholics from the park service and not hire any more. "I angrily refused," recounted Albright.[29] In Harlowton, Klansmen confronted the father of future associate justice of the Montana Supreme Court John C. Harrison. Dr. Francis Harrison was a dentist and, according to his son John, "didn't put up with the hooded boys." When members of the Wheatland Klan tried to convince him to join, he yelled, "Get your ass off my porch," and, upon reentering the house, declared "those SOBs tried to put the heat on me."[30] Alfred W. Eiselein, editor of the *Roundup Record*, who had asserted that the Klan's violent actions and anti-Americanism rejected everything for which America stood, also refused to yield to Klansmen's pressure, even when they warned him that his newspaper would fail within three months if he did not comply.[31] The Knights' threat proved hollow as Eiselein continued editing the *Record* until 1929, when he bought its rival, the *Roundup Tribune*, and combined the two papers into one.

Albright, Eiselein, and Harrison chose to stand their ground—they had friends and status in their respective communities. So did Gertrude Saxtorph's Danish husband, whom the Klan tried to run out of Lewistown.[32] Others decided it was not worth the risk. In Hardin, a recently arrived resident considered opening a lumber mill but was approached by some men who informed him that the only way he could build the mill was to own a gun, join the Masons, and join the Klan. He decided to return to the Midwest.[33] Verbal threats and intimidation, as well as burning crosses near Superior and Moccasin, compelled a number of residents to move.[34] The editor and owner of the Moccasin *Independent* claimed the Klan and its sympathizers conspired to withdraw their advertising, leading to the newspaper's demise.[35]

Whether by verbal or nonverbal threats, the pressure to conform or else leave the area often characterized the Klan's relationship with Montana communities. Not everyone was impressed with the Klan's tactics, however. Richard L. Schaertl of the Bitterroot Valley recalled an unexpected knock on the door late at night, and his older brother answered it. The two hooded and robed figures that stood silently in the "pitch black" surely did not anticipate his reaction: "What do you want, Al and Ed?" Chagrined, the two Knights disappeared back into the darkness.[36] Similar stories of mysterious visitors filtered throughout the primarily Catholic town of Stevensville, but the Klan's most visible appearance occurred at the annual Creamery Picnic and Pageant where, unexpectedly, marching Klansmen had slipped into the back of the parade. The crowd showed some curiosity, but the Knights were generally accepted as part of the larger show. The crowd reacted more viscerally in the evening pageant that celebrated the settling of the valley, the arrival of Jesuits, and the building of St. Mary's Mission. As a giant cross suddenly burst into flames, startled onlookers thought at first it was part of the ceremony. It quickly became clear that Klansmen had lit the match. Some of the audience, seething with anger according to the Schaertl family, raced toward the burning cross to accost the culprits, but the Knights escaped into the darkness. If they had been caught, Schaertl expressed certainty they would have been lynched, "as some of the pursuers were demanding."[37]

Vigilantism was hardly a new concept in Montana, and echoes of the state's bloody past continued to surface during the 1920s, if not in deed, then in word. The *Missoulian*, for instance, issued a remarkable statement in 1921 just as Kleagles were beginning to establish Klans in eastern Montana: "We do not see why it is necessary to import the Ku Klux Klan into the state. If it is necessary to tar and feather anybody . . . we Montanans can do the job and according to our own styles."[38] The *Missoulian* may have offered this as a throwaway satirical comment, but the association between vigilante justice and the Klan was not accidental. Neither was the implication that Montanans could revert to those traditional measures to satisfy a thirst for justice or revenge. Other newspapers also connected vigilantism with the 1920s Klan but made a different point. Vigilante committees "may have been justified" in the past, editor A. W. Eiselein wrote when the Klan arrived in Roundup, but they were no longer needed.[39] Both the *Butte Miner* and the *Great Falls Tribune* concurred, remarking that vigilante methods had been necessary when a structure of law enforcement had not been established in the territory.[40] In these modern times, however, state and local law officers were perfectly capable of handling criminal behavior. The *Butte Miner* added that the Klan had no business declaring itself the "law enforcing authority" in the state, as it had seemed to do recently when threatening alleged bootleggers.[41]

No evidence has been uncovered that organized Klan groups in Montana dispensed their version of frontier justice, but one individual Klansman, who was acting in his capacity as sheriff of Big Horn County, was directly involved in one of the most horrific incidents in the state. Sheriff Robert P. Gilmore and John MacLeod, an officer for the Office of Indian Affairs on the Crow Reservation, were murdered and Undersheriff Andrew L. Dorenberger seriously injured in a showdown with "a Crazed Negro," Hardin's *Searchlight* blared on November 3, 1926.[42] James Bolin, who had resided in Hardin for two years as a shoemaker, was "mistakenly suspected of petty theft" and had been warned to leave the county or face arrest for disturbing the peace.[43] Gilmore, in fact, had promised he "would rid the town of that nigger."[44] When Gilmore and Dornberger discovered that Bolin had disregarded the order to leave, they drove to his home and approached the front door. Likely understanding what could happen next when two white law officers with guns sought to apprehend him, Bolin retrieved his rifle, stepped outside, and started shooting. Gilmore was immediately killed, and Dornberger was injured. MacLeod arrived and tried to sneak into the Bolins' cabin via the back door and was also shot. The scene turned into a free-for-all with between two hundred and three hundred men rushing to the site armed with guns.[45]

Two of those men were Ann Scally Hokanson's father and brother. She remembered that as the scene unfolded, she was a child hiding in a store with her mother, and that in response to the shoot-out, someone had "draped a rope with a hangman's noose over the big cottonwood tree in front of the store."[46] One of the men surrounding the cabin where Bolin was hiding threw gasoline on a nearby barn and haystack. Flaming arrows, shot by either "Max Big Man," as Hokanson recalled, or by the many "Indian youths [who] had prepared flaming arrows," according to the *Billings Gazette*, ignited the haystack and forced Bolin to run out his door to escape the raging fire, where the awaiting men pierced his body with bullets.[47] Not content with leaving Bolin to die by gunfire, the crowd dragged him back into his burning cabin. "There was talk of a 'neck tie' party," the *Billings Gazette* casually remarked, "but instead, the negro was thrown into the flames and cremated."[48] After the frenzy, Hokanson's father took her and her mother "to the site of the still burning barn" and to where Bolin's body still lay. It was "very macabre," she remembered, and admitted that the image still haunted her.[49]

The overzealous ferocity of the conflict, along with the immediate mobilization of the town's men, spoke to the easy willingness of some Montanans to take the law into their own hands, especially toward a Black man who had been perceived as exhibiting some concerning behavior—one Native deputy observed that Bolin had "acted queerly" and was at times "quarrelsome."[50] It is a disturbing glance into a community where the *Searchlight* could scarcely even bring itself to refer to Bolin by his name, mentioning it only at the beginning and then dehumanizing him by referring to him only as "the negro" in the rest of the lengthy front-page article that described the tragedy.[51] Hardin's residents seemed to have followed Robert Fisk's philosophy: "We do not object so much to a decent, orderly lynching," he wrote in an 1883 editorial in the *Helena Daily Herald*, "when there is a particular atrocity in the crime and there can be no mistake as to the criminal . . ." Frederick Allen notes that Fisk's sentiment "represented a sincere belief among respectable citizens that vigilante justice was a workable, even indispensable tool of social order."[52] The commitment to law and order and the rejection of vigilante justice, as previously expressed by some Montana newspapers, collapsed in Hardin.

Charitable Giving and the All-Seeing Eye

Grand Dragon Lewis Terwilliger, who attended the elaborate funeral in Hardin for the murdered officers, understood that violence would not propel the Klan to political power, nor would it gain favor in the communities it was trying to impress. Thus, local Klans across the state sought legitimacy by publicly giving charitable gifts to Protestant churches, the Salvation Army, and other Realm-approved organizations. The Klan's message, cloaked in contradictions, asserted that worthy enterprises and individuals would receive the Klan's largesse (and presumably welcome it); yet the manner in which gifts were given, always by Knights wearing hoods and robes that ensured their anonymity, was unsettling and signified the power of a national organization unafraid to use force.

To convince the community at large that the Klan walked a benevolent path and people had nothing to fear from them, a common tactic was for Knights in full regalia to enter a local Protestant church during services, walk silently to the front of the congregation, and hand the reverend an envelope containing a gift of money and sometimes a note for him to read out loud. In turn, the reverend would welcome the Klan, thank them, and give an appreciative sermon acknowledging the order's generosity. The Knights would then depart as silently as they had entered. There was nothing spontaneous about these appearances. In most cases they were carefully scripted plans in consultation with the minister, who was likely already a member. Knowing that the *Helena Independent* would oblige by sending a reporter to investigate, for example, Kapitol Klan No. 32 made an anonymous phone call to the newspaper claiming that "a startling incident" would occur during the evening services at the Oak Street Methodist Church.[53] The $80 gift to the church earned praise as well as substantial space in the newspaper.[54]

The Klan understood the value of a dramatic entrance—the initial shock, the whispered conversations, sometimes curious, sometimes frightened, that would ensue. Publicity was what they desired, and the congregation could interpret Knights' presence however it wished. While the Klan hoped their gifts would be seen as gestures of goodwill, they were also content if their presence made people nervous. Ultimately, what mattered most was that they appeared to be doing good works. When Klansmen in Ronan donated $50 to the Ronan Methodist Episcopal church, as they had heard the church was "in need," the minister, with an eye toward making a favorable public impression, requested that the *Ronan Pioneer* print his response, in which he applauded the Klan's benevolence and "excellent constructive principles of Americanism and of Christian Ideals."[55] The next month, the Mission Valley Klan visited another Methodist Episcopal church, this time in St. Ignatius, with a $50 donation that prompted the reverend to say, "We appreciate the good work that is being done by the Klansmen, and we hope that greater things may be achieved" without elaborating on what that "work" or "greater things" entailed.[56] Montana Klansmen donated $40 to the Lewistown Salvation Army, gave an evangelist "a gift of money" at a revival meeting in Antelope, surprised the superintendent of Deaconess Hospital with "a sum of money" in Glasgow, and provided "$25 in crisp new bills" to the reverend at the Methodist church as well as a Christmas donation for a widow and her five children in Fromberg.[57]

Most charitable donations, at least those reported in newspapers, were made in 1922, just as Terwilliger was organizing the Realm. The Klan, hoping to persuade the community that it was a force for good, recognized that it needed to deflect uncomfortable questions or concerns about its violent actions in other parts of the country. "Don't be alarmed," one masked Klansman informed the Salvation Army captain in Missoula in the summer of 1922.

"We want to make a donation. Don't say anything," he said as another Klansman handed them an envelope with $50 and a note applauding the Salvation
Army's work.[58] Newspapers rarely reported Klan donations in later years.

A number of reasons could explain this absence. Grand Dragon Terwilliger's emphasis on frugality may have factored into local Klans' calculations,
as he often remarked that Knights should wisely manage their finances. "Our
enemies have plenty of money," he reminded them, and while charitable giving was a worthy gesture, it should not empty the Klan's bank account.[59]
The recent run of bank failures across the state likely troubled Terwilliger,
especially since the closing of Livingston's National Bank in August 1924 had
resulted in a loss for the Realm of around $200.[60] Klans may have become
thrifty out of necessity, or they may have simply lost interest in making public
donations, since much of the purpose of the donations was to announce their
presence in the community. Montana Knights may have sincerely believed
that they were doing good works, but even the most seemingly benign act,
such as a charitable gift, was permeated with a deep sense of superiority and
contempt toward others, empowered by the anonymity and secrecy the Klan
regalia provided them.

In one case in Montana, the Klan tried to convince outsiders that it harbored no ill feelings toward African Americans, which failed to fool anybody,
least of all the Black congregation at St. Paul's African Methodist Episcopal
church in Missoula. In the summer of 1923, "seven spectral figures" entered
the church and glided down the aisle to the pulpit, where one of them gave a
brief speech: "By this visit we want you to know that we are your friends and
are interested in your welfare." The envelope they handed to the minister contained a $20 gift to the church's building and operating fund.[61] One can only
imagine the fright of the congregation when the Klansmen appeared, but the
Imperial Nighthawk made a point of reporting it as if to prove the Klan had
kindly intentions.[62] Such donations to African American churches were not an
anomaly, as Thomas Pegram notes.[63]

Sometimes, gender determined who received the Klan's good wishes, as in
Missoula in 1922. With pride and a bit of fraternal mysticism, the University
City Klan proclaimed, "The all seeing eye has seen and the unerring ear has
heard the cry of the mother in distress." This referred to a mother of three who
needed to live in a warmer climate on advice from her doctor. It was "the good
wishes of this fraternity," asserted the Exalted Cyclops, to assist those in need,
and he contributed $25 toward her expenses.[64]

Usually, the Montana Klan offered only obligatory and abstract nods to safeguarding "exalted womanhood," as part of a long list of Klan principles, announcing the arrival of the organization in a community.[65] Key here was whether the woman was worthy of the Klan's benevolence and protection, as was the case in Missoula. Was she honorable? Virtuous? Grand Dragon Terwilliger expressed some doubt in a much more complicated situation in 1927.

Late that year, a letter from "a broken hearted mother," Mrs. Clare Rawlings of Butte, found its way to Terwilliger. Rawlings, as she told her tale, wanted to retrieve her son from a woman who had adopted him and who, Rawlings claimed, was physically abusing him, keeping him in filthy conditions, and threatening to kill him.[66]

Complicating matters for Terwilliger was that Rawlings had divorced her husband in 1921 and, according to reports, had lived with a man before "the officers of Livingston forced them to marry." Rawlings and her first husband were "not living right," asserted Mrs. Maggie Hathaway, the secretary of the Bureau of Child Protection for Montana, and "while they were having their good times," the state took their three children. Rawlings then divorced this husband (marrying him had been a mistake, she admitted) and successfully retrieved two of her boys from the state orphans' home. The third had already been adopted by a Mrs. Nelson in Butte. She then remarried her first husband in 1925. Now, a tearful Rawlings wanted her son back.[67]

Terwilliger tried to sift through the conflicting stories of Rawlings and Hathaway, who, although expressing some sympathy for the mother, noted that Rawlings "was a cigarette smoker [and] her fingers were badly colored." Moreover, according to an unnamed source of Hathaway's, Rawlings was incapable of reforming her life and would never be a good mother. After speaking with Hathaway, Terwilliger responded to Rawling and stressed that the Klan wanted her boys "cared for so that they will grow up into real American citizens." "We have investigated your past life," added Terwilliger, but he needed more information, and if Rawlings was "endeavoring to do the right thing now," the Klan would do what it could to see the family reunited.[68]

In the second letter, Rawlings seemed to understand what Terwilliger wanted to hear. Determined to draw a sharp contrast between herself and Mrs. Nelson, Rawlings emphasized that all she wanted to do was to "devote my life to my children." She then suggested that the Klan visit her at any time to see how clean she kept her home and how she raised her two other boys. Rawlings assured Terwilliger that her children were born in the United States, her husband was "a good man" with a steady job, and he did not drink. She alleged that Mrs. Nelson had at one time "grabbed the American flag" and "threw it down and stepped on it" in front of children and others. Clearly, Rawlings knew enough about the Klan to push the right buttons—Americanism, abstinence from alcohol, neat home, devoted mother.[69]

In the end, Terwilliger assigned the case to the Butte Klan, asking them to "quietly investigate this matter," particularly whether Rawlings was "now living a virtuous life and whether she has a good home." The welfare of the two boys also concerned Terwilliger and if they were being raised as loyal Americans.[70] How Rawlings came to the belief that the Klan could assist her is unclear, although the Klan's lofty statements about protecting white womanhood may have inspired her. She may have also talked about her situation with Klanswomen, since a women's auxiliary (the term used by the Kontinental Klan) did exist in the Butte area.[71] Nancy MacLean discovered in her study of the Klan that women in Georgia regularly called upon the Klan to assist them in dealing with domestic abuse or other kinds of troubles, many of them unable to receive satisfaction from the courts.[72] Rawlings did not receive the justice she sought. Although nothing more was mentioned of the case in letters, official circulars, or the minutes of meetings, the 1930 census reveals that only two boys, not three, were living with her and her husband.

Hoaxes and Victims

Some Montanans sought to create havoc and provoke animosities for their own reasons. Whether they burned crosses, sent threatening letters, or used blackmail, their actions echoed the intimidating tactics of the hooded order. Klan officials, lecturers, and members complained they were victims of hoaxes perpetrated by non–Klan members who engaged in criminal mischief in the Klan's name. Nevertheless, the organization still bore the larger responsibility for the range of threatening and violent behavior conducted by their members. The Klan, after all, was born out of the ravages of the Civil War to terrorize African Americans, and its campaign of violence had continued under Imperial Wizard William J. Simmons, who had revived the Klan in 1915, and his successor, Hiram W, Evans, the dentist from Dallas who assumed power in late 1922. While Evans publicly professed to seek a more respectable path by engaging in state and national politics, he could never entirely tamp down the nightriding and other acts of brutality, and some Klan observers claimed he still privately encouraged them.[73] "The very dynamics of the Klan dictated violence," notes David Chalmers. Thomas Pegram adds that "too often Klan officials tolerated violence in their pursuit" of their agenda.[74] What this meant for the Montana Klan was that Knights were often on the defensive.

Billings Klan No. 6, for instance, placed a full-page ad in the *Billings Gazette* in the fall of 1923 announcing that "so much vicious and slanderous misrepresentation" swirled about the order that they needed to set the record straight regarding the Klan's supposed penchant for violence and law-breaking. The Klan, Billings Knights argued, stood "foursquare for law and order" and "pure patriotism towards our glorious country." While "the organization's enemies" would have Americans believe that the Klan hated Jews, Catholics, and Blacks, nothing could be further from the truth.[75] The *Nation* scornfully dismissed the Billings Klan's attempt to defend itself, noting that Imperial Wizard Evans's speech in Dallas denigrated everyone who was not white and Protestant and pronounced that such people could never become real Americans.[76] The Klan's defensiveness appeared in Helena in early 1923, where Klansmen pleaded to the congregation at the Oak Street Methodist Church, "Judge not, that ye be not judged," while Bozeman Knights cried, "The Klansman is your best friend. Why kick him?"[77]

The claim of being the community's "best friend" rang hollow as cross burnings, the ultimate sign of the Klan's presence, appeared across Montana in the 1920s. Sometimes, well-attended initiation ceremonies accompanied the burning crosses. At other times crosses with no ceremonial function attached blazed for the sole purpose of attracting attention and issuing a warning, as when a giant cross "burst into flame" on Prospect Hill outside of Great Falls. "[C]onstructed of one-inch lead water pipe around which burlap was wrapped and saturated with oil" and twenty feet high, the cross burned for three hours and caused one man to grab his rifle and "rush to the hills." As he approached the burning cross and saw only a few men—no regalia was mentioned in the newspaper—he fired his rifle in the air.[78] Kascade Klan No. 19 was likely responsible for that incident, but it was a different story just south of Great Falls.

Law enforcement in Butte attributed the fifty-foot burning cross on St. Patrick's Day to "practical jokers who [were] possessed of a perverted sense of humor." The culprits left a sign crediting the deed to "Hillside Klan, No. 421" with a message: "The Cyclops orders the Kloranick mysteries to be conferred upon 4122 to 4211, inclusive. . . . You will see they are bound by the thrice binding oath and prepared for their journey through the mystic cave."[79]

A second, smaller cross burst into flames shortly after the Hillside cross. Both incidents caused a great deal of excitement in the Butte area. "The telephones in the office of the sheriff and the Miner were buzzing continually," noted the *Butte Miner*.[80] The Kontinental Klan of Butte and other nearby Klans probably had nothing to do with it. Hillside Klan No. 421 did not exist. The number of Klans in the state varied, but it likely went no higher than Ravalli County Klan No. 47 (which was probably a combination of the Hamilton and Stevensville Klans). Whoever wrote the sign also knew just enough about the Klan to guess some of the secret fraternal terminology.

While law enforcement passed the incident off as a joke and tried to calm residents' nerves, they also had to contend with anonymous letters that were far more personal and threatening. The *Anaconda Standard* warned in early 1923 that "Mysterious letters, written over the signature of crossed bones and signed 'Ku Klux' are spreading terror in Anaconda homes."[81] The newspaper reported, as did the *San Francisco Call* and the *Chicago Defender*, that the wife of the pastor for the African Methodist Episcopal Church received a menacing anonymous letter, ordering her to leave town or the "Ku Klux" would tar and feather her. Mrs. M. A. Clements expressed confusion and had no idea what she did to upset anybody in Anaconda. She turned the letter over to the county attorney, who dismissed it as "the work of practical jokers."[82] Another African American in Anaconda, "Slim," had a different response to a letter signed by the "Grand Wizard, District of Montana" with an accompanying "skull leering from a dripping-red parchment" warning him to "leave town in 24 hours or take consequences." The crude note elicited only derision from Slim. He retorted, "Those Ku Kluxers ain't goin' to get me and I'm staying right here in town." The Klan, Slim concluded, "ain't scaring nobody."[83]

In both cases, individual Klansmen may have been responsible, although it was likely the work of disgruntled racists who were not members of the Kontinental Klan. Moreover, Slim's reaction reflected Silver Bow County's dismissive attitude toward the hooded order. In nearby Lewis and Clark County, Representative Lester Lobel received two anonymous letters, one signed "K.K.K." and the other "3-7-77," the recognized signature of the early vigilantes in Montana.[84] A reaction to Lobel's resolution that called for an investigation of Prohibition officers who had been convicted of accepting bribes, the letters demanded that he cease his efforts.[85] "If you do not lay off the Rev Joseph Pope [the president of the Anti-Saloon League] and his men you will be taken out of town on a rail with a coat of tar and feathers. Signed in the sorrowful month in the sign of the Klug Kleagle."[86] Lobel stated he did not believe the Klan was responsible for the letters.[87] The *Meagher Republican* in White Sulphur Springs also reported on the "orgy of anonymous letter writers" in 1925 and that the writers, if not Klansmen, knew enough about the Klan's agenda to make the threats authentic. The editors declared that rattlesnakes "would be far more preferable" to these writers, at least snakes "look you square in the eye . . . and warn you to keep your distance."[88] If a skull and crossbones and warnings of tarring and feathering were not part of a Ku Klux Klan campaign, they certainly had the feel of one.

As with the Hillside Klan's burning cross, the authors of the anonymous letters knew just enough of the Klan's terminology to attempt to cast blame on the hooded order. The very nature of the Klan organization and the considerable weight it carried nationwide—three to four million members had joined Klans in every state and beyond, including Alaska and the Canal Zone—invited violence, or at least the threat thereof. Those who may have carried a grudge against particular residents in the community, or who wanted an avenue by which to express their racism and hostility, could do so confident in the knowledge that the Klan embraced those sentiments and, at times, acted upon them. The "dangerous character" of the Klan, the *Butte Miner* asserted in early 1922, allowed other organizations and individuals to act with impunity."[89] Even children took advantage of the Klan's unsavory reputation, as two Butte boys, twelve and thirteen years old, blackmailed a widow for $150. The note, signed "K.K.K.," demanded immediate payment from Mrs. Carrie Bennets or she would "be killed." Understandably frightened, she handed over the money to the boys, who promptly spent $125 of it on a motorcycle. The older boy regretted his actions, and Sheriff Duggan was able to retrieve the full amount taken and return it to Mrs. Bennets.[90]

The most dramatic hoax of all occurred at the University of Montana in Missoula in early 1923 when two students were allegedly kidnapped. The first student, who was a Yell Leader for the university and had written an essay criticizing the Ku Klux Klan, which prompted some threatening letters to him, was kidnapped "by several mysteriously dressed men" during halftime of a basketball game between the University of Montana and Montana State at Bozeman. Witnesses saw the four men, who wore "hooded suits of a flaming red color," shove the student in a car and drive away. After escaping, the student answered officials' questions but did not elaborate on the details, except to say the masked men took him to Greenough Park and "gave him a talking to." Two days later, the Associated Press reported that the president of the university and the Missoula police force had launched an investigation into the kidnapping. "The university people are in a near-panic," stated the newspaper, noting that another student received a menacing letter and applied for a gun permit. The second victim was a "university correspondent for the Missoulian," who asserted that he had learned the identities of some of the kidnappers. The kidnappers then grabbed him as "he was leaving his fraternity house to investigate an alleged clue promised through a mysterious telephone message." The University City Klan was upset enough about the incident to offer its services to law enforcement to capture the culprits behind the kidnapping and, if evidence warranted, pursue legal action. "An outrage," exploded the Exalted Cyclops, who also stated that the Klan was not responsible for threatening letters sent to students signed by "Tar and Feather Committee, Missoula Ku Klux Klan."[91]

About a week after the first kidnapping, it became clear that the events at the university were part of a giant hoax. Both of the alleged victims had agreed to a scheme hatched by members of the university band "to being abducted in order to arouse an interest in the student body." When hundreds of faculty, alumni, and students answered a call to meet in the university gym to discuss the recent kidnapping, the event "turned out to be a smoker with a large and varied program of entertainment for the purpose of securing a close cooperation among the students, faculty and alumni." It was, apparently, a rousing success.[92]

The presumably happy ending of the incident, which intended to foster male bonding and team spirit, must have further infuriated University City Klan No. 16. But Montana residents had already drawn their own conclusions about the Klan. They knew enough about the whippings, beatings, tarring and featherings, and other acts of brutality associated with the national Klan to conclude that the order was indeed violent, and it mattered little if Montana Klansmen were specifically engaged in such acts. Despite the Montana Klan's insistence that it stood for law and order, the University of Montana prank worked, at least for a few days, because the police, the press, university officials, and residents found the threat credible. The Klan may have protested the deception, but the violence inherent in the Klan movement would continue to damage the Realm and the national Klan through the 1920s.

CHAPTER 6

The Klan Collapses

Don't just sit back while others work; don't merely criticize;
Don't stand around and idly talk; don't ponder and surmise;
Don't say the cause is growing old; don't join the knocker's throng;
Don't say you can't, when asked to help boost work along.

Booster, Booster, Be a Booster,
Booster, Booster, Be a Booster,
Booster, Booster, Be a Booster.
                    "Boost for the Ku Klux Klan," c. 1925

G rand Dragon Lewis Terwilliger may not have written "Boost for the Ku Klux Klan," but he certainly agreed with its message. His skillful organizing efforts helped create the Realm in September 1923, and his leadership would define the hooded order's tenure in the state as he encouraged, warned, and pleaded with local Klans to understand the seriousness of the cause. Championing the interests of white Protestant Americans and ridding the state and country of its enemies took hard work. Terwilliger was ready for the challenge, as he had been since the beginning, and he expected the same level of commitment from his Knights. He would be disappointed.

A number of factors contributed to the downfall of the Montana Klan by the end of the decade. Part of the problem, ironically, may have been Terwilliger himself. His demands must have grown wearisome to local Klan officials as it became increasingly clear the extent to which the Realm and the Imperial Palace sought to micromanage local affairs. Interspersed throughout Terwilliger's steady stream of official circulars, for instance, were his requests, which became more urgent and exasperated as the decade wore on, that Kligrapps attend to the mundane details of keeping a secret fraternity together—such as the proper filing of quarterly reports. These reports (to be written on the "long, 14-inch, Form K-105" not the "old short, 11-inch form," reminded Terwilliger in the summer of 1924) were ostensibly tied to the national Klan's political success but were more accurately a way to gauge the amount of money flowing into the Realm's and, especially, into the Imperial Palace's treasuries.[1] Each report requested the essential facts about membership, including numbers of members in good standing—those who paid their dues on time, newly naturalized members, reinstatements, and transfers from other Klans. The second half of the form outlined the calculation of Imperial and Realm taxes. Terwilliger then compiled these reports from the forty-seven or so Klans in the state—the number varied as Klans disbanded or merged—and as time went on not all Kligrapps bothered to file reports with the Realm office. The result was the Grand Dragon's financial report that Terwilliger mailed to the Imperial Palace along with the Imperial taxes due. One can only imagine the paperwork in Atlanta, not to mention in Klaverns across the country.

The first Klans to hand in their reports on time made it to Terwilliger's Honor Roll—Columbus, Hardin, Missoula, and Thompson Falls were frequent recipients. Terwilliger did not tolerate delinquency, and those Kligrapps who failed to do their jobs, he warned, needed to be replaced by more competent officers in the local Klavern's next election. A late report meant that the Klan would lose its good standing and not receive vital passwords, countersigns, and other important information. "No Kligrapp worthy [of] the office" would allow this to happen, scolded the Grand Dragon. "Let us show the Imperial Office that Montana can be 100% in prompt and accurate reports."[2] It was a rare official circular in which he did not mention something about paperwork that had yet to be filed.

While Montana never reached that 100 percent—it is doubtful that any Realm in the Invisible Empire did so consistently—Terwilliger had reason to hope that the Realm could catch the notice of the Imperial Palace in other ways. In the early summer of 1924, he noted with some pride that Montana ranked second on the list of Realms in the Invisible Empire for reinstating lapsed members. Yet Terwilliger added that almost 23 percent of suspended

Klansmen "were allowed to drift off and perhaps become forever separated from the organization," thus placing the blame for lapsed members squarely on the shoulders of the local Klavern. That losing over a fifth of the Realm's membership was good enough to make second place means even greater numbers of Knights across the country did not consider membership in the Klan worthy of their time, energy, and money. Terwilliger continued to plead with local Klan officials to exert more effort to attract new members, as well as "keep up the interest and enthusiasm" of the old.[3] The following year's annual financial report noted that the Realm had increased its membership by just over a thousand, but whether those numbers reflected new members or reinstatements of old is unclear. Terwilliger, who would have been quick to share any recognition of Montana from the Imperial Palace, never mentioned it again.[4]

Terwilliger hoped that his time as Grand Dragon would be spent communing with like-minded Montana Knights, learning about and debating the finer points of Klankraft, planning the Realm's political agenda, and contributing to the larger success of the Invisible Empire. He was proud to participate in the movement, telling Knights that he had "been called [back East] for two important National meetings" on one occasion, and, on another, "a sudden official call to Atlanta" took precedence over a planned trip around the Realm.[5] "To my mind," Terwilliger mused in the aftermath of the defeat of Al Smith in 1928, "the most important work of the Ku Klux Klan is the creating of a mind in America in favor of all that is good and right and against all that is evil and wrong."[6] His Manichean view may have provided a simple yet pleasing explanation of the Klan's broader goals and reasons for being, but there was no escaping the more complicated challenge of running the Realm when local Klans failed to do the tasks required of them. As the correspondence and official circulars reveal, his constant requests to Klan officials to hand in their quarterly reports on time, to make sure that the Imperial and Realm taxes were calculated correctly and paid in full—a constant problem with the Butte Klan and possibly other Klans—occupied more and more of his time. His honor roll of local Klans handing in their reports when due grew shorter as the decade progressed. He must have been dismayed by the lack of commitment to these jobs—not to mention the lack of competence in completing them—and disappointed that he had to spend so much time instructing Klans to do the menial but necessary jobs to keep the Klan functioning.

Yet Terwilliger continued to pile on the work. In 1927, he and the Klorero's resolutions committee ordered Montana Kligrapps to serve as "information bureaus" by collecting data about local politicians and community leaders, including their attitudes toward the Klan, and to send it to the Grand Dragon's office. The resolutions committee also commanded Kligrapps to provide Terwilliger with detailed copies of the minutes from meetings, "showing all motions, names of members making motions," as well as meticulous financial records.[7] These extra tasks, assured Terwilliger, were for the greater good of the Realm since the great distances and inadequate roads—one heavy rainfall would make roads unpassable—prevented him from making regular visits to local Klaverns for pep talks. The geographical challenges of living in Montana also prevented Knights from networking with each other, which had caused many to become "downhearted and lose faith in the work and lose their interest in the organization."[8] Thus, the more information Terwilliger received, the better he could inform Montana Knights what individual Klaverns were doing. The unspoken benefit for Terwilliger, probably understood among Klansmen, was that these new requirements would allow Terwilliger to keep close tabs on local Klans to ensure they were doing their due diligence. Although Terwilliger offered to submit extra bulletins highlighting individual Klaverns' activities and accomplishments in light of the new reports coming into the Realm office, no such bulletins have been discovered. The cost of mailing such bulletins would have been a factor—by 1929 only $3.13 remained in the Realm treasury.[9]

Paradoxically, in order to run an efficient business as expected by Terwilliger and the Imperial Palace, Terwilliger had to ensure that local Klans were doing what they needed to do. All information about local Klans' tenacity, work ethic, and clout flowed upward—the Realm demanded it, the Imperial Palace demanded it. At the same time, however, Knights may have interpreted Terwilliger's oversight as too intrusive, or perhaps some were simply embarrassed because they had not completed the work required of them. It was a balancing act that proved difficult to manage.

Moreover, Terwilliger found himself having to soothe hurt feelings as fraternal brotherhood was not a given. "I regret that it is impossible for you boys in Butte to work in harmony," remarked Terwilliger to Floyd Johnson, upon hearing of Johnson's resignation. (The Kontinental Klan had actually banished him, but perhaps Terwilliger did not know this.) "The only way in which we can continue to have the influence that we deserve in the state," Terwilliger continued, "is for us to put aside personal differences and work together for a common object."[10]

Terwilliger kept trying. In the spring of 1930, he shared his experiences in a recent national gathering of Grand Dragons, calling it "inspirational." "Papers were read upon every phase of Klankraft, and the discussions were eager and intense," he declared, giving proof that Realms in the Invisible Empire were still active and ready to chart America's path forward. "Out here in the West," admitted the Grand Dragon, "we do not quickly feel the inspiration that comes from the renewed activity of Klankraft in the more populous states and cities of the East." In the next breath, he pleaded with Klans to improve their organizing work and observed that some Klans had become "careless" in the quarterly reports—at least those who had bothered to turn them in.[11] But should the Realm office be doing all of the work? Terwilliger and the Klorero did not think so. Individual efforts were critical, and individuals were more powerful and more influential than they thought, proclaimed the Klorero in 1927. "A personal attitude of pride and interest in personal and group power is the requisite for the success of Klancraft," the resolutions committee declared.[12] Several years later, Terwilliger praised a statement from a local Virginia Klavern asserting that local Klans had depended far too long on Realm and Imperial offices for help and needed to adopt a more vigorous can-do effort.[13] Surely, Terwilliger thought, Montana Knights could demonstrate the same spirit.

While Terwilliger received high praise and appreciation from the annual Kloreros, who consistently thanked him for his "faithful, untiring, business-like administration" and "pledge[d] to him our loyalty and support," some Knights grumbled about what they perceived as financial misdeeds of the Realm office.[14] In the spring of 1930, as disenchanted Klansmen continued to abandon the Invisible Empire, a dismayed Terwilliger countered charges that he was receiving a hefty salary as Grand Dragon but failing in his obligation to Klans across the Realm. Terwilliger retorted that nothing could be further from the truth, as for the past sixteen months "the salary of the Grand Dragon had amounted to exactly $3.05," after paying expenses for some travel and for maintaining the Realm office. As he stated: "Please understand that I am not complaining about this. I am perfectly willing to serve and sacrifice without salary. If I were wealthy I would be glad to sacrifice money also for the good of the cause. As it is, every cent received from the Realm is used for Klan purposes." His refusal to go into debt necessitated that he stay in Livingston, although "nothing would please me more," he affirmed, than if he could visit every Klan in the Realm on a regular basis.[15]

Concerns about financial obligations crept into the Klorero's deliberations even as early as 1924, when Terwilliger admitted that, despite his conservative approach, the Realm was not "in a flourishing condition financially."[16] The next year, Terwilliger informed the body that he was authorized to require members who had lapsed in their payments to pay one quarter's dues plus "two quarters in advance," thus sealing their financial commitment to the order. The attendees concluded that such a requirement, which would end up hurting local Klans more than helping, "would be inadvisable."[17] At least one Klavern had complained about the cost of Realm taxes, as Kontinental Klansmen voted to raise the issue at the next Klorero.[18] Paying heed, the attendees at the annual meeting in 1929 slammed Realm and Imperial taxes that were "excessive in proportion to the dues that can be levied."[19] High taxes were the reason why Montana Klans were in bad financial shape and why many Klans had disbanded, concluded the Klorero.[20]

Besides paying the quarterly taxes to Imperial and Realm headquarters and dues to the local Klavern, the toll on Klansmen's pocketbooks included the ten-dollar Klecktoken, or initiation fee, the purchase of the robe and helmet, and the extra costs for advanced degrees. Klansmen were also expected to contribute to political and fraternal funds and subscribe to the *Kourier* and other Klan-operated or Klan-endorsed publications. Early hints of trouble had appeared in 1924 when Knights rejected the *Montana Klansman*, the short-lived newspaper for the Realm, for financial reasons as well as concerns about secrecy. The cost of belonging, in other words, added up in a hurry.[21] Piling these expenses on top of demands made by other fraternities would force any financially strapped Klansman to reconsider his membership and to question whether belonging was worth the price. Many decided it was not. In late 1927, one Butte Klansman crystalized the dilemma that Montana Knights undoubtedly faced:

> Now Mr. Jones I do not want the boys to think I am trying to side step my duties or obligations, but I am not in a position to keep up my payments. . . . I have had to drop all but my Masonic order and I am not paid up with them. . . . So if the Boys will grant me a withdrawal card I certainly appreciate it then when I feel able to go on I will join again.[22]

He never did. Besides revealing that he could no longer afford to pay his dues, Orrell's choice of fraternities indicated that the more established and well-respected Masons registered a notch higher on the fraternal hierarchy than the Klan.

In fact, the membership numbers for the Masonic orders increased during the 1920s, only to decline after 1930. Other secret fraternities' numbers fluctuated, as both the Independent Order of Odd Fellows and the Knights of Pythias lost, regained, and then lost some more by the end of the decade.[23] Even for those who remained in secret fraternities, carving time out of their busy lives proved a difficult task, as the Harlowton IOOF's "Old Timers' Night" in late 1926 indicated. The "old timers" who showed up apologized for being "unable to attend lodge as much as they would have liked" and expressed hope that they could participate more regularly in the future.[24] Perhaps they did.

Like other secret fraternities, the Ku Klux Klan was competing in a losing battle with mass entertainment and other options for socializing. Americans were sampling new forms of recreation by the mid-1920s, including cars, radio, sports, and movies. These readily available and increasingly popular activities beckoned to those who wanted to keep in time with a changing American society. The Klan could not keep up. Even as the dynamic culture of the 1920s permeated the Klan movement's attempt to influence Americans via mass media outlets, new and old, as Felix Harcourt notes, the rank and file of the Klan were moving on.[25] Recreational and sports clubs were cheaper than fraternities and often offered the added bonus of socializing in the Montana outdoors. The rapidly growing network of service clubs, such as the Lions, Kiwanis, and Rotary clubs, also provided alternatives for those who desired camaraderie as well as the chance to make new business contacts, but who wanted to dispense with the time-consuming rituals of secret fraternalism.

Each week and each season ushered in different activities as men simply became too busy to give the attention to secret fraternities that they or their fathers had in the past. This trend was most notable among younger men. Miguel Hernandez states that older Masons worried about the new generation of members in the 1920s, since many wanted to rush through the introductory degrees straight to "one of the prestigious 'higher degrees' like the Scottish and York Rights," thus dismissing the established code that those degrees were earned over a span of time by demonstrating knowledge of and commitment to the fraternal mysteries of the order.[26] "Increasingly," Hernandez states, "membership in clubs and fraternities was used as a symbolic assessment of their social standing.[27] Secret fraternities had once provided a traditional rite of passage from youth to manhood and depended on a steady supply of young people to replenish the ranks. Now, instead of learning "the masculine message of the rituals," rituals that glorified and emphasized conventional values,

young men looked to their peers for approval and for guidance. As Mark
Carnes remarks in his study of secret fraternalism, "the movement was dying
of old age."[28]

The constant pursuit of enemies must have also been draining. Almost every
official circular sent by Terwilliger warned Klaverns to stand guard against
threats and remain dutiful to the Invisible Empire. In an almost desperate
appeal in 1929, he beseeched, "If we get careless about our local organizations,
it gives our enemies just that much greater chance of winning in local fights.
Boys, don't weaken our influence."[29] Yet what local fights Terwilliger meant
remained vague and amorphous. Just who these enemies were, how many
of them existed, and what kind of damage they could possibly inflict upon
Montana Knights' day-to-day existence was never clearly revealed. The Klan's
demands on their time and money required more effort than it was worth,
despite Terwilliger's plea that the Klan still had "special work to do" and that
its "principles are worthy and Truth will prevail."[30]

The community reaction to the Ku Klux Klan was also telling. The obvious ease with which the pranksters in Missoula deceived people into thinking that the Klan had kidnapped two students indicated that while the Klan
still stoked enough fear among Montanans that the kidnappings seemed real,
the hooded order was also treated as a joke, a stage prop for the larger purpose of festive male bonding in the university. For an organization that took
itself as seriously as the Klan, jokes at its expense must have been galling and
humiliating. Moreover, to wound Knights and put them on the defensive,
nothing could sting more than scorn, of which there was plenty, especially in
the mining city of Butte. The editors of the *Butte Miner* described the Klan as
a "farce comedy," a "consummate sham," and suggested that the secret order's
"conception of 100 per cent Americanism . . . appear[ed] to be largely based
on hate."[31] Butte's *Labor Bulletin* stated that some Montana residents "fear[ed]
the wrath of the Klowns" but they should rest assured that the Klan would not
be a permanent fixture in the country—it "will run its course, a cowardly and
dastardly one, it is true, but run it swiftly."[32]

That prediction's moment of truth appeared with the arrest of the Invisible
Empire's most powerful Grand Dragon, David C. Stephenson of Indiana, for
the kidnapping, rape, and eventual death of his secretary, Madge Oberholtzer,
making a mockery of the Klan's claim that it elevated white womanhood,
adhered to Prohibition (Stephenson had been drinking), and disavowed
violence. He was eventually convicted of second-degree murder in a highly

publicized trial and sent to prison.[33] The whippings, lynchings, and other brutal and malicious acts conducted by Klansmen made front-page news; they
also revealed that the Klan was not simply a Protestant fraternal order looking
out for the interests of all Americans, as it had long insisted. The pretense of
championing American principles while inflicting terror on those who failed
to meet the Klan's narrow definition of what it meant to be an American further contributed to the order's demise.

Other factors included the passage of the Immigration Act of 1924, which
eliminated one of the main rallying cries of the Ku Klux Klan. The sheer
opportunism of national leaders and some state leaders, who saw the Invisible
Empire only as a means of acquiring wealth and power, was hardly a recipe
for creating financially viable Realms or Klaverns. Finally, the Klan's attempts
to purge communities of bootlegging, immoral activities, corruption, and,
especially, of Catholics who held positions in government and education
failed miserably. The Klan could not prevent Al Smith's nomination as standard bearer for the Democratic Party in 1928. People still drank. Gambling and
prostitution still existed. And Catholics, along with an increasing number of
second-generation immigrants, were settling down nicely, adjusting to American society as Americans were adjusting to them. Montana Klansmen likely
shifted uncomfortably in their robes as they witnessed these changes. Just
because some members had turned more toward the secret fraternal aspects
of the order or abandoned the order to focus on the communal and business
interests of their town did not mean that they closed their eyes to the world
around them, nor did it mean that they were any less anti-Catholic or racist.
In the end, the Klan offered no long-term, cohesive, and positive program and
instead catered to the worst prejudices of Americans. Larger problems that
affected Montanans' daily lives and well-being, such as the massive number
of bank closings throughout the state, were not addressed. Membership in
the Invisible Empire provided Montanans a temporary outlet to express their
bigotry and to ostensibly assert a measure of control over communities and
over people they did not like.

Montana Knights' apathy toward the order was reflected in the minutes
of the last two Realm Kloreros in 1929 and 1930. Perhaps they were worn out
after the fervor of the Al Smith campaign, as the number of attendees at the
1929 Klorero was so small that the resolutions committee, which had consisted of five to six members in previous years, had only three members. Also,
the credentials committee did not exist, and nominations were made from

the body as a whole instead of by committee. Moreover, the names of officers nominated to serve the Realm had remained the same in the last two years, indicating that only a very small number of Knights expressed interest in administrative duties. Others who remained in the order were only too willing to let their colleagues try to help Terwilliger rebuild the Realm.[34]

In the last available official circular, issued in early January 1931, the Grand Dragon made a final plea to Montana Knights. "Where the local Klan has become inactive," Terwilliger stated, loyal Klansmen "may become members of the Grand Klan of Montana." Knights needed only to pay $6.00 for dues, which included bulletins from the Grand Dragon "together with pertinent literature from time to time. We need your assistance, and you need the close touch that membership in the Grand Klan will give you." His request to make checks payable to him indicated his continued commitment to engaging Montana Knights in the struggle, and that the Realm had devolved into a one-man operation.[35]

Terwilliger died in 1948, and unsurprisingly, his obituary said nothing about his leadership in the Klan: no mainstream newspaper would have dared to mention such an association even if editors knew about it and family members acknowledged it. Regardless, of the multiple organizations in which Terwilliger had participated, most of which were listed in the lengthy obituary, it was the Ku Klux Klan that most captured his devoted allegiance in the 1920s.[36]

Epilogue

What Bill, my telephone correspondent, could not have predicted in 2006 was the extent to which the ideology of the "buffoons [and] neo-Nazis" of the 1990s radical right would permeate politics and society in the 2010s and 2020s. Indeed, Bill may have derided those "young kids from Seattle," but he said it was due more to their perceived incompetence in charting goals and crafting a plan on how to achieve them than to their prejudices. White nationalism, in other words, has metastasized from the fringes of the radical right into much of the political mainstream, in the Make America Great Again (MAGA) movement and the Republican Party and its base, giving bigotry not only an organizational structure but also a powerful platform with a national reach.

Much had happened between the slow disintegration of Grand Dragon Lewis Terwilliger's Realm and the emergence of the radical right in Montana. As he packed into cardboard boxes his official circulars, letters, and other materials from his years serving as the leader of the Realm, the Invisible Empire had already started to implode, damaged by the D. C. Stephenson scandal in Indiana and unable to hold on to members, who were trying to survive the economic collapse of the Great Depression. The Klan remained embedded in patches across the United States during the 1930s and 1940s, particularly in the Midwest and the South, but the numbers had greatly diminished.[1] The Klan never emerged again as a singular national force. After World War II, the Klan was joined by other white supremacist groups that formed in response to the growing civil rights movement.[2] African Americans and their slow yet steady progress toward achieving the civil and political rights that were their due were seen as the gravest threat to the social order, not Catholics or the Roman Catholic Church. Economic woes of the 1970s, the divisions left in the wake of the Vietnam War, and the success and visibility of the women's rights movement and other social movements, added to many whites' unease and, for some, resentment and a perception that they were being left behind.[3]

In Montana, that resentment was reflected in two cross burnings, the ultimate warning sign of the hooded order. In 1979, a Bridger high school teacher woke up to see the smoldering remains of a sturdily built cross placed in his front yard. A shocked Jerry Scott, who was white, believed he had been targeted because of his active participation in the teachers' union, the Montana Education Association. Scott stated a "vocal minority" thought that Bridger's schools and teachers were receiving too much funding. That minority included a school board member who claimed the school administration had "padded" the data to make the community more sympathetic to the contract negotiations that had taken place the previous year. He resigned from the school board and joined the newly formed Bridger Taxpayers' Association, which opposed the financing of the school system, a reflection of the broad taxpayer protests that swept across the United States in the 1970s. Although the former school board member declared the cross burning to be "reprehensible," the Bridger community remained on edge.[4]

Four years later in another small town, a Black man, Cameron Dillingham, and a white woman, Rayetta Orr, woke up to the remnants of a burned cross in front of their house. The two friends asserted that they had been "harassed and threatened" since Dillingham's arrival in Troy. The crudely written note attached to a nearby tree accused them of racial mixing and warned Dillingham to leave immediately. Later that day, Dillingham was arrested for attacking a man with a baseball bat, who had arrived at Orr's home with a friend and threatened Dillingham and who Dillingham believed was behind the cross burning. Casually brushing off the cross burning and note as simple episodes of vandalism instead of a racially inspired threat, one of the patrolmen of Troy expressed that his "biggest fear is that the Friday and Saturday night drinking crowd might make more of the incident then there really is."[5]

The 1990s: Montana Quest and Skinheads

These two isolated events were acts of individuals and unconnected to a Klan organization in the state. The weight of the terror embedded in those cross burnings was directed at specific residents of their respective communities. One was triggered by hostility toward public school teachers seeking control over their own livelihoods, and the other, anger toward a Black man and a white woman transgressing against an unwritten racial code. The 1990s Ku Klux Klan that Bill derided as "nothing" aimed its hostility toward multiple constituencies. The Montana chapter of the Knights of the Ku Klux Klan, one of the many new renditions of the Klan headquartered in Arkansas, appeared in Billings in 1993, preceded by the arrival of racist literature in Montana's largest city in October.[6] The trigger for the Klan, or Montana Quest as it sometimes called itself, was a Community Walk on January 18, 1993, in honor of Martin Luther King Jr., sponsored by the Montana Association of Churches. After the event, white supremacists, including the Klan and Northwest United Skinheads, who had appeared in Billings around the same time, papered Billings churches with hate flyers.[7]

Montana Quest tried to forge a link to Terwilliger's Realm of the 1920s, but it was a feeble attempt. Its initial, and perhaps only, newsletter copied newspaper articles dated 1923 and 1925 about cross burnings on Square Butte, near Laurel, and on the rimrocks overlooking Billings to remind Montanans of the undeniable former presence of robed and hooded Knights in the state. But this was no official circular in the style of Terwilliger, who spoke to thousands of Knights across the Realm, reminded them of their patriotic and financial duty to the Klan and to America, and laid out the Invisible Empire's political agenda and how to accomplish it. While Terwilliger pointed to Catholic political power and influence as the Realm's gravest threat, Quest's newsletter zeroed in on other targets. Especially egregious was what the editor considered the immorality and dangers of homosexuality, and that "the radical left wing" and "white liberals" were teaching children about anal sex and race-mixing. "We are at a crossroads," cried Montana Quest, "we are engaged in a war."[8] It was a war that Terwilliger would not have recognized, although it reverberates in today's troubling political climate.

The most dangerous of enemies, Quest pronounced, centered on the recently formed Montana Human Rights Network (MHRN). Quest claimed that "rich Jews" operated the Billings chapter of the "Montana Homo Rights Network" and formed a "Pro-Faggot Triad" along with the Montana Association of Churches (MAC), which championed "pro-gay" and "anti-white" policies, and Police Chief Wayne Inman. Quest charged that MHRN, MAC, and Inman conspired to advance a "secret homosexual agenda," reflecting the larger persistence of homophobia in the United States during the 1980s and 1990s. Moreover, the media could not be trusted since the *Billings Gazette* was "controlled" by Jews, echoing Terwilliger's suspicions about newspapers, if not the culprit behind them.[9] The Klan expanded its distribution of anti-LGBTQ, anti-Semitic, and white supremacist literature through the rest of 1993 and into 1995. It touched down in Bozeman, where someone left a business card with the slogan "Racial Purity is America's Security" in a bookstore. Klan pamphlets appeared in Missoula and Red Lodge, and in Hardin white supremacist literature was distributed by the Klan and the racist and anti-Semitic Church of the Creator, likely in response to a Native American–sponsored conference on cultural diversity.[10]

Northwest United Skinheads focused on terrorizing Billings, as they chalked graffiti on top of the Rimrocks, posted a swastika on a stop sign near a Billings synagogue, and attempted to recruit teenagers at a local concert. "Racial slurs [and] death threats," plus incidents of skinheads chasing minorities, continued through the spring of 1993. Anti-Semitism took a more vicious turn that fall, however. After the hundred or so members of the small Jewish community in Billings received hate mail, threatening phone calls, and a bomb threat against the Congregation Beth Aaron synagogue, vandals desecrated the synagogue's cemetery. More frightening was a series of attacks in late 1993 that began when a brick was thrown into a child's bedroom window. After the *Billings Gazette* published a full-page image of a menorah and urged residents to display it in their windows in a show of support for the Jewish community, two Billings churches and six homes, which had posted those images, were vandalized. One church's windows were broken, and another church's door was "shattered." In the meantime, Jewish families answered their ringing phones only to hear anti-Semitic taunts to look outside their windows where their newly damaged cars sat parked.[11]

Flyers distributed by Montana Quest ("We are the Klan—Bringing Back the Dream!") included crude additions and comments such as handwritten swastikas, "The Holocaust never happened," and "Adolf Hitler was right," but executive director of the MHRN Ken Toole believed that the anti-Semitic vandalism was the work of skinheads, "the type of activity that skinheads are renowned for."[12] When asked how many skinheads were in Billings, nineteen-year-old Steve claimed that Northwest United Skinheads had "'not less than 50 and not more than 100.'" The group did not coordinate efforts with Montana Quest, as he defiantly declared, "I'm a skinhead for life in my heart," although

Steve acknowledged their ideas overlapped.[13] My conversation with Bill in 2006 also revealed that it was easy enough to conflate the two, especially in light of each group's blatant anti-Semitism.

White Nationalism in the West

As the example of Northwest Skinheads United shows, the Ku Klux Klan in the 1990s was facing competition from more radical organizations with a greater potential for violence and a willingness to use it. By the 1990s and 2000s, Montana was often the state of choice. The demographics of Montana were a natural attraction to the radical right. The state is, and has been, predominantly white with fewer than seven people per square mile in 2012, while the average density for the United States was over a dozen times higher that same year. Crowded multicultural cities are nowhere to be found. The state's largest urban center is Billings, which stood at 91,950 in 2000 and fewer than 118,000 in 2021.[14] Added to the mix are a general suspicion of and sometimes open hostility to the federal government, lax gun laws, a libertarian attitude of live and let live, a fierce sense of privacy, and a belief that the West and especially Montana represent the last vestiges of a vanishing frontier. In 2010, for example, assuming that Montana would be fertile territory for his brand of anti-Semitism and anti-government hostility, Chuck Baldwin moved his eighteen family members from Florida to Montana. A leader in the Patriot movement, he established himself as pastor of Liberty Fellowship in Kalispell, which counted among its congregants Randy Weaver from the Ruby Ridge, Idaho, shoot-out in 1992. He explained his decision to create a home in Flathead Valley in a letter to his followers: "We know there is a fight coming. We know there is a line being drawn in the sand and we want to be in the right place. The good ground is right here in Montana."[15]

Montana Quest had recognized the possibilities. So did others, including the militia, a broad-based movement that believed, among other things, that the US government was conspiring to take away their guns. Many also embraced Christian Identity, the anti-Semitic and white supremacist theology that hails white people as God's chosen race and views Jews and Black people as subhuman.[16] Around the same time that the Klan was posting hate flyers in Billings, John Trochmann of Noxon, who liked to invoke Ruby Ridge and the Waco, Texas, siege as reasons militias needed to be formed, was busily founding his own Militia of Montana.[17] Bill sang the praises of the Militia of Montana, of which he was a proud member. The militia was home to *"real*

men," he told me, and he added, "I go to all the gun shows." The Montana
Freemen, a racist and common-law group that disavowed all federal and state
laws and thus refused to follow them, also appeared in the mid-1990s. Armed
to the teeth, the Freemen hid in their 960-acre farm rather than surrender
to federal authorities. The FBI laid siege to the self-named Justus Township,
which ended peacefully after eighty-one days. In 1999, the leaders of the Freemen were convicted and sentenced to long prison terms for breaking a host of
federal laws.[18]

Creating a space where like-minded people could gather was not much of an
issue with the Invisible Empire of the 1920s. Terwilliger's Klan assumed white
supremacy was a given, and much of American society in the 1920s agreed. By
the 1980s and 1990s, however, that mindset had changed as most of American
society began to recognize, accept, and at times embrace diversity as a positive
good. The radical right rejected that premise and, while a scattered few talked
nostalgically of restoring that time when white supremacy reigned throughout
the country, most white nationalists championed more revolutionary strat-
egies. Creating an all-white homeland within the United States became the
prominent characteristic of white nationalism and a common thread weaving
radical right-wing groups together as they sought to seal themselves off from
a multicultural and urban society.

The most dominant white nationalist organization in the country during
the 1980s and 1990s lived just over the Montana border in Hayden Lake,
Idaho. The Hayden Lake compound was home to Aryan Nations, which
became a "communal campfire of the right," as James Ridgeway noted, and
welcomed an assortment of neo-Nazis, skinheads, and Klansmen under its
roof.[19] Founded by Richard Butler in 1977 and informed by the tenets of Christian Identity, which have permeated much of the radical right, Aryan Nations
pursued what Butler called the Northwest Territorial Imperative, the move to
establish an all-white ethnic state in the Pacific Northwest. The idea captivated
the leader of Montana Quest, John Abarr. He fondly remembered attending
an Aryan Nations Congress in 1988 when he was around eighteen years old;
especially memorable was the heady experience of participating in his "first
Cross Lighting Ceremony." Yet, Abarr was more drawn to the Ku Klux Klan,
believing it to be more of an American organization, which it most certainly
was, than Aryan Nations, with its clear homage to Nazism.[20]

White nationalism took a more violent turn in 1983 when Robert Mathews
organized Aryan Nation's militant offshoot, the Order, after conferring with

like-minded others at the compound. The idea of the Order (or the Silent Brotherhood) came to Mathews after reading the futuristic novel *The Turner Diaries* by William Pierce, the founder of the violent neo-Nazi National Alliance. (Mathews was the National Alliance's Pacific Northwest leader.) *The Turner Diaries*, which had already "achieved cult status" among the radical right and would later inspire Timothy McVeigh, the terrorist behind the Oklahoma City bombing, described in chilling detail a vicious race war.[21] The Order sought to instigate that war with the aim of establishing an all-white homeland in the Pacific Northwest, which would then secede from the United States.[22] David Lane, a former organizer for the Ku Klux Klan who thought the white nationalist movement had grown too tame, welcomed Mathews's invitation to join the Order. Lane would go on to coin the "14 Words" ("We must secure the existence of our race and a future for White children"), the instantly recognizable slogan of white nationalists. The Order was responsible for a series of violent crimes, including bank heists, a bombing of a synagogue, and the murder of a Jewish radio host in Denver who had openly mocked white supremacists and Christian Identity on his show. Several years after federal agents killed Mathews in a shoot-out on Whidbey Island, Washington, John Abarr organized a memorial for his special hero: "His Memory Shall Live On! Hail the Order."[23]

The Order collapsed shortly after Mathews's death, and surviving members landed in prison. Aryan Nations began to fracture by the end of 2000 after Southern Poverty Law Center's (SPLC) successful lawsuit against the order won the plaintiffs $6.3 million in damages, leaving it financially insolvent. After Richard Butler died in 2004, internal squabbling over the rightful successor and direction of the organization led to its final collapse.[24] Some Aryan Nations followers had already started to cross the border into Montana. The National Alliance, too, was part of the migration, as it started targeting Montana in 2004 by distributing literature in most of the major cities in the state.[25]

By that time, a dream of an all-white homeland evolved in at least one sector of the white nationalist movement. H. Michael Barrett's *Pioneer Little Europe (PLE) Prospectus*, published in 2001, advised white nationalists to "terraform the old white community," by driving out "ordinary whites" who were afraid to take a stand. PLE's objective was to foster "Uncontrolled White Nationalist Culture," an imperative to create a new society, a new way of living, being, and acting. He advised adherents to start small by becoming embedded into the community in multiple ways instead of seeking to claim the entire northwest

in one gulp, as sought by the Order and Aryan Nations, or James Wesley Raw-
les's later rendition, called "The American Redoubt," composed of Montana,
Wyoming, Idaho, and the eastern sections of Oregon and Washington, where
true white conservative Christians could defend the faith.[26]

April Gaede was interested. A former member of the National Alliance
and the Creativity Movement, Gaede moved from California to the Flathead
Valley in Montana in 2006 to create that all-white community. She started
advertising on the largest white nationalist platform at the time, Stormfront,
inviting white nationalists to move to the Flathead region to create their Pioneer Little Europe. Authorities estimated that because of Gaede's promotion
of PLE, around fifty white nationalists moved to Kalispell and Whitefish,
joined by another seventy or so with extreme anti-government leanings. Her
twin adolescent daughters, whom Gaede started promoting as the "young face
of white nationalism" when they were nine years old, started their short-lived
musical career when they were twelve, performing at Holocaust denial and
National Alliance events under the name of Prussian Blue, the color of Zyklon
B residue in Nazi gas chambers. In 2011, both young women had disavowed
white nationalism.[27]

That same year, Richard Spencer, one of the most influential white nationalists in the country, moved his pseudo-intellectual National Policy Institute
(NPI) to Whitefish, Montana, where his mother lived. Spencer created the
term "alt-right" in an attempt to give the radical right a veneer of respectability, shouted "Hail Trump" in 2016 to the Nazi-saluting crowd at the annual
conference of NPI, and was a leader in the violent Unite the Right rally in
Charlottesville, Virginia, in 2017. Spencer championed the idea of a white
homeland, declaring in 2013 that he "had a dream" to create a "white state . . .
on the North American continent." The diverse and multicultural America
that exists today, insisted Spencer, was not what the founding fathers had
envisioned. Instead, the United States had been conceptualized "for more
than 300 years" as "a nation ruled by and for Whites" and the country needed
to return to that sensibility.[28] By June 2022, Spencer had slipped quietly away
to Dallas, Texas, his NPI think-tank in "disarray" and his financial situation
in question after the successful *Sines v. Kessler* decision in late 2021 that found
the white nationalist perpetrators in Unite the Right, including Spencer, liable
for damages.[29] He was discovered on the Bumble dating app, portraying himself as a political moderate. When questioned by a writer for *Jezebel*, Spencer

declared that he was no longer a white nationalist and requested that people respect his privacy.[30]

Spencer's professed change of heart will not fool those who are paying attention. The same is true of Montana Quest's John Abarr. Like Spencer, Abarr had long supported building an all-white homeland. He continued to absorb white nationalist talking points after his visit to Aryan Nations at Hayden Lake by working on William Daniel Johnson's campaign in a special congressional election in Wyoming in 1989 to replace Dick Cheney, who had just been nominated for secretary of defense. Johnson, who wanted to deport all non-European whites from the United States, received less than 1 percent of the vote. After the failed campaign, Abarr spent some time in Los Angeles, California, where he realized that Johnson's idea of deportation was "totally unrealistic." He returned to Montana, settling in Great Falls, warning the public to wear masks to protect themselves against AIDS during an annual Pride! celebration in Bozeman, and running unsuccessfully for various political offices. One of those times was in 2011, when he decided to run as a Republican for the state legislature, a deception MHRN's Christine Kaufman recognized immediately. It was not a new ploy.

David Duke, neo-Nazi and former Grand Wizard of the Louisiana Ku Klux Klan, was the first white nationalist to trade in his hood and robe for a three-piece suit and a clean-cut visage when he won a special election for a seat in the Louisiana state legislature in February 1989. Duke's electoral victory was his only one, as he lost in multiple races for the US Senate, the Louisiana governorship, and the US presidential primaries. Yet, Duke had "blazed a path that other candidates . . . would follow in years to come."[31] Abarr strode that path, as have other white nationalists such as Spencer, even if they do not run for political office, by tossing aside outward trappings of Klan regalia and camouflage garb. Blending in has become more important, more effective, and more insidious as the ideology of the radical right has permeated the mainstream.[32]

The pervasive ideological thread of white nationalism that linked the Invisible Empire to the extreme right of the 1980s and beyond is also a characteristic of the MAGA movement under former president Donald Trump. Though often diluted from the hardcore white nationalism of the radical right, the decades-long connections between the Republican Party and extremism have been well documented.[33] More recently, in the wake of the 2008 presidential election when Americans chose Democrat Barack Obama to lead the country, the "paranoia, racism, and rage" that defined the newly formed Tea Party infiltrated the GOP. That force, as David Corn explains, continued to ferment during the Obama years and eventually formed the base of the MAGA movement.[34] Some Republicans may have dismissed with a wave the radical right's glee when Trump was elected in 2016, but there was no question that white nationalists knew the score. "Our Glorious Leader has ascended to God Emperor. . . . The White race is back in the game," exclaimed Andrew Anglin. "White Nationalists all over the world are celebrating!" added Brad Griffin, while David Duke crowed, "Make no mistake about it, our people played a HUGE role in electing Trump!"[35] Trump's claim that "some very fine people" were among those who spearheaded the violent Unite the Right rally in 2017 made it clear where he stood, a position that has only strengthened after his defeat in the 2020 presidential election.[36] As Peter Wehner put it, the GOP "is more MAGA friendly *after* his [Trump's] defeat in 2020 than it was during his presidency . . . it's hard to overstate how radicalized and anarchic the base of the Republican Party remains."[37]

White nationalism and MAGA also intersect with Turning Point USA (TPUSA), an organization formed in 2012 by Charlie Kirk that is committed to spreading right-wing propaganda on college campuses and in high schools, including those in Montana. TPUSA has captured the attention of the MHRN, not only because the organization serves as a way "to introduce young people to racist concepts who can then be moved to harder white nationalist platforms," but also because of the involvement of the Montana Republican Party: The GOP in Yellowstone and Flathead Counties invited Kirk to give a presentation in the spring of 2020.[38] Greg Gianforte, a wealthy Republican who is currently serving as Montana's governor and who won praise from President Trump in 2017 for body-slamming a reporter, donated some initial funding to TPUSA.[39] While more hardcore activists and Holocaust deniers such as Nicholas J. Fuentes have criticized TPUSA for being too "scared" to vigorously advocate white nationalist ideas, TPUSA's continued fealty to the former president signals support of his bigotry.[40] One veteran of TPUSA in Montana is Republican Braxton Mitchell from Columbia Falls, who was elected to the Montana legislature in 2020 and who has offered multiple bills that adhere to the MAGA line. One of them, which failed, sought to designate Antifa as a terrorist organization, yet others, such as prohibiting minors from attending drag shows, have either been signed into law by Governor Gianforte or are making their way through the legislative process.[41]

It would be a mistake, however, to include all Montana Republicans in the MAGA camp. Two prominent Republicans, for instance, former Republican National Committee chairman, state governor, and attorney general Marc Racicot and former secretary of state and state senate president Bob Brown, denounced Donald Trump on the eve of the 2022 election: "Trump destroys the bonds of our union by exploiting our human insecurities, resentments and fears, and then supplants our better angels with malice, slander, grievances, cruelties, vengeance, and scorn. In doing so, he has desecrated the Constitution and poisoned the political life of America." Both Racicot and Brown then announced their support of Democrat Monica Tranel in the race for one of two Montana seats in the US House of Representatives. Tranel lost to Republican Ryan Zinke, who had served as Trump's secretary of the interior for two years before resigning due to an "avalanche of investigations into his conduct."[42]

Similarities and Differences

Notwithstanding the great gulf of time and historical context that separates Terwilliger's Klan of the 1920s and the extreme right and the MAGA movement of today, they share some distinct similarities. Most obviously, Terwilliger's declaration that "white civilization shall be maintained" has crept into the current mainstream of one political party, as Donald Trump's tenure in the White House has shown, and his hold over the Republican Party continues. Senator Tommy Tuberville (R-Alabama) sees nothing wrong with being called a white nationalist, and those who identify as such he calls "Americans" and "Trump Republicans." In the Montana state legislature, Republicans denied in 2021 that white nationalist groups existed in the state and voted down a resolution that "would have labeled white supremacist neo-Nazi violence as domestic terrorism," even as a 2020 SPLC report "found that Montana [had] more hate groups per capita than any other state."[43] Refuting the presence of such groups only allows their racist and anti-Semitic ideology, which informs acts of harassment, vandalism, and terror, to become embedded in Montana society. Indeed, the number of recorded anti-Semitic incidents has risen sharply in Montana, doubling between 2021 and 2022 from seven to fourteen, a troubling trend in a state with such a small population.[44]

Another similarity between the Klan of the 1920s and the recent variations of white nationalist organizations and individuals today is a visceral hostility toward an enemy. Terwilliger and the Klan showed no subtlety in determining who was evil and who was not, and the menu of bigotry was vast.

Those who were not with them were against them. As Michael Kazin explains in the *Populist Persuasion*, the "us versus them" language has reverberated throughout the twentieth century and into the twenty-first.[45] It is also a common sentiment within the continuum of right-wing activity and beliefs over time as expressed by the Klan, Aryan Nations, and militia movement, as well as MAGA, TPUSA, Moms for Liberty, and others. Whether the enemy is the Catholic Church, Jews, Muslims, African Americans, the federal government, or the LGBTQ community, white Americans on the far right are fighting, so they believe, for a just and patriotic cause. Imperial Wizard Hiram Wesley Evans's anti-immigrant hostility in his 1923 speech in Dallas has transitioned to Richard Spencer's call for "peaceful ethnic cleansing." Anti-Catholicism has dissipated, but the anti-Semitism that was always present in the Klan's worldview has become more pernicious and more violent.[46] The catchphrase of today's political right is "wokeness," a vague term that Terwilliger would have puzzled over, but after discovering that "wokeness" simply meant progress toward and support of political, social, and economic equality and justice since the civil rights era, the Grand Dragon would have agreed that this was the new enemy to fight. Republican Speaker of the House Matt Regier's statement in March 2023, "The House understands that Montana has become a state for families fleeing from 'woke' extremism," reveals disturbing parallels with the words of white nationalist Chuck Baldwin upon moving to Kalispell in 2010 ("the good ground is right here in Montana.")[47] Thus, as James Madison notes in his recent study of the Klan in Indiana, the questions that the 1920s Klan posed are back.[48] White nationalists, whether they identify as such or not, are drawing clear lines about who belongs in America and who does not, who has full rights and privileges, and who does not.

The differences between the 1920s Klan and today's white nationalists and MAGA movement are also notable. Terwilliger's Klan was the most dominant nativist organization in the country—no other organization of its kind even came close. Its political, social, and cultural impact reached far beyond the three to four million dues-paying members nationwide and the over 5,100 members in Montana. The current Klan is fractured into multiple groups, ranging from True Invisible Empire Knights to Loyal White Knights of the Ku Klux Klan, which was the most widespread in the country in 2015. In 2021, the SPLC noted the continued decline of the Ku Klux Klan "as younger extremists move into newer groups that do not carry the same stigma as a group long associated with white supremacist terror. In 2020, Klan chapters dwindled to

25, down from 47 in 2019 and down significantly from years past, when there were typically about 150 chapters in any given year."[49]

Since the flow of information is vastly different than in the 1920s, radical right groups enjoy far easier access to those younger extremists. Stormfront, Daily Stormer, VDare—the reach of white nationalist social media is long, and even as they are often de-platformed, they regroup and find other ways to connect with their followers. The swift mobilization of the crowds, ranging from individual and anonymous MAGA supporters to the Proud Boys and Oath Keepers, that gathered at the capitol on January 6, 2021, to violently prevent the peaceful transfer of power from Trump to the newly elected Democrat Joseph Biden demonstrates that reach. It also emerged in the ferocity and quickness of the troll storm that Andrew Anglin, founder of the Daily Stormer website, which boasts millions of followers, unleashed on a Jewish family in Whitefish in 2016 and 2017. While SPLC won a $14 million lawsuit against Andrew Anglin in 2019, the damage done to the Gersh family in the interim was enormous.[50] More subtly, but just as pernicious, are the MAGA outlets on social media, radio, and television that decry "wokeness" in an attempt to turn back the clock: Truth Social, NewsMax, One America Network, and many others exhort variations of the same message—one full of grievance, victimhood, hostility, and fear about losing power in an increasingly multicultural and diverse society.[51] The 1920s Klan aired a similar narrative, but without the sweeping scope of today's media platforms.

Another difference between the Klan of the 1920s and the hate groups that appeared in Montana during the 1990s and beyond is the swift resistance to them. When Montana Quest and Northwest United Skinheads arrived in Billings in the spring of 1993, for example, Police Chief Wayne Inman immediately declared that bigotry demanded a firm and public response. Residents agreed and created an ad hoc committee to confront the hate groups in the area. Their response included a march attracting over eight hundred people.[52] Ken Toole, the director of the MHRN at the time, remarked that residents in Billings responded to the challenges "extraordinarily well." Toole expressed optimism that the strong resistance would hold steady, and that around the state, communities had answered.[53]

MHRN continued to work with local communities to strategize appropriate responses, recognizing that there was not one blueprint to follow. When Matt Hale's Church of the Creator planned to hold its annual conference in Superior in the fall of 1999, the residents of Superior decided to act. In previous years, concerned citizens had conducted counterprotests to the Creators' presence. This time, the recent shooting rampage in the Midwest against minorities by an acolyte of Hales, who murdered two people, injured ten, then killed himself, prompted worries about safety and resulted in a different approach to avoid confrontation. Superior residents decided to celebrate a "Day of Harmony" two weeks before the scheduled conference, making clear to everyone that the Church of the Creator did not represent the town's values. Missoula took a different approach and wanted to do something, as MHRN director Travis McAdam stated, "edgier." MHRN worked with the local affiliate to organize a block party in front of Creator Dan Hassett's house in Missoula. And a party it was, with around two hundred people attending, local businesses donating food, and a local band providing music. Hassett came outside, engaged in a conversation with one of the attendees, and tried to convince her that the Holocaust was a hoax. Having participated in the Dutch resistance against the Nazis during World War II, she firmly set him straight.[54]

As MHRN continues to foster relationships with various single-issue groups in communities and to emphasize a message of hope and perseverance, the battle for justice continues throughout the state. As Rachel Carroll Rivas, co-director of MHRN, stated in 2021:

> The line between Far-Right activists and lawmakers has become too blurred, leaving regular Montanans locked out of the seats of power in what is hailed as a citizen legislature. This session we've seen testimony limited during bill hearings and other such manifestations of the Far Right's influence. This happens when the Far Right is able to exert control over democratic processes. Democracy begins to suffocate as authoritarianism and conspiracies shape how policy is considered and made.[55]

A vivid example of Rivas's concerns occurred in the spring of 2023, when state representative Zooey Zephyr from Missoula, the first openly transgender lawmaker in Montana, was banned from the House floor by Republicans for passionately speaking out against a bill that would prohibit gender-affirming care for youth in the state. She was relegated to the hallway outside the chamber for the rest of the legislative session, unable to represent her eleven thousand constituents. She was also denied access to "capitol entrances, bathrooms and party workspaces" because her key card had been deactivated. Zephyr sued House Speaker Matt Regier and state house sergeant-at-arms Bradley Murfitt to return to the House to finish the legislative session. She was unsuccessful.

Republicans passed the trans health-care bill, and Governor Gianforte signed it into law.[56] Extending beyond the state's capitol, the war on "wokeness" in Montana includes the Montana State Library Commission's withdrawal from the American Library Association because the president of the ALA, who serves for one year, self-identifies as a Marxist lesbian. Slaven Lee, the executive director of the Missoula Public Library, stated that "the president of the ALA has very little impact on what the actual organization does," making the decision by the Montana State Library Commission a purely political and cynical move. Not only is Montana the "first state in the nation to split from the ALA"; critics have also noted that the loss of affiliation with the national organization will "have an outsized impact on rural and tribal libraries" because funding is threatened, if not lost, for services such as broadband access.[57]

The echoes from the past are undeniable. While the Klan's vision of 100 percent Americanism demanded that only native-born Protestant teachers could teach in public schools, Moms for Liberty and their allies in state legislatures, governor's offices, and school boards vilify teachers if they display the colors of the rainbow in classrooms or assign books they deem inappropriate. These include *To Kill a Mockingbird*, *The Handmaid's Tale*, and other books with themes "centered on race, history, sexual orientation and gender."[58] Attacks on LGBTQ rights have accelerated, moving beyond the 1990s Klan's homophobia and becoming a central theme in the Republican Party. Effects range from a Supreme Court decision that allows businesses to discriminate against LGBTQ people and the state of Florida banning Advanced Placement (AP) Psychology because of its inclusion of gender and sexuality, to an Indiana school district's decision to table a request from a librarian to attend her state's annual library conference for fear of a possible "nefarious" agenda.[59] By May 2023, state legislatures across the country had introduced over 520 anti-LGBTQ bills, over 220 specifically targeting transgender and nonbinary people.[60] As another stark indicator of their hostility toward LGBTQ people, Republicans recently elected as House Speaker Louisiana representative Mike Johnson, who has a long history of leading efforts to criminalize gay sex and outlaw gay marriage, declaring that "homosexual marriage is the dark harbinger of chaos and sexual anarchy."[61]

While the Klan of the 1920s violently attacked and murdered African American men because of their suspected association with white women, a group of Mississippi police officers in 2023 brutally assaulted two Black men "because a white neighbor had complained that Black people were staying with a white woman who owned the house."[62] Florida's recent "Stop WOKE Act," signed into law by Governor Ron DeSantis in 2022, gave the green light to reject a new AP course in African American Studies, which was followed the next year by the Florida State Board of Education's approval of revising school textbooks to claim that slavery was a positive good for some enslaved people.[63] Talk of secession and a new civil war are also brewing among those in MAGA, ranging from Republican representatives in Congress such as Marjorie Taylor Greene from Georgia (who asserts that states should secede from the United States because of President Biden's "traitorous America last border policies") and Matt Gaetz from Florida (who warns there will be "bloodshed" if Trump is kept off state ballots in the 2024 election), to former Arkansas governor Mike Huckabee declaring on his talk show that if Trump does not regain the presidency in 2024, "it is going to be the last American election that will be decided by ballots rather than bullets."[64]

The rhetoric of violence has become reality in the racially motivated mass shootings of African Americans in Buffalo, New York (2022), and Jacksonville, Florida (2023), and of Hispanics in El Paso, Texas (2019), to name just three incidents. Radical right violence toward the LGBTQ community has also increased, especially toward transgender people, as the mass murder at Club Q in Colorado Springs, Colorado, in the fall of 2022 demonstrates.[65] Conventional portrayals of the shooters as "lone wolves," an image that Kathleen Belew strikes down in *Bring the War Home*, deflects responsibility from the wider white nationalist culture that has nurtured and amplified their beliefs.[66]

As Republican and former secretary of state Bob Brown mused in an op-ed for Montana newspapers in which he drew connections between the Montana Klan of the 1920s and the events of today, "a strong strain of hostility among us" exists, "held by those who see differences as a threat [and who] see tolerance and compromise as weakness and disloyalty."[67] He urged Montanans to rally against that hostility and to reject the radical right's intolerance. Hopefully, Montanans, and all Americans, will listen.

Appendix

Montana Klans and Knights' Occupations

Montana Klans by City

Note: Not all Klans could be identified, therefore some entries remain blank.

No. 1—Havre (Havre Klan)

No. 2—Laurel (Laurel Klan)

No. 3—Columbus (Columbus Klan)

No. 4—

No. 5—Glasgow (Valley County Klan)

No. 6—Billings (Billings Klan)

No. 7—Big Timber (Big Timber Klan)

No. 8—Lewistown (Lewistown Klan)

No. 9—Livingston (Livingston Klan)

No. 10—Bozeman (Bozeman Klan)

No. 11—Helena (Helena Klan)

No. 12—Ronan (Mission Valley Klan)

No. 13—Polson (Lake City Klan)

No. 14—Red Lodge (Red Lodge Klan)

No. 15—

No. 16—Missoula (University City Klan)

No. 17—

No. 18—Roundup (Roundup Klan)

No. 19—Great Falls (Kascade Klan)

No. 20—Terry (Terry Klan)

No. 21—Miles City (Miles City Klan)

No. 22—Kalispell (Kalispell Klan)

No. 23—Bridger (Bridger Klan)

No. 24—Glendive (Glendive Klan)

No. 25—Choteau (Choteau Klan)

No. 26—Thompson Falls (Power City Klan)

No. 27—

No. 28—Superior (Superior Klan)

No. 29—Harlowton (Wheatland Klan)

No. 30—Butte (Kontinental Klan)

No. 31—Deer Lodge (Powell County Klan)

No. 32—Helena (Kapital Klan)

No. 33—Plentywood (Big Muddy Klan)

No. 34—

No. 35—Hardin (Hardin Klan)

No. 36—

No. 37—Stevensville (Fort Owen Klan)

No. 38—Townsend

No. 39—Conrad

No. 40—

No. 41—

No. 42—

No. 43—

No. 44—Bainville (Robin Hood Klan)

No. 45—

No. 46—Scobey

No. 47—Ravalli County Klan

Note: Belgrade (Gallatin County) also had a Klan, but it is unclear what number it was. Moccasin and Hysham might have also been on this list. Most of the entries on this list are from the Knights of the Ku Klux Klan, Kontinental Klan Records, Microfilm 457,

Appendix C, Montana Historical Society. The Ravalli County Klan may have been a combination of two Klans: Stevensville and Hamilton.

Knights' Occupations

Butte

ashman—1
auditor—1
baggageman—1
baker—3
barber—2
blacksmith—1
bookkeeper—3
broker—1
butcher—3
carman—1
carpenter—6
cashier—4
certified public accountant—1
clerk—21
collector—1
commissioner—1
conductor—6
coroner—1
dairyman—1
driver—7
electrician (3 chief)—4
engineer—5
expressman—1
farmer—1
fireman—1
foreman—2
grocer—2
insurance agent—2
janitor—1
laborer—4
lawyer—1
lineman—1

machinist—13
mail carrier—1
manager/proprietor—6
mechanic—4
merchant—1
mine boss—2
miner—20
oil service attendant—1
paper cleaner—1
president of Montana Motors—1
president of Sweet Bros., Inc.—1
printer—1
Prohibition agent—1
railway agent—3
rancher—3
real estate agent—1
salesman—9
shoemaker—1
switchman—1
teacher—3
teamster—4
telegraph operator—2
teller—1
trammer—2
vice president (Stilwell Grocery)—1
warehouse man—1
water inspector—1
welder—1

Unknown—23
Total—201

Harlowton

abstractor—1
auto driver—1
barber—1

blacksmith—1
boiler maker—4
bookkeeper—1

bridge and building foreman—1
butcher—1
car inspector—1
car repairer—6
carpenter—2
cashier—4
chief of police—1
clerk—11
conductor—5
coroner—1
county employee—7
dairyman—1
dentist—2
drayman—1
druggist—1
electrician—8
engineer—4
expressman—1
farmer—13
garage man—4
insurance agent—1
laborer—4
lawyer—2
lineman—1
machinist—4
manager/proprietor—13
mechanic—4
merchant—5

miller—4
minister—3
oil agent—1
oil man—1
park supervisor—1
physician—1
postmaster and editor—1
printer-publisher—1
railroad worker—6
railway car foreman—1
rancher—19
real estate agent—1
roadmaster—1
roundhouse foreman—1
salesman—2
storekeeper—2
student (high school)—1
switchman—3
teacher—2
telegraph operator—2
truck driver—2
water inspector—1
welder—1
well driller—1
yard master—3

Unknown—12
Total—192

Roundup

auto agent—1
auto salesman—3
auto worker—1
banker—1
barber—4
blacksmith—3
bookkeeper—2
brakeman—1
butcher—2
carpenter—2
cashier—2
chief of police—1
clerk—25

cook—1
coroner—1
county employee—3
dentist—4
driver—2
druggist—6
electrician—2
elevator man—1
engineer—6
farmer—36
furniture dealer—1
grocer—2
iceman—1

insurance agent—1

janitor—2

laborer—6

launderer—1

lawyer—5

lineman—5

lumberman—2

machinist—1

mail carrier—2

manager/proprietor—14

meat cutter—2

mechanic—4

merchant—4

mine boss—2

miner—34

mining salesman—1

minister—3

moving picture operator—1

musician—1

oil driller—1

oil salesman—2

painter—2

physician—6

plumber—2

pool hall worker—1

president Roundup National Bank—1

printer *Roundup Record*—1

probation officer—1

pumpman—2

railroad man—5

railway agent—1

rancher—2

real estate agent—4

retail salesman—4

stock buyer—1

student (high school)—1

switchman—1

tea agent—1

teacher—2

teamster—2

telegraph operator—2

tinsmith—1

U.S. postmaster—2

vice president Citizens Bank—1

Unknown—28

Total—282

Notes

Introduction

Epigraph: "Come Join the Knights of the Ku Klux Klan," in Crew, Ku Klux Klan Sheet Music, 37.

1. Interview with Bill [last name withheld], March 27, 2006 (notes in author's possession).

2. Lewis Terwilliger, official document No. 1, 1923, F163, Publications, MF457, Kontinental Klan, Montana Historical Society (hereafter MHS).

3. Chalmers, *Hooded Americanism*, 88; Goldberg, "Denver: Queen City of the Colorado Realm," in Lay, *The Invisible Empire in the West*, 39–40.

4. Grand Dragon of Wyoming, "Operation of Klankraft in the West," Papers Read at the Meeting of Grand Dragons, Knights of the Ku Klux Klan, First Annual Meeting, Asheville, NC, July 1923, 109–110.

5. Chalmers, *Hooded Americanism*, 220–21.

6. Lay, "Introduction," in Lay, *The Invisible Empire in the West*, 11.

7. Jackson, *The Ku Klux Klan in the City, 1915–1930*; Alexander, *The Ku Klux Klan in the Southwest* (1965) and Chalmers's *Hooded Americanism* (1st edition, 1965) were the first studies to challenge that traditional view. See also Robert Goldberg, *Hooded Empire*, and Gerlach, *Blazing Crosses in Zion*. As yet, there is no comprehensive study of the Klan in California, although there are a number of local studies, such as Cocoltchos, on the Klan in Anaheim, in *Invisible Empire* and Rodriquez, "No Ku Klux Klan for Kern."

8. Gordon, *The Second Coming of the KKK*, 3.

9. Pegram, *One Hundred Percent American*, 6.

10. Fox, *Everyday Klansfolk*; Madison, *The Ku Klux Klan in the Heartland*. Other recent scholarship includes Harcourt, *Ku Klux Kulture*; Barnes, *The Ku Klux Klan in 1920s Arkansas*; Rice, *White Robes Silver Screens*; Richard, *Not a Catholic Nation*.

11. Pegram, *One Hundred Percent American*.

Chapter 1. The Klan Comes to Montana

Epigraph: "He's a Knight of the Ku Klux Klan," in Crew, *Ku Klux Klan Sheet Music*, 80.

1. Lewis Terwilliger, Official Circular No. 1, n.d., c. 1923, F163, Publications, MF457, Kontinental Klan, MHS.
2. For example, the records from the Harlowton Klan and obituaries show that 112 Klansmen were born in the Midwest, 16 in the South, 13 in the Northeast, and 6 in the west. Roundup revealed similar ratios: 160 in the Midwest, 10 in the South, 24 in the Northeast, and 19 in the West. Membership records, Knights of The Ku Klux Klan, Wheatland Klan, No. 29 (Harlowton, MT) 1923–1928, SC 2223 MHS.
3. *Harlowton Times*, February 24, 1927.
4. Harlowton Woman's Club, *Yesteryears and Pioneers*, 26.
5. Gutfeld, *Montana's Agony*, 93. See State Department of Agriculture and Publicity, *The Opportunities and Resources of Montana*, 26.
6. Gates, "Homesteading in the High Plains," 125.
7. Harlowton Woman's Club, *Yesteryears and Pioneers*, 51.
8. Harlowton Woman's Club, *Yesteryears and Pioneers*, 160, 230.
9. Quoted in Stearns, *A History of the Upper Musselshell Valley (to 1920)*, 82.
10. Meyers, "Homestead on the Range," 219. Eastern Montana was home to 38 percent of the state's population in 1900 and 57 percent of the state's population in 1920; Gates, "Homesteading in the High Plains," 124–25.
11. The rural population in the state jumped from 242,633 in 1910 to 376,878 in 1920. Fourteenth Census of the United States, 1920, Volume III, Population, Table 1.
12. State Department of Agriculture and Publicity, *The Opportunities and Resources of Montana*, 7–8.
13. Chicago, Milwaukee, and St. Paul Railway, *Montana, Along the New Line to the Pacific Coast*, 1.
14. Dr. S. K. Campbell, for instance, had "extensive farming and cattle interests in Wheatland County." Stout, *Montana: Its Story and Biography*, 653.
15. Malone, Roeder, and Lang, *Montana*, 177–84.
16. Harlowton Woman's Club, *Yesteryears and Pioneers*, 5.
17. Toole, *Twentieth-Century Montana*, 92. Toole added that because of the county-splitting, the cost of running county administrations increased by 149 percent. See also Malone, Roeder, and Lang, *Montana*, 249–252.
18. *Helena Independent*, January 19, 1923, Diocese Scrapbooks, XXVI, Diocese of Helena, Montana, 50.
19. Kinzer, *An Episode in Anti-Catholicism*, 40. Kinzer notes that the groundwork was already laid for the APA (by 1892) with the presence of other nativist groups, such as the Junior Order of United American Mechanics and the Patriotic Order of the Sons of the America, 59–62; 71. Also see Higham, *Strangers in the Land*, 81–82.
20. *Examiner* (Butte, MT), March 26, 1896. The *Examiner* was founded in 1895. Kinzer, *An Episode in Anti-Catholicism*, 95.
21. Wallace, *The Rhetoric of Anti-Catholicism*, 120, 123, 128–29; Kinzer, *An Episode in Anti-Catholicism*, 180. The APA originated in Clinton, Iowa, a city with a large number of immigrant Catholics. Membership in the APA, like the Klan, is difficult to

determine because of the secret nature of the order. Humphrey J. Desmond suggests that membership hovered around one million at its peak; Wallace agrees. Desmond, *The A.P.A. Movement*, 12, 70, 71. Wallace, *The Rhetoric of Anti-Catholicism*, 76. The *Examiner* (Butte, MT) claimed that two million had joined by the beginning of 1895 and the number had grown to 3.5 million at the beginning of the next year. *Examiner*, March 26, 1896, 4. The APA was particularly strong in the Midwest, but it also found favor in the West, especially California, Washington, and Colorado. Hunt, "The Heyday of the Denver APA, 1892–1894," 74.

22. Kinzer, *An Episode in Anti-Catholicism*, 93–94.
23. Higham, *Strangers in the Land*, 82.
24. Higham, *Strangers in the Land*, 82.
25. Cuddy, "The Irish Question and the Revival of Anti-Catholicism in the 1920's," 251.
26. Hunt, "The Heyday of the Denver APA," 74; Kinzer, *An Episode in Anti-Catholicism*, 180; Cuddy, "The Irish Question and the Revival of Anti-Catholicism in the 1920's," 251.
27. Higham, *Strangers in the Land*, 59. Also Wallace, "The Heyday of the Denver APA"; The Roman Catholic Diocese of Helena, diocesehelena.org/about; Kinzer, *An Episode in Anti-Catholicism*, 23; Emmons, *The Butte Irish*, 98.
28. See Pegram, *One Hundred Percent American*, 77, for more on the oath.
29. Wallace, *The Rhetoric of Anti-Catholicism*, 50; Ander, "The Swedish American Press and the American Protective Association," 165–166; Pegram, *One Hundred Percent American*, 77–78. The *New York World* reprinted in part the bogus Knights of Columbus Oath (September 14, 1924), ACLU Reel 36 Vol 252.
30. Kinzer, *An Episode in Anti-Catholicism*, 64–65.
31. Wallace, *The Rhetoric of Anti-Catholicism*, 139–140.
32. Kinzer, *An Episode in Anti-Catholicism*, 58.
33. *Examiner*, April 9, 1896.
34. Kinzer, *An Episode in Anti-Catholicism*, 78, 140–41.
35. Hunt, "The Heyday of the Denver APA," 77, 79.
36. Hunt, "The Heyday of the Denver APA," 79.
37. Political affiliations are hard to come by, but obituaries and newspaper articles from Harlowton, Roundup, and other parts of the state reveal that thirty-two members were known Republicans, nine were Democrats, and one was an Independent. Considering the tight association between Irish Catholics and the Democratic Party in Butte, most certainly Kontinental Klansmen voted Republican.
38. Strong, *Our Country*, 57. Introduction by Austin Phelps, iii.
39. Kinzer, *An Episode in Anti-Catholicism*, 92, 103–4. Bowers would remain very active in the APA.
40. *Examiner*, June 15, 1895, 1.
41. Kinzer, *An Episode in Anti-Catholicism*, 103–4; *Examiner*, May 18, 1895.
42. *Examiner*, May 18, 1895; December 15, 1895. For a lively and detailed accounting of the riot, see Writers Project of Montana, *Copper Camp*, 57–60. The *Daily*

Intermountain (Butte), July 5, 1894, tartly reported "the occupants of the saloon resented the liquid refreshments offered and returned the compliment by firing bullets filled with gunpowder and lead back at the firemen." Also see Kinzer, *An Episode in Anti-Catholicism*, 103–4.

43. Kinzer, *An Episode in Anti-Catholicism*, 104.

44. *Examiner*, July 16, 1896.

45. The APA's decline was due mostly to the stress of the presidential election in 1896. Kinzer, *An Episode in Anti-Catholicism*, 176, 240. Higham, *Strangers in the Land*, 178–181. For other historical works on the APA not already mentioned, see Jo Ann Manfra, "Hometown Politics and the American Protective Association, 1887–1890," 138–166; Kennedy, "Pulpits and Politics"; Frink, "'God Give Us Men!'"49–63.

46. As Pegram states, "The robust patriotism of the war years generated a lingering postwar suspicion of labor unionists, political radicals, recent immigrants, southern black migrants, and other Americans then considered marginal." Pegram, *One Hundred Percent American*, 11.

47. Toole, *Twentieth-Century Montana*, 139.

48. Quoted in Gutfeld, *Montana's Agony*, 61.

49. Zellick, "Patriots on the Rampage," 37–38. "Liberty Committees were organized in practically all the small towns of the state and became the local arbiters of patriotism. Billings even boasted a "Third Degree Committee" whose function was to round up and punish "financial slackers" and "pro Germans." Toole, *Twentieth-Century Montana*, 140. From the limited data on Klan membership, two Klansman from the Wheatland Klan (Judith Gap and Hedgesville) served on the Wheatland County Council of Defense. "County Councils of Defense," Montana Council of Defense, RS 19, Box 4, Subject File: County Councils of Defense, Folder 3, MHS; W. N. Smith to Chas D. Greenfield, Harlowton, September 24, 1918, Montana Council of Defense, RS 19, Box 3, F13, MHS.

50. Malone, Roeder, and Lang, *Montana*, 278; Toole, *State of Extremes*, 139.

51. Gutfeld, *Montana's Agony*, 68; Toole, *Twentieth-Century Montana*, 187; Malone, Roeder, and Lang, *Montana*, 278; *Harlowton Times*, May 2, 1918.

52. Office of the Superintendent, Harlowton Public Schools, to C. D. Greenfield, May 3, 1918.

53. *Harlowton Times*, July 18, 1918; August 8, 1918. See Letter to Mr. W. N. Smith, April 19, 1918, in Montana Historical Society, Montana Council of Defense, RS 19, Box 3, File 19 (Wheatland County Defense Council). Also see W. N. Smith to Chas. D. Greenfield, September 24, 1918, File 13; Office of the Superintendent, Harlowton Public Schools, May 3, 1918, to C. D. Greenfield; and "Local Councils are Organizing," n.d., in File 13. Many thanks to Steve Sabol for his assistance with the MCD records.

54. F. M. Wall, Roundup, to M. M. Donohue, Pres., Federation of Labor, Butte, n.d., Montana Council of Defense, Box 2, File 10, MHS.

55. Toole, *Twentieth-Century Montana*, 142.

56. Malone, Roeder, and Lang, *Montana*, 270.
57. Gutfeld, *Montana's Agony*, 13.
58. *Harlowton Times*, September 13, 1917.
59. The murder of Little inspired almost all of the newspapers in the state to attack the IWW as a radical organization and condemn it for its anti-war stance. Gutfeld, *Montana's Agony*, 48.
60. Huppert, *Looking Back*, 72.
61. Interview of Norma Hanson Gilmore by Anna Zellick, Lecturer at College of Great Falls at Lewistown College Center, May 30, 1978, Lewistown Public Library; Donovan, *The First Hundred Years*, 103.
62. Dissly, *History of Lewistown*, 77; Montana Council of Defense, RS 19, Montana, Various State Boards and Agencies, Box 2, Folder 12, MHS.
63. In Donovan, *The First Hundred Years*, 103. Also see Zellick, "Patriots on the Rampage," 30–43.
64. Interview with George L. Ruckman by Anna Zellick, Lewistown Public Library, July 11, 1978, 5–6. George Ruckman was a student at the school and witnessed the event. Interview with Gertrude Margretta Klein Saxtorph by Anna Zellick, 1978, OH 1704, MHS. Dr. Fred A. Attix's involvement in the Klan seemed to be a well-known fact in Lewistown.
65. *Harlowton Times*, January 26, 1922.
66. Pegram, *One Hundred Percent American*, 7, 8.
67. *Great Falls Tribune*, December 31, 1922, 9.
68. "The Great American Play," *Butte Miner*, February 11, 1923.
69. As Rice notes, *The Birth of a Nation* "became useful for social and political organizations like the Klan, which looked to exploit the mass media to define, promote, and position themselves with the American mainstream." Rice, *White Robes Silver Screens*, xvi.
70. Most book-length studies discuss the national organization, at least for a bit. For the most complete, see Chalmers, *Hooded Americanism*, for the general outline of events.
71. *Billings Gazette*, November 15, 1924, 1.
72. *Billings Gazette*, November 15, 1924, 1.
73. Estimates of Klan membership were numerous, but all fell within the same general range. Chalmers estimated over 3 million. Chalmers, *Hooded Americanism*, 291. Jackson estimated over 2 million. Jackson, *The Ku Klux Klan in the City, 1915–1930*, 23. Former Kleagle Edgar I. Fuller, writing under the pseudonymn Marion Monteval, estimated 5 million members. Marion Monteval [Edgar I. Fuller], *The Klan Inside Out*, 45. *The New Republic* stated in 1923 that 2.5 to 4.5 million people had joined. "Why They Join the Klan," 32. Membership numbers for Montana were derived from the yearly Realm taxes. Each member was taxed 25 cents per quarter equaling $1.00 per year. In 1924, the Realm reported $4,036 in Realm taxes; thus, approximately 4,036 Montanans were members of the Klan in 1924. This number

is approximate and is on the low side because of the nature of the tax system and the fluctuating membership rolls. One estimate of membership of over 6,000 was given to the *Billings Gazette* in 1923. *Billings Gazette*, September 25, 1923, 5.

74. *Progressive Men of the State of Montana*, 883.

75. *Progressive Men of the State of Montana*, 883.

76. Livingston Enterprise, *Centennial Scrapbook: Livingston 1882–1982*, 57.

77. *History of Park County, Montana*, 469.

78. Stout, *A History of Montana*, 234; *The Choteau Acantha* (Choteau, MT), August 24, 1920.

79. Obituary, *Park County News* (Livingston, MT), October 14, 1948.

80. See "The Geography of Montana" at Netstate, http://www.netstate.com/states/geography/mt_geography.htm.

81. Montana State Highway Commission, *History of Montana State Highway Department*, 60 and 73. (The number increased from 60,650 in 1920 to 135,168 in 1930).

82. Diary, August 26, 1923, Fred A. Attix Papers, Reel 74C, MHS; Margaret Rumsey, Diary, June 1916, cited in Montana Historical Society, *Not in Precious Metals Alone*, 206–7.

83. Wyss, *Roads to Romance*, 29.

84. Birney, *Roads to Roam*, 162. "The road was atrocious," Birney went on, "the scenery superb." As *Newsline*, the newsletter of the Montana Department of Transportation, put it, "Montana soon gained the reputation of having the worst highways in the nation." "Gas Tax History," *Newsline* June 2017, 1.

85. Montana State Highway Commission, *History of the Montana State Highway Department 1913–1942*, 100–101.

86. Montana State Highway Commission, *History of the Montana State Highway Department 1913–1942*, 27. Crossing the Continental Divide during winter would have been impossible—mountain passes received anywhere from 150 inches to 400 inches of snow, 101.

87. Fergus County Bi-Centennial Heritage Committee, *The Heritage Book of the Original Fergus County Area*, 249.

88. Fergus County Bi-Centennial Heritage Committee, *The Heritage Book of the Original Fergus County Area*, 249. Stories are plentiful about the poor conditions of Montana roads during the 1910s and 1920s. Even Montana governor Joseph Dixon acknowledged the "bad condition of the main highway from Butte to Helena." Dixon to John E. Corett, June 21, 1921, Montana Governors' Papers, MC 35, Box 30, General Correspondence, Highway Commission, Dixon Administration, MHS.

89. Wyss, *Roads to Romance*, 29.

90. Spritzer, *Roadside History of Montana*, xii-xiii.

91. Malone, Roeder, and Lang, *Montana*, 182.

92. See the Montana State Highway Commission Highway Map of Montana 1926, https://www.mdt.mt.gov/other/mdtexrepo/maps/1926_MT_HWY.JPG.

93. Lay, *The Invisible Empire in the West*. See pages 39 (Colorado), 67 (Texas), 103 (California), 128 (Utah), and 154 (Oregon).

94. *Fallon County Times* (Baker, MT), June 16, 1921.
95. *Harlowton Times*, June 9, 1921.
96. Membership records, Knights of The Ku Klux Klan, Wheatland Klan, No. 29 (Harlowton, MT) 1923–1928, SC 2223, MHS.
97. *Great Falls Tribune*, July 24, 1921, 3.
98. *Anaconda Standard*, October 8, 1922, Diocese Scrapbooks, XXV, p. 78.
99. *The Producer News* (Plentywood, MT), August 12, 1921; *Butte Bulletin*, July 21, 1921.
100. *Kalispell Times*, May 18, 1922; *Glasgow Courier*, May 19, 1922; *Butte Miner*, May 19, 1922; *Roundup Record*, June 23, 1922; *Anaconda Standard*, October 8, 1922; *Great Falls Tribune*, December 22, 1922.
101. *Helena Independent*, January 29, 1923; *The Daily Missoulian*, June 22, 1923.
102. *Imperial Nighthawk*, October 3, 1923.
103. Kloreo, September 16, 1923, F97, Kontinental Klan, MF457, MHS.
104. Terwilliger, Official Circular, June 2, 1924, F163, Kontinental Klan, MF 457, MHS.
105. *Big Timber Pioneer*, November 11, 1923; *Roundup Tribune*, June 1, 1922; "Ku Klux Klan Has Hold in Livingston," *Great Falls Tribune*, September 9, 1922.
106. "Ku Klux Klan is in Evidence Here," *Glasgow Courier*, May 19, 1922.
107. *The Choteau Acantha*, June 1, 1922.
108. Ku Klux Klan is in Evidence Here," *Glasgow Courier*, May 19, 1922; *The Choteau Acantha*, June 1, 1922.
109. *Harlowton Times*, January 26, 1922.
110. "Practically everyone who attended was listed," stated the paper. *Big Timber Pioneer*, April 10, 1924.
111. Higham, *Strangers in the Land*, 80. Higham notes the APA's founder, Henry F. Bower, was "a devoted Mason." Further, Protestants made up the bulk of Masonic membership, although some Catholics did join in defiance of the Roman Catholic Church's position.
112. Schmidt, "Fraternal Organizations," 122. According to Schmidt, 155 new fraternities emerged between 1877 and 1903, with an additional 98 new orders between 1904 and 1925.
113. Grand Master Arthur D. Prince, *Butte Miner*, June 17, 1922, 2.
114. *Butte Bulletin*, January 5, 1923.
115. Chalmers, *Hooded Americanism*, 34.
116. Data are from newspaper articles, obituaries, and county histories. This is a larger number than reported in my article about the Harlowton Klan—*Proceedings of the Grand Lodge of Ancient Free and Accepted Masons of the State of Montana 1924–1925* has added more names to the list of Klansmen who were also Masons. Note that *Proceedings* includes only Master Masons, not Apprentices and Journeymen.
117. A contemporary source on the Klan's money-making machine is William G. Shepherd, "Ku Klux Koin." The combined moneys from the "mandatory robe purchases, membership fees, and annual taxes" meant that Imperial headquarters raked in "at least $25 million in 1924." Pegram, *One Hundred Percent American*, 16. Also, see Alexander, "Kleagles and Cash."

118. Chalmers, *Hooded Americanism*, 34.
119. Knights of the Ku Klux Klan, Inc., *Kloran [of the] Knights of the Ku Klux Klan*, 5th edition, (1916), 49 Publications, F138, Kontinental Klan, MF 457, MHS.
120. *Harlowton Times*, March 20, 1924.
121. Pegram, *One Hundred Percent American*, 22.
122. Pegram, *One Hundred Percent American*, 22.
123. "Why They Join the Klan," 321.
124. William J. Jameson, "Ku Klux Klan in Montana," n.d., Jameson papers, Jameson Law Library, University of Montana School of Law.
125. Minutes, Kloreo, Billings, August 24, 1924, F98, MF457, Kontinental Klan, MHS.

Chapter 2. Secret Fraternalism and Klankraft

Epigraph: "The Mystic City," in Crew, *Ku Klux Klan Sheet Music*, 185.

1. Examples include the Junior Order United American Mechanics, the Order of the Little Red Schoolhouse, and the Guardians of Liberty. See Higham, *Strangers in the Land*, 80; Kinzer, *An Episode in Anti-Catholicism*, 34–35.
2. Merz, "Sweet Land of Secrecy," 329.
3. *Polks City Directory*, Butte, 1923, 94–99.
4. *Polks City Directory*, Livingston, 1925, 15.
5. *Helena Independent*, August 16, 1927, Diocese Scrapbooks, XXXII, p. 50.
6. The Klan was not consistent in its spelling of Klankraft (or Klancraft). I use Klankraft throughout the book, since it was the original spelling, unless in a direct quote. (Usually Evans spelled it with a "c.")
7. Clawson, *Constructing Brotherhood*, 131–132. Also, see Gist, "Secret Societies," 129.
8. One consequence of the "whites only" clauses was the growth of all-Black fraternities. Clawson, *Constructing Brotherhood*, 132.
9. *Ideals of the Ku Klux Klan*, n.d. (1925?), 3, F129, Publications, Kontinental Klan, MF457, MHS.
10. Lewis Terwilliger to Albert W. Jones, November 15, 1927, F10, Correspondence, Kontinental Klan, MF457, MHS.
11. An unnamed Kligrapp to Albert W. Jones, November 11, 1927, F10, Correspondence, Kontinental Klan, MF457, MHS.
12. Terwilliger, Proposed Amendment to Article 2, Section 1, March 4, 1929, F89, Organizational Records, Kontinental Klan, MF 457, MHS.
13. *The Kloran*, 1916, 26. Also see *Constitution and Laws of the Knights of the Ku Klux Klan*, Atlanta, Georgia, Membership, Article IV, Section 1, 1926, 9. F138 and F126, Publications, Kontinental Klan, MF457, MHS.
14. Higham, *Strangers in the Land*, 80; Wallace, *The Rhetoric of Anti-Catholicism*; Kinzer, *An Episode in Anti-Catholicism*, 41, 49.
15. Quoted in Wallace, *The Rhetoric of Anti-Catholicism*, 61.
16. Terwilliger, Official Circular, December 22, 1928, F166, Publications, Kontinental Klan, MF457, MHS.

17. Minutes, May 26, 1925, F106, Organizational Records, Kontinental Klan, MF457, MHS.

18. Terwilliger announced in late 1924 that the Royal Riders of the Red Robe would change its name to the Krusaders. Terwilliger, Official Circular, October 24, 1924, F163, Publications, Kontinental Klan, MF457, MHS.

19. Letter from J. B. Kula to Lewis Terwilliger, April 27, 1924, F1, Correspondence, Kontinental Klan, MF457, MHS.

20. Condensed Minutes of the Annual Kloreo for the Realm of Montana, Great Falls, August 14, 1927, F100, Organizational Records, Kontinental Klan, MF457, MHS.

21. Condensed Minutes of the Annual Kloreo for the Realm of Montana, Great Falls, August 14, 1927, F100, Organizational Records, Kontinental Klan, MF457, MHS.

22. Minutes of the Kloreo, Helena, Montana, June 16–17, 1928, F101, Organizational Records, Kontinental Klan, MF457, MHS.

23. *Examiner* (Butte), April 9, 1896, and July 16, 1896; Kinzer, *An Episode in Anti-Catholicism,* 45.

24. Terwilliger, Official Circular, December 6, 1924, F163, Organizational Records, Kontinental Klan, MF457, MHS.

25. Terwilliger, Official Circular, June 13, 1924, F163, Organizational Records, Kontinental Klan, MF457, MHS.

26. Terwilliger, Official Circular, June 13, 1924, F163, Organizational Records, Kontinental Klan, MF457, MHS.

27. Minutes of the Klorero, Billings, Montana, August 24, 1924, F98, Organizational Records, Kontinental Klan, MF457, MHS.

28. Minutes of the Klorero, Helena, Montana, September 6, 1925, F99, Organizational Records, Kontinental Klan, MF457, MHS.

29. Terwilliger, Official Circular, June 13, 1924, F163, Publications, Kontinental Klan, MF457, MHS.

30. "Real Men Wanted," *Imperial Nighthawk,* June 20, 1923, 7.

31. Quoted in *Great Falls Tribune,* May 31, 1922, 7; Brown Harwood, Imperial Klazik, Grand Dragon papers, July 1923, 4.

32. Hiram W. Evans, "The Klan in Action," 1929, 3. F133, Publications, Kontinental Klan, MF457, MHS; *Imperial Nighthawk,* June 20, 1923, F133, Publications, Kontinental Klan, MF457, MHS.

33. "Real Men Wanted," *Imperial Nighthawk,* June 20, 1923, 7.

34. Hiram W. Evans, "The Klan in Action," 1929, 3. F133, Publications, Kontinental Klan, MF457, MHS.

35. Terwilliger, Official Circular, June 13, 1924, F163, Publications, Kontinental Klan, MF457, MHS.

36. *Examiner* (Butte, MT) October 5, 1895.

37. *Examiner* (Butte, MT), June 29, 1895. See also Frink, "God Give Us Men!"

38. *Examiner* (Butte, MT) November 23, 1895.

39. Terwilliger, Official Circular, October 24, 1924, F163, Publications, Kontinental Klan, MF457, MHS.

40. Terwilliger, Official Circular, August 3, 1924, F163, Publications, Kontinental Klan, MF457, MHS.
41. "K.K.K. Stages State Meeting," *Billings Gazette*, September 3, 1923.
42. "Klan Ceremony near Billings, *Billings Gazette*, September 21, 1923; *Butte Miner*, September 21, 1923.
43. William J. Simmons, Naturalization Ceremony, *The Kloran* (1916), 22, F138, Publications, Kontinental Klan, MF457, MHS.
44. See Blumer, "Introduction to Social Movements," 9.
45. Terwilliger mentioned in his Official Circular, January 26, 1929, that the fourth degree had not yet been completed, but as soon as it was, Klansmen would be informed. F102, Publications, Kontinental Klan, MF457, MHS.
46. William Simmons, *Kloran*, Knights of the Ku Klux Klan, K-Uno, fifth edition (1916), 13, F138, Publications, Kontinental Klan, MF457, MHS.
47. Simmons, *Kloran*, 30, 38, 40.
48. Simmons, *Kloran*, 26, 29. See Gist, "Secret Societies," 95–96, for a brief discussion of punishments in secret fraternities. Secret fraternities typically included such threats in their oath, some considerably more graphic than the Klan's.
49. Simmons, *Kloran*, 49.
50. Gist, "Secret Societies," 70–79. Secret fraternities often recited romantic and mythical tales of the order's origins. This served as one tactic for attracting and retaining members.
51. Gist, "Secret Societies," 115.
52. Simmons, *Kloran*, 12. Louise Rasmussen of Roundup, Montana, remembers that when she was a child the Klan burned a cross up the street. Her parents pulled her out of bed and wanted her to remember the event "with horror." Louise G. Rasmussen, interview by Laurie Mercier, OH812, Tape 1, October 11, 1984, MHS.
53. Gist, "Secret Societies," 66–67.
54. Hiram W. Evans, "The Klan in Action," 1929, 32, F133, Publications, Kontinental Klan, MF457, MHS.
55. Clawson, *Constructing Brotherhood*, 228.
56. Terwilliger, Official Circular, November 6, 1929, Official Circular, December 22, 1928, F102 and F101, Publications, Kontinental Klan, MF457, MHS.
57. Terwilliger, Official Circular, September 15, 1928, F101, Publications, Kontinental Klan, MF457, MHS. For more on symbolism see Gist, "Secret Societies," 30, 68–69. Gist, "Secret Fraternities," 30; Clawson, *Constructing Brotherhood*, 232.
58. Monteval, *The Klan Inside Out*, 46, 59.
59. Alexander's opening line in "Kleagles and Cash" quotes a Kligrapp after his local chapter disbanded: "I am convinced that the Ku Klux Klan is the greatest graft organization in history." "Kleagles and Cash," 348.
60. Terwilliger, Official Circular, October 29, 1924, F98, Publications, Kontinental Klan, MF457, MHS.
61. Terwilliger, Official Circular, October 29, 1924, and March 10, 1928, F98 and F101, Publications, Kontinental Klan, MF457, MHS. Also, see *Constitution and Laws of*

the Knights of the Ku Klux Klan, Atlanta, Georgia, Membership, Article IV, Section 1, 1926, 47. F138 and F126, Publications, Kontinental Klan, MF457, MHS. "The Klan in Action" (1929) noted in the section "Advanced Klancraft" that Ku-Duo was now "Knights of the Great Forest" and K-Trio was "Knights Kamelia." Hiram W. Evans, "The Klan in Action," 1929, 32, F133, Publications, Kontinental Klan, MF457, MHS.

62. Knights of the Ku Klux Klan, Inc., *Kloran of the Knights of the Great Forest*, K-Trio, 1928, 25. F137, Publications, Kontinental Klan, MF457, MHS.

63. *Kloran of the Knights of the Great Forest*, 10, 24, 28–29.

64. *Kloran of the Knights of the Great Forest*, 28.

65. Pegram, *One Hundred Percent American*, 207–209.

66. Chalmers, *Hooded Americanism*, 288–289; *Helena Independent*, September 14, 1926, 1.

67. *Kloran of the Knights of the Great Forest*, 31.

68. *Kloran of the Knights of the Great Forest*, 39.

69. *Kloran of the Knights of the Great Forest*, 20.

70. Terwilliger to "Faithful and Esteemed Klansman," January 18, 1928; Terwilliger to Albert W. Jones, February 10, 1928, F11, Correspondence, Kontinental Klan, MF457, MHS.

71. *Kloran of the Knights of the Great Forest*, 42–43.

72. William Joseph Simmons, *First Lesson in the Science and Art of Klankraft*, Imperial Instructions Document No. 1, Atlanta, Georgia; *Knights of the Ku Klux Klan*, 1918, Beinecke Rare Book and Manuscript Library, Yale University Library, New Haven, CT.

73. Hiram W. Evans, "Where the Klan Stands Today," Fourth Imperial Klonvokation, Chicago, IL, July 17, 18, 19, 1928, Ku Klux Klan Collection, SC 112, Ball State University Archives and Special Collections.

74. Terwilliger, Official Circular, January 1925, F164, Publications, Kontinental Klan, MF457, MHS.

75. Terwilliger, Official Circular, March 31, 1928, and Official Circular, June 14, 1927, F101 and F100, Publications, Kontinental Klan, MF457, MHS.

76. *Imperial Klaliff Bulletin*, October 7, 1926, 3. F141, Publications, Kontinental Klan, MF457, MHS.

77. Terwilliger, Official Circular, January 1926, F99, Publications, Kontinental Klan, MF457, MHS. Felix Harcourt notes that by 1923, the *Fellowship Forum* "was clearly governed by the Klan"; indeed, the Grand Dragon of Texas had joined the board of directors. See Harcourt, *Ku Klux Kulture*, 31–51.

78. Terwilliger, Official Circular, July 15, 1927, F100, Publications, Kontinental Klan, MF457, MHS.

79. Terwilliger, Official Circular, July 15, 1927, F100, Publications, Kontinental Klan, MF457, MHS.

80. James S. Vance to Albert Jones, October 18, 1928, F12, Correspondence, Kontinental Klan, MF457, MHS.

81. See William Lloyd Clark, *The Story of My Battle with the Scarlet Beast* and *The Rail Splitter Catalogue* (Milan, Illinois: The Rail Splitter Press, n.d.), F160, Publications, Kontinental Klan, MF457, MHS.

82. W. W. Casper, Editor and Business Manager, *The Montana Klansman*, Belgrade, MT. n.d. Summer 1924, F7, Correspondence, Kontinental Klan, MF457, MHS.

83. Minutes of the Klorero, Billings, August 24, 1924, F98, Correspondence, Kontinental Klan, MF457, MHS.

84. Terwilliger, Official Circular, October 24, 1924, F163, Publications, Kontinental Klan, MF457, MHS.

85. Terwilliger, Official Circular, October 24, 1924, F163, Publications, Kontinental Klan, MF457, MHS. Also see W. W. Casper, Editor and Business Manager, *The Montana Klansman*, Belgrade, MT. n.d. (Summer 1924), F7, Correspondence, Kontinental Klan, MF457, MHS.

86. W. W. Casper to Floyd F. Johnson, October 7, 1924; W. W. Casper, Editor and Business Manager, *The Montana Klansman*, Belgrade, MT. n.d. (Summer 1924), F7, Correspondence, Kontinental Klan, MF457, MHS.

87. Terwilliger, Official Circular, October 24, 1924, F163, Publications, Kontinental Klan, MF457, MHS.

88. Terwilliger, Official Circular, February 1925, F164, Publications, Kontinental Klan, MF457, MHS.

89. Terwilliger, Official Circular, March 1925, F164, Publications, Kontinental Klan, MF457, MHS.

90. Terwilliger, Official Circular, March 1925, F164, Publications, Kontinental Klan, MF457, MHS.

91. *Imperial Nighthawk*, June 20, 1923, 7.

92. Terwilliger, Official Circular, January 1925, F164, Publications, Kontinental Klan, MF457, MHS.

93. Terwilliger, Official Circular, March 1925, F164, Publications, Kontinental Klan, MF457, MHS.

94. Terwilliger, Official Circular, January 1925, F164, Publications, Kontinental Klan, MF457, MHS.

95. Terwilliger, Official Circular, October 6, 1925, F164, Publications, Kontinental Klan, MF457, MHS.

96. Terwilliger, Official Circular, October 6, 1925, F164, Publications, Kontinental Klan, MF457, MHS.

97. Terwilliger, Official Circular, January 1925, F164, Publications, Kontinental Klan, MF457, MHS.

98. Minutes of the Klorero, Great Falls, August 14, 1927, F100, Organizational Records, Kontinental Klan, MF457, MHS.

99. Terwilliger, Official Circular, May 31, 1929, F167, Publications, Kontinental Klan, MF457, MHS.

100. Terwilliger, Official Circular, February 16, 1929, April 13, 1929, F167, Publications, Kontinental Klan, MF457, MHS.

NOTES TO CHAPTER 3

101. Terwilliger, Official Circular, June 1925, F164, Publications, Kontinental Klan, MF457, MHS.
102. *Belle Fourche Bee*, May 28, 1925, July 9, 1925. Also see *Belle Fourche Bee*, June 11, June 18, and July 2, 1925. An estimated 760 robed and hooded Klansmen, 93 of them on horses, marched in the parade.

Chapter 3. Fighting Enemies

Epigraph: "The Battle Hymn of Klandom," in Crew, *Ku Klux Klan Sheet Music*, 32.
1. Pegram, *One Hundred Percent American*, 9.
2. Terwilliger, Official Circular, May 10, 1928, F166, Publications, Kontinental Klan, MF457, MHS.
3. See, for example, *Kloran* (1916), 14. F138, Publications, Kontinental Klan, MF457, MHS.
4. See MacLean, *Behind the Mask of Chivalry*, 161, for a discussion of Evans's brand of muscular Christianity and its influence on "civilizing" the country.
5. Grand Dragon of Mississippi, "A Spiritual Interpretation of Klankraft," KKK Papers, Annual Meeting, 1923, North Carolina, July 1923, 52.
6. Laura McCall, "Introduction," in Basso, McCall, and Garceau, *Across the Great Divide*, 1–5.
7. State Department of Agriculture and Publicity, *The Opportunities and Resources of Montana*, 5.
8. Grand Dragon of Wyoming, "Operation of Klankraft in the West," Papers Read at the Meeting of Grand Dragons, Knights of the Ku Klux Klan, First Annual Meeting, Asheville, NC, July 1923, 110.
9. *Spokane Review*, August 6, 1926. The occasion was the Realm's annual Korero and a visit from Imperial Wizard Evans. There was a parade of "nearly 400 robed marchers" in Livingston. The next day, the Klan planned to visit Yellowstone. "Klansmen Assemble at Official Entrance Yellowstone Park," *Imperial Nighthawk*, August 13, 1924. For a discussion of Flathead Lake, see *Klorero* (1927). The idea was scrapped by 1929 because there was not enough money. *Klorero* (1929).
10. Flint, "Introduction," *Spaces of Hate*, 2–3; Kathleen Blee, "The Geography of Racial Activism: Defining Whiteness at Multiple Scales," in Flint, *Spaces of Hate*, 50.
11. Evans, "The Menace of Modern Immigration," 6, 10.
12. Evans, "The Menace of Modern Immigration," 16.
13. Evans, "The Menace of Modern Immigration," 22, 24. Also see Spiro, *Defending the Master Race*, 171.
14. There was no need to read Grant's and Stoddard's books in full; popular magazines and newspaper editorials quoted them liberally and gave credence to their eugenic arguments. Higham, *Strangers in the Land*, 273. See also Evans, "The Klan's Fight for Americanism" and Jacobson, *Whiteness of a Different Color*, 75–79.
15. Jacobson, *Whiteness of a Different Color*, 7.
16. *Imperial Nighthawk*, August 15, 1923.
17. *Imperial Nighthawk*, August 15, 1923.

18. Evans, "The Menace of Modern Immigration," 8, 23.
19. *Imperial Nighthawk*, February 14, 1924, reported on Terwilliger's speech to the Bozeman Klan.
20. No newspaper given, October 28, 1923, Diocese Scrapbooks, XXVIII, p. 36.
21. "A Peep behind the Hood," no newspaper given, November 3, 1923, Diocese Scrapbooks, XXVIII, p. 42.
22. "What Might Have Happened," *Missoulian*, October 30, 1923, Diocese Scrapbooks, XXVIII, p. 41.
23. *Harlowton Times*, January 27, 1921.
24. *Billings Gazette*, August 10, 1924.
25. *Park County News* (Livingston), March 28, 1924, 8.
26. H. W. Evans, Greetings to Klansmen, 1925. F8, Kontinental Klan, MF457, MHS.
27. Table 6: Country of Birth of Foreign-born Whites, Fourteenth Census of the United States, 1920, Volume III, Population, 577. Irish in Montana: 7,260, Silver Bow County: 3,370, with another 1,000 in Deer Lodge County.
28. Addison K. Lusk, Federal Prohibition Director, to Governor Joseph M. Dixon, May 16, 1923, Montana Governor's Papers, Box 32, F15: General Correspondence, Prohibition, MC35, MHS.
29. *Great Falls Tribune*, April 17, 1923, 8.
30. No liquor awaited the homesteaders as a reward for their services, but the lucky ones "received a five dollar bill." Mathison, *Echoes from the Breaks*.
31. Donovan, *The First Hundred Years*, 125; Gertrude "Trudy" Klein Saxtorph, interviewed by Ann Zellick, September 8, 1979, OH1704, MHS; Roy History Committee, *Homestead Shacks over Buffalo Tracks*, 149. "Twenty-five to thirty miles an hour; top speed!" declared the same resident.
32. Wilson, *Honky Tonk Town*, 2.
33. *Kalispell Times*, May 18, 1922; Spritzer, *Roadside History of Montana*, 47.
34. Wilson, *Honky Tonk Town*, 78; Spritzer, *Roadside History of Montana*, 47.
35. Rustebakke and Southland, *Millennium Memories*, 56.
36. *Kalispell Times*, September 7, 1922, 4. Also, see Malone, *The Battle for Butte*, 74 and Writers Project of Montana, *Copper Camp*, 10. Montana enacted its prohibition law in January 1919, and, just a few hours later, officers arrested a liquor dealer. *Copper Camp*, 6. Butte was quick to violate the Volstead Act. The *Butte Evening News* reported on January 1, 1919, that two saloons were raided, one where over thirty men were drinking. The *Butte Miner* noted in 1924 that Butte wanted "a cleanup of the bootleggers for it is heartily tired of the way bootleggers have been cleaning up here," April 11, 1924.
37. Murphy, "Bootlegging," 178. Murphy points out that Prohibition in Butte "allowed ethnic groups and women to capitalize on the underground economy by launching new business in the manufacturing and sale of liquor."
38. Murphy, *Mining Cultures*, 54.
39. James Blakely, interviewed by Ray F. Calkins, oral history transcript, Silver Bow Archives, November 15, 1979, 3, 4.

40. *Butte Miner*, September 26, 1923.
41. Addison K. Lusk, Federal Prohibition Director, to Governor Joseph M. Dixon, May 16, 1923, Montana Governor's Papers, Box 32, F15: General Correspondence, Prohibition, MC35, MHS. Kalispell and Libby, on the other hand, were characterized by acting federal prohibition officer John H. Metcalf as "perhaps the driest [*sic*] towns in the state." *Kalispell Times*, December 28, 1922, 1.
42. Minutes, November 9, 1927, F108, Kontinental Klan, MF457, MHS.
43. Minutes, September 16, 1925, F106, Kontinental Klan, MF457, MHS.
44. *Butte Miner*, May 19, 1922; *Fallon County Times*, June 22, 1922.
45. Harlowton Woman's Club, *Yesteryears*, 42.
46. "Moonshiners Have Troubles Galore: Big Horn Sheriff Makes Life Miserable for all Offenders," *The Searchlight* (Hardin), February 4, 1925; County Sheriffs Get Real Haul of Moon," *The Searchlight* (Hardin), June 3, 1925; Bi-Centennial Committee of the Big Horn County Historical Society, *Lookin' Back*, 303.
47. *Harlowton Times*, January 13, 1921; August 5, 1921; March 30, 1922; November 26, 1925.
48. *The Daily Missoulian*, January 22, 1923; *Helena Record*, January 22, 1923, Diocese Scrapbooks, XXVI.
49. "Ku Klux in Cabal with Lanstrum to 'Get' Slattery," December 16, 1925, no paper identified, Diocese Scrapbooks, XXXI, 7; *Fergus County Argus* (Lewistown), December 24, 1925, 1. Slattery had been in office since the summer of 1921. He then opened a law office in Great Falls. "District Attorney is Great Falls Attorney," *Big Timber Pioneer*, February 4, 1926, 2.
50. "Ku Klux Klan Seen in Montana: Try to Unseat U.S. Attorney John M. Slattery, Charges Helena Independent," *Spokane Review*, December 20, 1925.
51. *Helena Independent*, December 16, 1925; *Powder River County Examiner* and the *Broadus Independent*, December 25, 1925, 1. Also see *Spokane Review*, December 20, 1925, Reel 4, F 190.
52. Malone, Roeder, and Lang, *Montana*, 265; Waldron, *Atlas of Montana Elections*, 107.
53. "Montana Klan Vote Factor," *Spokane Review*, September 21, 1926, F190, Clippings, Kontinental Klan, MF457, MHS.
54. See *Harlowton Times*, August 24, 1922; May 1, 1924; June 17, 1926; October 28, 1926.
    When the voting was done, 73.4 percent of Silver Bow County voted in favor of repeal, followed closely by Glacier (71.6) and Deer Lodge (70.5). Waldron, *Atlas of Montana Elections*, 110.
55. Waldron, *Atlas of Montana Elections*, 110. Wheatland County opposed the state initiative with 54 percent of the vote.
56. Governor Erickson to Edward Galloway, Hardin, December 1, 1927, F10 General Correspondence Prohibition, Box 52, Erickson administration, Montana Governors' Papers, MC35, MHS.
57. Terwilliger to Ed Davis, February 6, 1928, F11, Correspondence, Kontinental Klan, MF457, MHS.

58. Malone, Roeder, and Lang, *Montana*, 265.
59. Terwilliger, Official Circular, August 30, 1924, F163, Publications, Kontinental Klan, MF457, MHS.
60. Terwilliger, Official Circular, October 24, 1924, F163, Publications, Kontinental Klan, MF457, MHS.
61. Terwilliger, Official Circular, August 3, 1924, F163, Publications, Kontinental Klan, MF457, MHS. The phrase "without fear or favor" was used in Klan publications, such as the *Fiery Cross* (Indianapolis). See volume 3, September 12, 1924, for instance. Hoosier State Chronicles: Indiana's Digital Historic Newspaper Program.
62. Terwilliger, Official Circular, August 3, 1924, F163, Publications, Kontinental Klan, MF457, MHS.
63. Terwilliger, Official Circular, September 30, 1928, F166, Publications, Kontinental Klan, MF457, MHS.
64. State Candidates, Primary Election, July 17, 1928, and State Candidates, General Election, November 6, 1928, F166, Publications and F184, Miscellany, Kontinental Klan, MF457, MHS. The two other candidates in the Republican primaries who were identified as Klansmen or former Klansmen by the Realm's political committee ran for governor and treasurer. Neither was successful in gaining the party's nomination.
65. State Candidates, Primary Election, July 15, 1930, F168, Publications, Kontinental Klan, MF457, MHS.
66. *Butte Miner*, October 4, 1921, 1.
67. Walsh also condemned the Klan during a Tolerance mass meeting held in Washington, DC, and attended by Protestant, Catholic, and Jewish clergymen. Walsh gave the main address. No newspaper listed, December 1922, Diocese Scrapbooks, XXV, 138. See also Bates, *Senator Thomas J. Walsh of Montana*.
68. "Information Regarding Political Candidates," 1924, F163, Publications, Kontinental Klan, MF457, MHS.
69. "5 Mountain States Still Uncertain," *New York Times*, October 12, 1924; "Montana Troubles All Party Leaders," *New York Times*, October 11, 1924.
70. "Montana Troubles All Party Leaders," *New York Times*, October 11, 1924.
71. Coolidge won the popular vote by an almost 2–1 margin. Morris, *Encyclopedia of American History*, 335. Also, see Chalmers, *Hooded Americanism*, 202–215 and Pegram, *One Hundred Percent American*, 19–20, 213–215 for more discussion of the 1924 presidential campaign.
72. *Spokane Review*, September 11 and 12, 1924, F190, Clippings, Kontinental Klan, MF457, MHS. "Democrats Hit K.K.," *Helena Independent*, September 11, 1924.
73. Waldron, *Atlas of Montana Elections*, 102.
74. *Billings Gazette*, November 8, 1924, 4. Walsh won 89,681 votes to Linderman's 72,000. Waldron, *Atlas of Montana Elections*, 97.
75. See lists for the 1928 and 1930 elections: F166 and F168, Publications, Kontinental Klan, MF457, MHS.

76. Fisher, "Montana: Land of the Copper Collar"; "Democrats Hit K.K.," *Helena Independent*, September 11, 1924.

77. Higham, *Strangers in the Land*, 82; Manfra, "Hometown Politics and the American Protective Association," 164; Kinzer, *An Episode in Anti-Catholicism*, 203.

78. See Emmons, "The Orange and the Green in Montana," 236–237.

79. Lewis Terwilliger to Floyd Johnson, n.d., 1924, F7, Correspondence, Kontinental Klan, MF457, MHS.

80. *Harlowton Times*, August 21, 1924.

81. *Big Timber Pioneer*, March 6, 1924.

82. *Helena Independent*, March 12, 1922.

83. See McDonald, *Red Corner*, 59–60.

84. Steele, *Wellington Rankin*, 113.

85. Waldron, *Atlas of Montana Elections*, 101.

86. Malone, Roeder, and Lang, *Montana*, 230, 288. Montana voters did pass Dixon's initiative to institute a graduated mine tax. Other successful progressive reforms championed by Dixon included "initiat[ing] new methods of assessing railroads and utilities thus increasing their taxable value" and instituting an old-age pension law. Also see Small, *A Century of Politics on the Yellowstone*, 67; Waldron, *Atlas of Montana Elections*, 97.

87. Terwilliger, Official Circular, November 11, 1924, and December 6, 1924, Publications, F163, Kontinental Klan, MF457, MHS.

88. Terwilliger, Official Circular, November 11, 1924, F163, Publications, Kontinental Klan, MF457, MHS.

89. Waldron, *Atlas of Montana Elections*, 98.

90. Terwilliger, Official Circular, October 31, 1928, F166, Publications, Kontinental Klan, MF457, MHS.

91. Terwilliger, Official Circular, March 1925 (note: there are two official circulars labeled March 1925), F164, Publications, Kontinental Klan, MF457, MHS.

92. Albert Jones to Lewis Terwilliger, November 20, 1928, F12, Correspondence, Kontinental Klan, MF457, MHS.

93. Terwilliger, Official Circular, March 1925, F164, Publications, Kontinental Klan, MF457, MHS.

94. Svingen, "Jim Crow, Indian Style," 276.

95. Terwilliger, Official Circular, December 6, 1924, F163, Publications, Kontinental Klan, MF457, MHS.

96. The state legislature continued to ensure, indirectly, that Indians would not be represented at the county level in 1927 and in 1937. No Indians in Big Horn County who ran for state and county seats between 1924 and 1934 won. See Svingen, "Jim Crow, Indian Style," 278–79 for further explanation. Kristin Inbody adds that the state constitution was amended "to disenfranchise as many Indian voters as possible, limiting voting rights to taxpayers in 1932—knowing those who lived on reservations were exempt from some taxes. Later laws aimed to make voter

registration and polling difficult to impossible on reservations." Kristen Inbody, "Montana Moment: Forged in War, Citizenship Extends to Indians," *Great Falls Tribune*, June 14, 2014, https://www.greatfallstribune.com/story/life/my-montana /2014/06/15/montana-moment-forged-war-citizenship-extends-indians/10501851/.

97. The Kontinental Klan agreed and endorsed Hardin's resolution. Minutes, December 6, 1924, F105, Organizational Records, Kontinental Klan, MF457, MHS.

98. *Butte Miner*, April 3, 5, 6, 1924.

99. Minutes, May 6, 1924, F105, Organizational Records, Kontinental Klan, MF457, MHS.

100. *Billings Gazette*, April 8, 1924.

101. "Ku Klux Klan Wins in School Board Contest," *Hardin Tribune*, April 11, 1924; *Billings Gazette*, April 6, 1924.

102. *Billings Gazette*, April 3, 1924.

103. "Klan at Billings, *Butte Miner*, April 8, 1924; William J. Jameson, "Ku Klux Klan in Montana," n.d., Jameson Papers, Jameson Law Library, University of Montana School of Law.

104. Lewis Terwilliger, Official Circular, October 20, 1927, F165, Publications, Kontinental Klan, MF457, MHS.

105. Small, *A Century of Politics on the Yellowstone*, 71.

106. William J. Jameson, "Ku Klux Klan in Montana," n.d., Jameson Papers, Jameson Law Library, University of Montana School of Law.

107. "Klan Asks Judge to Send All Delinquent Girls to State Vocational School," *Montana Record-Herald*, c. November 23, 1927, Diocese Scrapbooks, XXXII, p. 78; Home of the Good Shepherd, Vertical Files, MHS.

108. Kinzer, *Episode*, 95–96.

109. Terwilliger, Official Circular, June 24, 1927, F165, Publications, Kontinental Klan, MF457, MHS.

110. Terwilliger, Official Circular, June 24, 1927, F165, Publications, Kontinental Klan, MF457, MHS.

111. Baumler, "The Florence Crittenton House."

112. Minutes of the Klorero, Great Falls, August 14, 1927, F100, Organizational Records, Kontinental Klan, MF457, MHS; *Montana Record-Herald*, c. November 23, 1927, Diocese Scrapbooks, XXXII, 78; Terwilliger to the Judge of the District Court, November 18, 1927, F10, Correspondence, Kontinental Klan, MF457, MHS. "Klan Asks Judge to Send All Delinquent Girls to State Vocational School," *Montana Record-Herald*, c. November 23, 1927, Diocese Scrapbooks, XXXII, 78; See H.B. No. 295, *House Journal of the Twenty-first Legislative Assembly of the State of Montana*, Helena, Montana, State Publishing Co., January 7, 1929–March 7, 1929, 463; Baumler, "The Florence Crittenton House"; Terwilliger, Official Circular, March 6, 1929, F167, Publications, Kontinental Klan, MF457, MHS.

113. "'Saving Girls.'" Reformers began to make some changes to the school in the 1950s.

114. "'Saving Girls.'"

115. Hiram W. Evans to Faithful and Esteemed Klansman [Albert Jones, Butte], January 18, 1928, F11, Correspondence, Kontinental Klan, MF457, MHS.
116. Terwilliger, Official Circular, October 10, 1927, F165, Publications, Kontinental Klan, MF457, MHS.
117. Terwilliger, Official Circular, September 7, 1927, F165, Publications, Kontinental Klan, MF457, MHS.
118. Terwilliger, Official Circular, December 5, 1927, and December 12, 1927, F165, Publications, Kontinental Klan, MF457, MHS.
119. Bozeman Kligrapp, July 18, 1928, Terwilliger, Office of the Grand Dragon, January 18, 1928.
120. Albert Jones to Terwilliger, October 25, 1928, F12, Correspondence, Kontinental Klan, MF457, MHS.
121. Editorial, *Harlowton Times*, January 19, 1928.
122. Letter, "A few objections to an editorial appearing in the Butte Miner of June 27, 1928," Kontinental Klan, July 3, 1928, F12, Kontinental Klan, MF457, MHS.
123. Terwilliger to Faithful and Esteemed Klansman [Albert Jones, Butte], January 18, 1928, F11, Correspondence, Kontinental Klan, MF457, MHS.
124. Terwilliger to Faithful and Esteemed Klansman [Albert Jones, Butte], February 1, 1928, F11, Correspondence, Kontinental Klan, MF457, MHS.
125. Terwilliger, Official Circular, April 27, 1928, F166, Publications, Kontinental Klan, MF457, MHS.
126. Terwilliger, Official Circular, July 14, 1928, F166, Publications, Kontinental Klan, MF457, MHS.
127. James S. Vance to Albert Jones, October 18, 1928, F12, Correspondence, Kontinental Klan, MF457, MHS.
128. Jones to *Fellowship Forum*, October 25, 1928, F12, Correspondence, Kontinental Klan, MF457, MHS.
129. Solicitation for membership, International Protestant Foundation, Inc., (New York), October 20, 1927, F 10, Correspondence; Membership card, *The Rail Splitter Catalogue*, The Rail Splitter Press, Milan, Illinois, F160, Publications; Membership card, Society of Protestant Americanism, F179, Miscellany, Kontinental Klan, MF457, MHS.
130. Lewis Terwilliger to Mrs. D. Cohen, January 23, 1929, F13, Correspondence, Kontinental Klan, MF457, MHS.
131. Terwilliger to Albert Jones, January 23, 1929, F13, Correspondence, Kontinental Klan, MF457, MHS.
132. Terwilliger, Official Circular, September 30, 1928, F166, Publications, Kontinental Klan, MF457, MHS.
133. Silver Bow, Deer Lodge, and Glacier counties chose Smith. Waldron, *Atlas of Montana Elections*, 113, 115, 118. Wheeler, *Yankee from the West*, 296. Democrats objected to Smith's Catholicism (especially), but also his urban background and his criticism of Prohibition. Pegram, *One Hundred Percent American*, 218.
134. Terwilliger, Official Circular, November 7, 1928, F166, Publications, Kontinental Klan, MF457, MHS.

135. Terwilliger, Official Circular, December 3, 1928. Also see Official Circular, November 7, 1928, F166, Publications, Kontinental Klan, MF457, MHS.
136. Terwilliger, Official Circular, December 22, 1928, F166, Publications, Kontinental Klan, MF457, MHS.
137. Terwilliger, Official Circular, January 31, 1929, F167, Publications, Kontinental Klan, MF457, MHS.
138. Terwilliger, Official Circular, March 6, 1929, F167, Publications, Kontinental Klan, MF457, MHS.
139. Terwilliger, Official Circular, May 14, 1929, F167, Publications, Kontinental Klan, MF457, MHS.
140. Albert Jones to Terwilliger, January 31, 1928, F11, Correspondence; Terwilliger, Official Circular, May 14, 1929, and May 31, 1929, F167, Publications, Kontinental Klan, MF457, MHS.
141. Hiram Wesley Evans, "Greetings," February 1929, F13, Correspondence, Kontinental Klan, MF457, MHS.
142. Hiram Wesley Evans, "Greetings," February 1929, F13, Correspondence, Kontinental Klan, MF457, MHS.
143. Albert Jones to Terwilliger, October 3, 1928, F12, Correspondence, Kontinental Klan, MF457, MHS.
144. Terwilliger, Official Circular, December 22, 1928, F166, Publications, Kontinental Klan, MF457, MHS.
145. A Montana Klansman, "Honorable Klannishness," *Kourier Magazine* (May 1925): 31. Bureau of the Census, *Fifteenth Census of the United States: 1930, Population*, 7.
146. *Great Falls Tribune*, August 3, 1930, 6; Terwilliger, Official Circular, January 1926, F164, Publications, Kontinental Klan, MF457, MHS.
147. Terwilliger, Official Circular, October 29, 1930, F168, Publications, Kontinental Klan, MF457, MHS. Walsh swept to his third term in a race that was never close, winning 106,274 votes to Galen's 66,724. Waldron, *Atlas of Montana Elections*, 120.
148. Pegram, *One Hundred Percent American*, 211–12.

Chapter 4. Three Communities

Epigraph: "Keep the Crosses Burning," in Crew, *Ku Klux Klan Sheet Music*, 116.
1. The available documents concerning Butte include, among other items, membership lists, minutes from meetings, and letters between the Butte Kligrapps and Terwilliger. Membership cards with names, occupations, and other personal information comprise the Harlowton Klan records. For Roundup, only a published list of names is available. Much of the information concerning Butte and Harlowton is derived from my two articles "'Kluxer Blues': The Ku Klux Klan Confronts Catholics in Butte" and "'Come Join the K.K.K. in the Old Town Tonight': The Ku Klux Klan in Harlowton."
2. *Butte Bulletin*, July 21, 1921; *Butte Miner*, July 22, 1921; *Spokesman Review*, October 23, 1923.
3. Charter membership list, membership records, Kontinental Klan, MF457, MHS.

4. The La Grande, Oregon, Klan, with 362 members, also fluctuated greatly in attendance, although that was more understandable since the chapter met once a week
instead of twice monthly. See Horowitz, *Inside the Klavern*.

5. Minutes, Klonklaves, 1926, Reel 2, F107, Kontinental Klan, MF457, MHS.

6. Kligrapp's Quarterly Reports, Kontinental Klan, MF 457, MHS.

7. See Emmons, "The Orange and the Green in Montana," 236–37. The Orange Order
is a long-standing fraternal society created in Northern Ireland, dedicated to
upholding and championing Protestantism.

8. Table 32: Members in Selected Denominations by Counties: 1926, U.S. Department
of Commerce, Bureau of the Census, *Religious Bodies: 1926*, vol. 1: Summary and
Detailed Tables, United States: Government Printing Office, 1930, 639.

9. Terwilliger to A. W. Jones, October 28, 1927. File 10, Correspondence, Kontinental
Klan, MF457, MHS.

10. Minutes from meetings, May 7, 1923; November 21, 1923; March 26, 1924; July 15,
1924; July 19, 1924; February 14, 1925 (regular and special meetings); March 9, 1926;
May 22, 1929, F104–107, 110, Organizational Records; Rental Receipts in Financial
Records. Also see J. S. Kula to Charles Steele, April 30, 1925, F8, Correspondence,
Kontinental Klan, MF457, MHS.

11. Knights of Columbus, Minutes from Meetings, Council No. 668, 1922–1927, OC034
Silver Bow Archives; Ancient Order of Hibernians Volumes 5 and 6, 1913–1932,
OC012 Silver Bow Archives.

12. Albert Jones informed the *Rail Splitter* that he had not received the October shipment
and wondered "if someone have [sic] destroyed them." The *Railsplitter* replied saying
that they "sent 100 papers with the Oct. Mailing and they must have gone astray if
you have not received them . . ." Jones to the *Rail Splitter* and reply by Mrs. W. L.
Clark, October 17, 1927, F10, Correspondence, Kontinental Klan, MF457, MHS.

13. *Examiner* (Butte), July 6, 1895.

14. Floyd Johnson to Lewis Terwilliger, October 10, 1924, F7, Correspondence, Kontinental Klan, MF457, MHS.

15. Floyd Johnson to Dr. L. D. Johnson, Grand Dragon of Wyoming, March 29, 1924,
F7, Correspondence, Kontinental Klan, MF457, MHS.

16. Kligrapp to Imperial Palace, Form K-114, January 10, 1925, F7, Correspondence,
Kontinental Klan, MF457, MHS.

17. For reasons that are unclear, the Klan lifted the banishment two years later. Minutes, January 20, 1925, and February 9, 1927, F106, F108, Organizational Records,
Kontinental Klan, MF457, MHS.

18. Albert Jones to Lewis Terwilliger, February 13, 1928, F11, Correspondence, Kontinental Klan, MF457, MHS.

19. Lewis Terwilliger to Albert Jones, December 9, 1927, and January 6, 1928, F10
and F1, Correspondence. The Kontinental Klan records also hold an obituary
of Mrs. Ann Klassan, who served as the "postmistress" of Silver Bow County. A
handwritten note on the obituary declares "a wrecker of the Klan." F191, Clippings,
Kontinental Klan, MF457, MHS.

20. Terwilliger to Mr. W. J. Sullivan, June 21, 1928, F11, Correspondence, Kontinental Klan, MF457, MHS. Although "Butte, Mont." was typed in the header of the letter, it was signed Ku Klux Klan, Box 607, Livingston, Montana, which was Terwilliger's and the Realm's post office box.
21. Kontinental Klan to Terwilliger, March 3, 1925, F8, Correspondence, Kontinental Klan, MF457, MHS.
22. Minutes, November 28, 1928, F109, Organizational Records, Kontinental Klan, MF457, MHS.
23. Minutes, December 14, 1927, F108, Organizational Records, Kontinental Klan, MF457, MHS.
24. James L. Parker to Albert Jones, January 10, 1929, F13, Correspondence, Kontinental Klan, MF457, MHS.
25. Minutes, June 9, 1925, July 1, 1927, and February 22, 1924, are just three examples. F105, F106, F108, Organizational Records. Mrs. Jones to "Albert's friends," January 9, 1929, F13, Correspondence, Kontinental Klan, MF457, MHS.
26. Other Klans established similar funds. The Klan Komfort Fund, a Realm initiative in Oregon, ran into some scrutiny by the Imperial Palace in Atlanta, indicating, as David Horowitz points out, some "controversy over the program." LeGrande seemed not to be impressed, but, like the Butte Klan, they took care of their own. See Horowitz, *Inside the Klavern*, 69, 107–08.
27. Relief Committee Report, February 24, 1924; Minutes, February 13, 1924; February 22, 1924; March 12, 1924; Special, March 26, 1924, F105, Organizational Records, Kontinental Klan, MF457, MHS. Fraternal benevolence was common among Klans—see, for instance, the minutes of the La Grande Klan in Oregon in Horowitz, *Inside the Klavern*, 69.
28. Minutes, October 13, 1925, F106, Organizational Records, Kontinental Klan, MF457, MHS.
29. Minutes, January 20, April 14, November 24, 1925, F106, Organizational Records, Kontinental Klan, MF457, MHS.
30. Minutes, October 21, 1924, F105, Organizational Records, Kontinental Klan, MF457, MHS.
31. Minutes, March 23, 1927, F108, Organizational Records, Kontinental Klan, MF457, MHS.
32. Minutes, March 23, 1927, F108, Organizational Records, Kontinental Klan, MF457, MHS.
33. Floyd Johnson to Hiram W. Evans, January 4, 1925, F7, Correspondence, Kontinental Klan, MF457, MHS.
34. Bylaws and amendments, F89, Organizational Records, Kontinental Klan, MF457, MHS.
35. Bylaws and amendments, F89, Organizational Records, Kontinental Klan, MF457, MHS.
36. Minutes, July 1, 1928, F109, Organizational Records. C. U. Brown to Albert Jones, August 3, 1928, F12, Correspondence, Kontinental Klan, MF457, MHS.

37. Jones to Terwilliger, February 14, 1931, F14, Correspondence, Kontinental Klan, MF457, MHS.
38. Musselshell was created from Fergus, Meagher, and Yellowstone counties. Stout, *Montana*, 469, 794; Hougardy et al., *Horizons O'er the Musselshell*, 171.
39. Stout, *Montana*, 796–797; Spritzer, *Roadside History of Montana*, 307, Zellick, "Fire in the Hole," 18. Mine Number One operated for only a short time. Spritzer, *Roadside*, 307–08.
40. Zellick, "Fire in the Hole," 18.
41. Zellick, "Fire in the Hole," 16; Stout, *Montana*, 796–97; Malone, Roeder, and Lang, *Montana*, 338; Knapp, Abstract, Devil's Basin Oilfield, Musselshell County. "The excitement was terrific and lasted for several years before petering out," remembered Louise Rasmussen about nearby Devil's Basin in 1919, "the first wildcat discovery of oil in Montana." Ultimately, it was not commercially successful. Louise Rasmussen speech, n.d., provided by Tim Schaff, Roundup.
42. Zellick, "Fire in the Hole," 18.
43. Spritzer, *Roadside*, 309; Zellick, "Fire in the Hole," 19; Spritzer, *Roadside*, 308; Hougardy et al., *Horizons*, 163.
44. *Fourteenth Census of the United States, 1920*, Volume III, Population, 581.
45. Zellick, "Fire in the Hole," 26; Zellick, *Anna: A Memoir*.
46. *Roundup Record*, June 23, 1922.
47. *Roundup Record*, June 23, 1922.
48. Hougardy et al., *Horizons*, 179; Joe Vicars, OH813, Tape 1, Sides A and B, MHS.
49. Hougardy et al., *Horizons*, 179; Joe Vicars, OH813, Tape 1, Sides A and B, MHS.
50. Biography of G. F. Jeffries in Stout, *Montana*, 820–21; Delbert Walker interview by Laurie Mercier, May 11, 1982, OH278, Tape 2, Side B, MHS; Tim Schaff, correspondence, September 27, 2006. Some of the men on the membership list were not from Roundup or Klein; instead, they hailed from a puzzling array of towns and cities, such as Miles City, Great Falls, and Glendive, all many miles away from Roundup but accessible by rail. Perhaps these Knights were only passing through town and, on a friend's recommendation, participated in the naturalization ceremony. They likely played no active role in the Roundup Klan, since those communities (and others) had chapters of their own.
51. The available records for members in professions: Butte 9/153, Harlowton 12/183, Roundup 26/254.
52. Zellick, "Fire in the Hole," 27.
53. Author's interview with Chat and Mac Oliver, August 2, 1990. Notes in possession of author.
54. 1924 and 1925 Proceedings of the Grand Lodge of Ancient Free and Accepted Masons of the State of Montana. 64/188 Master Masons were Klansmen.
55. Louise E. Rasmussen, OH812, Tape 1, Side A, OH812 MHS; Rasmussen speech.
56. St. Benedict's Catholic Parochial School was built in 1923, and many of the South Slavs preferred to send their children to that school. Zellick, "Fire in the Hole," 16–17, 29.
    Rasmussen, OH812, Tape 1, Side A; Joe Vicars, OH813, Tape 1, Sides A and B, MHS.

57. Rasmussen, OH812, Tape 1, Side A; Joe Vicars, OH813, Tape 1, Sides A and B, MHS; Delbert Walker interview by Laurie Mercier, May 11, 1982, OH78 Tape 2, Side B, MHS.
58. Loewen, *Sundown Towns*, 4.
59. Dale Alger and Tim Schaff to author, summer 2006. Loewen cites another example of African American railroad crews unable to spend the night in a sundown town, Niantic, Illinois. *Sundown Towns*, 8. "Eleven Montana counties had no blacks at all" in the 1930 census. Loewen, *Sundown Towns*, 9.
60. Author's interview with Chat and Mac Oliver, August 2, 1990. Notes in possession of author.
61. Editorial, *Roundup Record*, December 23, 1921.
62. *Fourteenth Census of the United States,* 1920, 581; *Fifteenth Census of the United States,* 1930, 18. Total Black population in the state was 1,658 in 1920; in 1930, 1,256.
63. Stephen Tighe to Walter Oleson (Butte), April 12, 1924, F5, Correspondence, Kontinental Klan, MF457, MHS.
64. Interview with Chat and Mac Oliver, August 2, 1990. Notes in possession of author.
65. *Roundup Record*, February 23, 1923.
66. "Ku Kluxers Make Second Public Appearance in Roundup," *Roundup Record*, June 1, 1923.
67. *Roundup Tribune*, July 5, 1923; "Fiery Cross is 4th Spectacle," *Roundup Record*, July 6, 1923. County Attorney Charles Huppe also took notice; the next chapter explores that story.
68. Dalich, "Shelby's Fabled Day in the Sun," 4.
69. "Montana Klansmen Opposing Fight," *Imperial Nighthawk*, June 6, 1923.
70. Dempsey won in a fifteen-round decision. Three Montana banks that had been closely associated with the fight failed. "Although bank officials generally insisted that the fight had no connection" to the bank failures, both the mayor of Shelby (who was also the president of First State Bank) and George Stanton, of Stanton Trust and Savings Bank of Great Falls, held hefty financial interests in the fight, and both lost spectacularly. Dalich, "Shelby's Fabled Day in the Sun," 6, 22. Thanks to Benton Gates for sharing his knowledge about the Dempsey fight.
71. *Roundup Tribune*, August 30, 1923.
72. *Roundup Record*, July 6, 1923.
73. *Lewistown Democratic News*, September 3, 1923.
74. *Billings Gazette*, December 25, 1923; *Roundup Record*, December 28, 1923.
75. "K.C. Council is Organized Here," *Roundup Record*, April 27, 1923.
76. Louise Eiselein Rasmussen, OH812, Tape 1, Side A, MHS; Vicars, OH813, Tape 1, Sides A and B, MHS; Jameson, "Ku Klux Klan in Montana," n.d. Jameson Papers, Jameson Law Library, University of Montana School of Law.
77. Zellick, "Fire in the Hole," 30.
78. Hougardy et al., *Roundup on the Musselshell*, 69; Malone, Roeder, and Lang, *Montana*, 283.

79. Louise Eiselein Rasmussen, OH812, Tape 1 Side A, MHS; Hougardy et al., *Horizons*, 63.
80. Hougardy et al., *Horizons*, 67.
81. Malone, Roeder, and Lang, *Montana*, 283.
82. Rasmussen, speech.
83. Stearns, *A History of the Upper Musselshell Valley*, 154.
84. Quoted in Stearns, *A History of the Upper Musselshell Valley*, 184.
85. *Harlowton Times*, January 16, 1919; Stearns, *A History*, 172, 185, 187.
86. Between 1909 and 1925, the state legislature doubled the number of counties, from 28 to 56. Malone, Roeder, and Lang, *Montana*, 249–51. Also see Stearns, *A History of the Upper Musselshell Valley*, 185, 193. For the battle over creating Wheatland County, see Stearns, 144–94.
87. *Harlowton Times*, April 6, 18, 1918; May 30, 1918; February 7, 1918; January 2, 1919.
88. Mahon, *History of the Militia and the National Guard*, 157. Also see Chambers, *To Raise an Army*, 153. The *Harlowton Times* recognized the "necessity" of creating such a group, which was sure to be "one of the best organizations in the state of Montana." August 23, 1917. While some states legalized the Home Guard, the Montana state legislature rejected Governor Stewart's move to do the same. Gutfeld, *Montana's Agony*, 43.
89. Wheatland Klan, Membership records, SC2223, MHS.
90. Wheatland Klan, Membership records, SC2223, MHS.
91. Eckard V. Toy, "Robe and Gown: The Ku Klux Klan in Eugene, Oregon," 165; David A. Horowitz, "Order, Solidarity, and Vigilance: The Ku Klux Klan in La Grande, Oregon," 194 and Robert A. Goldberg, "Denver: Queen City of the Colorado Realm," 52, both in Lay, *The Invisible Empire in the West*. I used Goldberg's numbers for early joiners, since those dates correlated more closely with the Wheatland experience.
92. Harlowton was the eastern endpoint where "electric locomotives were exchanged for steam and later diesel-powered engines." Wilkerson, "Lines West," 24.
93. Many Masons warned of the influx of the Klan. See, for example, Lay, "Imperial Outpost on the Border: El Paso's Frontier Klan No. 100" in *The Invisible Empire in the West*, 73–74. *Harlowton Times*, December 7, 1922; September 4, 1924; November 20, 1924; June 29, 1922. For instance, in 1923 seven out of ten new officers installed in the Harlowton Chapter No. 22, Royal Arch Masons, were Klansmen. Of the nine offices listed in the Palestine Commandery in 1922, seven were Klansmen. In January 1926, the Musselshell Lodge A.F. and A.M. installed new officers—nine of twelve, Klansmen. At the end of the year, the Lodge held another round of elections—ten of twelve went to Klansmen. The Musselshell Lodge of Masons No. 69 elected ten of twelve Klansmen as officers in 1926, while the Harlowton Chapter No. 28 Royal Arch Masons chose eight of twelve as officers. *Harlowton Times*, January 11, 1923; December 21, 1922; December 24, 1925; January 7, 1926; December 23, 1926. Elections for the Palestine Commandery Knights Templar

in May 1926, for example, show that seven of twelve officers were Klansmen. See *Harlowton Times*, May 20, 1926.

94. *Harlowton Times*, October 19, 1922; December 21, 1922; October 18, 1923; September 22, 1921.

95. Roundup, Lewistown, and Big Timber had Klans. It seems likely that White Sulphur Springs had one, but the records are not clear. Kleagles generally tried to organize (at the very least) the county seat of each county. See the list of known Montana Klans in Appendices, Kontinental Klan, MF457, MHS; Kloreo, Livingston, September 16, 1923, F98, Organizational Records, Kontinental Klan, MF457, MHS.

96. *Harlowton Press*, September 20, 1923; Janet E. Thomson, *News About Our Families Who Lived in Harlowton, Montana, 1908–1939: Husband, Thomson, Boifeuillet, Lunney, Gaines, and Knudson Families* (Great Falls, MT, 2003), 91.

97. *Harlowton Press*, November 8, 1923; Thomson, *News About Our Families*, 93. Soliciting the Protestant churches for support was a common tactic of the Klan.

98. *Harlowton Press*, November 8, 1923; Thomson, *News About Our Families*, 93; *Harlowton Times*, November 8, 1923.

99. John Rietz, "Stories of My Life," compiled and edited by Joann (Rietz) Peta, et.al., 1993, Upper Musselshell Historical Society. Goldberg notes in his study of Denver that Catholics also launched their own boycotts. Goldberg, "Denver: Queen City of the Colorado Realm," in Lay, *The Invisible Empire in the West*, 60. Certainly, the Klan initiated its own consumer boycotts while practicing "vocational Klannishness" (frequenting Klan-owned businesses). See, for example, Blee, *Women of the Klan*, 147; Goldberg, *Hooded Empire*, 130; MacLean, *Behind the Mask of Chivalry*, 78. Attempts to discover Sears and Roebuck records regarding Harlowton failed.

100. *Harlowton Times*, February 3, 1921.

101. *Harlowton Times*, October 20, 1921.

102. *Harlowton Times*, October 27, 1921.

103. *Harlowton Times*, October 19, 1922.

104. Knights of the Ku Klux Klan, Inc. *Kloran [of the] Knights of the Ku Klux Klan*, 5th edition (1916), 49. Publications, F138, Publications, Kontinental Klan, MF457, MHS.

105. Wheatland opposed the state initiative to end state prohibition with 54 percent of the vote. Waldron, *Atlas of Montana Elections*, 110.

106. *Harlowton Times*, April 19, 1923.

107. Klansmen were represented in the Chamber of Commerce in Magna, Utah, and in Orange County, California, for example. Lay, "Imperial Outpost on the Border: El Paso's Frontier Klan No. 100," in *Invisible Empire*, 76 and Christopher N. Cocoltchos, "The Invisible Empire and the Search for the Orderly Community: The Ku Klux Klan in Anaheim, California," in Lay, *Invisible Empire*, 107.

108. *Harlowton Times*, March 16, 1922; *Harlowton Times*, March 30, 1922; *Harlowton Times*, April 19, 1923 (38 of 70 on the Chamber's committees were Klansmen). See the *Harlowton Times*, for example, March 13, 1924; March 26, 1925; March 10, 1927; March 17, 1927; May 7, 1925.

109. *Harlowton Times*, November 19, 1925.

110. *Harlowton Times*, January 7, 1926; also see November 12, 1925; December 21, 1922.

111. *Harlowton Times*, June 5, 1924.

112. *Harlowton Times*, May 29, 1924; April 9, 1925. In 1892, the National League for Good Roads was organized "to consolidate local and state activities in the 'Good Roads Movement.'" National Archives, Records of the Bureau of Public Roads, http://www.archives.gov/research/guide-fed-records/groups/030.html. *Harlowton Times*, November 5, 1925.

113. Waldron, *Atlas of Montana Elections*, 107, 111. The initiative passed handily with 73.1 percent approving, most from the western section of the state.

114. *Harlowton Times*, May 8, 1924.

115. *Harlowton Times*, February 10, 1921.

116. Stout, *Montana*, 653; Chalmers, *Hooded Americanism*, 281.

117. See, for instance, *Harlowton Times*, September 1, 1921; May 11, 1922; March 18, 1924; April 3, 10, 1924; December 4, 1924.

118. *Harlowton Times*, September 1, 1921; January 24, 1924; June 4, 1925; April 21, 1927; August 24, 1922; December 4, 11, 1924; April 23, 1925; January 14, 1926; June 22, 1926.

119. *Roundup Record*, November 30, 1923.

120. *Harlowton Times*, April 21, 1921; February 3, 1921; June 30, 1921; August 5, 1921; January 12, 1922; February 1, 1923.

121. *Harlowton Times*, March 27, 1924; April 17, 1924; August 14, 1924.

122. *Harlowton Times*, December 1, 15, 1921. "Is the World Getting Better?" was the topic of another Klansman's talk in early 1924. *Harlowton Times*, January 14, 1924.

123. *Harlowton Times*, September 8, 1927.

124. "Whiskers continue to flourish in and around Harlowton," *Harlowton Times*, July 22, 1926; August 5, 1926; August 19, 1926.

125. Lewis Terwilliger to Mrs. D. Cohn, January 23, 1929, F13, Correspondence, Kontinental Klan, MF457, MHS.

126. Harlowton's list of members was more detailed than Roundup's and included dates and payments of taxes, so one could tell how many members remained in the order by the end of the 1920s.

127. "Ku Klux Klan in Butte," *Butte Bulletin*, July 21, 1921; "Suggestion for Target Practice," *Butte Bulletin*, September 23, 1921.

Chapter 5. Kluxing Montana

Epigraph: "When the Kluxers Klux Up Yonder," in Crew, *Ku Klux Klan Sheet Music*, 34.

1. Charles F. Huppe to Wellington D. Rankin, July 13, 1923, Montana Attorney General Records, Group 76, Docket 4, Case 337, Box 98, F49, MHS.

2. *Roundup Record*, July 13, 1923.

3. "Fiery Cross is 4th Spectacle," *Roundup Record*, July 6, 1923.

4. Charles F. Huppe to Wellington D. Rankin, July 13, 1923, "Quick Verdict for Defendant in Klan Case," *Roundup Tribune*, December 20, 1923.

5. "Quick Verdict for Defendant in Klan Case," *Roundup Tribune*, December 20, 1923.

6. Charles F. Huppe to W. D. Rankin, July 13, 1923.

7. Raymer, *Montana*, 612.

8. Charles F. Huppe to Stephen Tighe, July 7, 1923, Montana Attorney General Records Group 76, Docket 4, Case 337, Box 98, F49, MHS.

9. *Roundup Record*, August 3, 1923 (the *Record* printed both Huppe's and the Roundup Kligrapp's letters); *Roundup Tribune*, July 26, 1923.

10. Charles F. Huppe to W. D. Rankin, July 13, 1923. The Justice of the Peace does not appear on the membership list of the Roundup Klan. Edgar J. Baker to W. D. Rankin, July 26, 1923, Montana Attorney General Records Group 76, Docket 4, Case 337, Box 98, F49, MHS; Gertrude Klein Saxtorph, interview by Anna Zellick, transcript, 9, 1978, OH1704, MHS.

11. Joe Vicars, OH813 Tape 1 Sides A and B, MHS.

12. Warrant of Arrest, July 12, 1923, The State of Montana vs. Chas. F. Huppe, 487 15 Judicial District, Musselshell County, Montana, No. 290, Montana Attorney General Records Group 76. Docket 4, Case 337, Box 98, F49, MHS; *Roundup Tribune*, August 2, 1923; *Roundup Record*, August 3, 1923.

13. Complaint of A. J. Whipple, The State of Montana vs. Charles F. Huppe, July 11, 1923. District Court, 15th Judicial District, State of Montana, county of Musselshell, No. 290; Montana Attorney General Records Group 76, Docket 4, Case 337, Box 98, F49, MHS. Instructions to the Jury, The State of Montana vs. Charles F. Huppe, Montana Attorney General Records Group 76, Docket 4, Case 337, Box 98 F49, MHS.

14. "Quick Verdict for Defendant in Klan Case," *Roundup Tribune*, December 20, 1923; Verdict in the District Court of the Fifteenth Judicial District of the State of Montana in and for the County of Musselshell, The State of Montana vs. Chas. F. Huppe, Montana Attorney General Records Group 76, Docket 4, Case 337, Box 98, F49, MHS.

15. Raymer, *Montana*, 612. Huppe continued to face legal challenges. In 1931, multiple charges were filed against Huppe by district judge of the 15th Judicial District G. F. Jeffries. Then Huppe filed his own charges against Jeffries and A. G. McNaught, a former law partner of Jefferies. The charges on both sides included bitter accusations of perjury, collusion, destruction of evidence, and conspiracy. The Montana Supreme Court would dismiss charges against Huppe, who died in June 1932. While the legal trouble did not involve the Klan, both Jeffries and McNaught had been Knights in the Roundup Klan. "County Attorney of Musselshell Returns Fire," *Independent Record* (Helena), November 21, 1931; "Big Law Cases to Higher Court," *Melstone Messenger*, February 11, 1932; "Objections Are Filed to Recommendation to Suspend Huppe," *Billings Gazette*, April 2, 1932; "Charles Huppe, Roundup, Dies," *Great Falls Tribune*, June 13, 1932.

16. *Roundup Record*, August 3, 1923.
17. *Harlowton Times*, March 20, 1924.
18. *Ronan Pioneer*, April 4, 1924.
19. Terwilliger, Official Circular, November 1, 1927, F165, Publications, Kontinental Klan, MF457, MHS. Klansmen did occasionally pursue their own agendas without the sanction of Klan leaders, as in the case of a violent beating of a Georgia attorney. The Grand Dragon of Georgia disavowed the act, asserting that the culprits may have worn hoods and robes, but they "were not in any sense Klansmen." Quoted in Pegram, *One Hundred Percent American*, 168.
20. Terwilliger, Official Circular, November 1, 1927; December 5, 1927, F165, Publications, Kontinental Klan, MF457, MHS. Also, see Pegram's discussion of violence in the South, *One Hundred Percent American*, 169–70.
21. *Harlowton Times*, April 7, 1921.
22. Pegram, *One Hundred Percent American*, 179.
23. See Pegram's chapter "The Problem of Hooded Violence: Moral Vigilantism, Enemies, and Provocation" in *One Hundred Percent American*, 157–183.
24. Pegram, *One Hundred Percent American*, 161–70.
25. *Helena Independent*, 1923, Diocese Scrapbooks, XXVI, 69.
26. "First Appearance of Ku Klux Klan," Montana News Association, Inserts, Vol 5, page 234, appeared in Montana newspapers the week of July 10, 1922; *Powder River County Examiner*, July 21, 1922.
27. See the chapter "The Klan Rides, 1865–71" in Chalmers, *Hooded Americanism*; "Klan Moving its Forces in State," *Anaconda Standard*, October 8, 1922, Diocese Scrapbooks, XXV, 78.
28. "Klan Gives Message to Corvallis Church," *Anaconda Standard*, October 8, 1922, Diocese Scrapbooks, XXV, 78.
29. Albright, "The Great and Near-Great in Yellowstone," 88.
30. Author's interview with John Harrison, June 29, 2005, notes in possession of author. When we reviewed the membership list of Harlowton Klansmen together, he was surprised to see Howard Squires's name on the list, and on seeing Dr. S. K. Campbell's name, he exclaimed, "Oh, that hurts!" Campbell was "a good country doctor."
31. *Roundup Record*, June 23, 1922. Tim Schaff to author, September 27, 2006. Also see Hougardy et al., *Horizons O'er the Musselshell*, 69.
32. Gertrude Klein Saxtorph, Interview by Anna Zellick, September 8, 1979, transcript, 10–11, OH1704, MHS.
33. Interview with Tim McCleary, July 9, 2006.
34. Deb Davis, "Days of the KKK," *Mullan Trail News*, September 3, 1986. The Committee for the Bicentennial, *Furrows and Trails in Judith Basin*, 10.
35. "Independent Quits—Plant to be Moved," *Independent* (Moccasin), May 8, 1924. According to the owner, it was because he had criticized the financial condition of the local public school.
36. Schaertl, *Echoes of the Past*, 27–29.
37. Schaertl, *Echoes of the Past*, 27–29.

38. Quoted in the *Great Falls Tribune*, August 7, 1921.

39. *Great Falls Tribune*, August 7, 1921.

40. Editorial, *Great Falls Tribune*, August 1, 1921.

41. "Ku Klux in Montana," *Butte Miner*, January 18, 1922.

42. "Officers Killed by a Crazed Negro," *Searchlight* (Hardin), November 3, 1926, 1. Note: there are various spellings of Bolin's name in the newspapers and other documents—Bolden, Belden, and Bolin. I use "Bolin," which was originally in the *Searchlight* and in Timothy P. McCleary, "The Death of Officer John MacLeod and Sheriff Robert Gilmore: A Flash-Point in Big Horn County History," *Big Horn County News*, April 9, 1997.

43. Walter, "KKK: White Hoods Under the Big Sky," 74; The "evidence was insufficient to warrant his arrest" on burglary charges, stated the *Billings Gazette*, October 30, 1926.

44. Walter, "KKK: White Hoods Under the Big Sky," 74.

45. *Billings Gazette*, October 30, 1926.

46. Ann Scally Hokanson, "Biography of John William Scally," n.d., 9. Biography given to author by Timothy P. McCleary, July 2006.

47. *Billings Gazette*, October 30, 1926.

48. *Billings Gazette*, October 30, 1926.

49. Hokanson, "Biography," 9–10.

50. *Billings Gazette*, October 30, 1926.

51. "Officers Killed by Crazed Negro," *Searchlight*, November 3, 1926.

52. Allen, *A Decent, Orderly Lynching*, xviii.

53. *Helena Independent*, January 29, 1923, Diocese Scrapbooks, XXVI, 15.

54. *Helena Independent*, 1923, Diocese Scrapbooks, XXVI, 69.

55. *Ronan Pioneer*, March 13, 1925.

56. *St. Ignatius Post*, April 5, 1925.

57. *Great Falls Tribune*, December 19, 1922; Aasheim, *Sheridan's Daybreak*; *Glasgow Courier*, May 19, 1922; *Billings Gazette*, December 25, 1923.

58. *Great Falls Tribune*, July 2, 1922.

59. Terwilliger, Official Circular, December 6, 1924, F163, Publications, Kontinental Klan, MF457, MHS.

60. Malone, Roeder, and Lang, *Montana*, 283; Terwilliger, Official Circular, August (late, n.d.), 1924, F163, Kontinental Klan, MF457, MHS.

61. *Ronan Pioneer*, August 3, 1923. The Klansmen "stalked into a negro church" was how the *Wolf Point Herald* framed it. August 9, 1923.

62. *Imperial Nighthawk*, August 8, 1923, 5.

63. Pegram, *One Hundred Percent*, 24.

64. *Glasgow Courier*, December 1, 1922.

65. See MacLean, *Behind the Mask of Chivalry*, 114. *Great Falls Tribune*, December 22, 1922, 5; "Inside Facts as I Found Them" (Bozeman Klan) mentions upholding "virtuous womanhood," but it is only one line among many. More attention is paid to Klansmen being white, Christian, and "Anti-Nothing," n.d., F113, Publications, Kontinental Klan, MF457, MHS.

66. Letter from "A broken hearted mother," Mrs. Clare Rawlings, Butte. No salutation. November 1927; Rawlings to Knights of the Ku Klux Klan, November 30, 1927, F10, Correspondence, Kontinental Klan, MF457, MHS.

67. Hathaway to Terwilliger, November 26, 1927 (Hathaway's letter includes a type-written note from a Mrs. W. Trudeau, who also discussed the case), F10, Correspondence, Kontinental Klan, MF457, MHS.

68. Terwilliger to Mrs. Maggie Hathaway, November 25, 1927; Hathaway to Terwilliger, November 26, 1927; Terwilliger to Hathaway, November 28, 1927; Knights of the Ku Klux Klan to Rawlings, November 18, 1927, F10, Correspondence, Kontinental Klan, MF457, MHS.

69. Rawlings to Knights of the Ku Klux Klan, November 30, 1927, F10, Correspondence, Kontinental Klan, MF457, MHS.

70. Lewis Terwilliger to Albert W. Jones, December 1, 1927, File 10, Correspondence, Kontinental Klan, MF457, MHS.

71. There are several references to the women's Klan in Montana in the records; one reference in Butte in 1927 is a letter from Exalted Cyclops C. U. Brown of Jefferson Klan No. 40 in Cardwell/Whitehall to W. Aitken in Butte, August 12, 1927, asking Aitken to see if Terwilliger would allow "the ladies" to use the men's robes for an upcoming parade in Whitehall, asking for an extra forty robes, F10, Correspondence, Kontinental Klan, MF457, MHS.

72. MacLean, *Behind the Mask of Chivalry*, 121–22. "The Georgia Realm office . . . reported receiving an average of twenty letters *each week* from women inviting the order to threaten or use violence against people whose conduct they disapproved of." 121.

73. Pegram, *One Hundred Percent*, 182–83.

74. Chalmers, *Hooded Americanism*, 297; Pegram, *One Hundred Percent American*, 183.

75. *Billings Gazette*, September 30, 1923.

76. "The Klan and the Bottle," 570.

77. *Helena Independent*, January 29, 1923, Diocese Scrapbooks, XXVI, 15; Bozeman Klansman, "How to Tell a Klansman: Inside Facts as I Found Them," F113, Publications, Kontinental Klan, MF457, MHS.

78. "Cross of Fire Burns High on Prospect Hill," *Great Falls Tribune*, May 27, 1924.

79. "Fiery Crosses Are Seen Upon Heights, *Butte Miner*, March 18, 1924.

80. "Fiery Crosses Are Seen Upon Heights, *Butte Miner*, March 18, 1924.

81. *Anaconda Standard*, February 6, 1923.

82. *Anaconda Standard*, February 6, 1923; *Chicago Defender*, February 17, 1923, and *San Francisco Call*, February 6, 1923, ACLU, Vol. 23, Reel 31.

83. *Anaconda Standard*, March 23, 1923.

84. Allen, *A Decent, Orderly Lynching*, 357–60; Malone, Roeder, and Lang, *Montana*, 80–81.

85. *Kalispell Times*, January 18, 1923. Also see *Milwaukee Leader*, January 17, 1923, ACLU Files, Vol 231, Reel 31; *Helena Independent*, January 16, 1923.

86. *Milwaukee Leader,* January 17, 1923, ACLU Files, Vol 231, Reel 31.
87. *Bozeman Courier,* January 17, 1923.
88. *Meagher Republican,* January 16, 1925.
89. *Butte Miner,* January 18, 1922.
90. *Harlowton Times,* September 13, 1923; "Youths Employ K.K.K. Threat," *Wolf Point Herald,* September 13, 1923.
91. Diocese Scrapbooks, XXVI, 33; Diocese Scrapbooks, XXVI, 15; "Missoula Klan Will Help Hughes Probe," *Missoulian,* January 29, 1923. The students subsequently "armed themselves with revolvers."
92. "Campus Kidnapping Mystery Revealed to Men at Smoker," *Missoulian,* February 2, 1923; "K.K. Scare Just Fake," Diocese Scrapbooks, XXVI, 13, c. February 2, 1923.

Chapter 6. The Klan Collapses

Epigraph: "Boost for the Ku Klux Klan," in Crew, *Ku Klux Klan Sheet Music,* 183.
1. Terwilliger, Official Circular, June 14, 1924, F163, Publications, Kontinental Klan, MF457, MHS.
2. Terwilliger, Official Circular, June 14, 1924, F163, Publications, Kontinental Klan, MF457, MHS.
3. Terwilliger, Official Circular, June 3, 1924, F163, Publications, Kontinental Klan, MF457, MHS.
4. The official circulars from 1926 and the Grand Dragon's Financial Reports from 1925 to 1927 are missing.
5. Terwilliger, Official Circular, August 3, 1924, and May 1925, F163 and F164, Publications, Kontinental Klan, MF457, MHS.
6. Terwilliger, Official Circular, December 3, 1928, F166, Publications, Kontinental Klan, MF457, MHS.
7. Klorero, Great Falls, August 14, 1927, F100, Organizational Records, Kontinental Klan, MF457, MHS.
8. Klorero, Great Falls, August 14, 1927, F100, Organizational Records, Kontinental Klan, MF457, MHS. Low attendance was blamed on the roads after it had rained.
9. "Financial Report of the Grand Dragon of the Realm of Montana," June 1, 1928, to October 1, 1929, Financial records, Kontinental Klan, MF457, MHS.
10. Terwilliger to Floyd F. Johnson, January 14, 1925, F7, Correspondence, Kontinental Klan, MF457, MHS
11. Terwilliger, Official Circular, April 9, 1930, F167, Publications, Kontinental Klan, MF457, MHS.
12. Klorero, Great Falls, August 14, 1927, F100, Organizational Records, Kontinental Klan, MF457, MHS.
13. Terwilliger, Official Circular, June 10, 1930, F167, Publications, Kontinental Klan, MF457, MHS.
14. Minutes from the Kloreros, 1924–1930, F98-F103, Organizational Records, Kontinental Klan, MF457, MHS.

15. Terwilliger, Official Circular, May 20, 1930, F167, Publications, Kontinental Klan, MF457, MHS.

16. Klorero, Billings, August 24, 1924, F98, Organizational Records, Kontinental Klan, MF457, MHS.

17. Klorero, Helena, September 6, 1925, F99, Organizational Records, Kontinental Klan, MF457, MHS.

18. Minutes, June 13, 1928, F109, Organizational Records, Kontinental Klan, MF457, MHS.

19. Klorero, Missoula, October 20, 1929, F102, Organizational Records, Kontinental Klan, MF457, MHS.

20. Klorero, Missoula, October 20, 1929, F102, Organizational Records, Kontinental Klan, MF457, MHS.

21. For a short time, the cost of a robe was added on to the Klectoken, for a total of fifteen dollars. Terwilliger, Official Circular, November 11, 1924; June 24, 1927, F163 and F165, Publications, Kontinental Klan, MF457, MHS; By-Laws of Kontinental Klan No. 30, December 26, 1923, and *Constitution and Laws of the Knights of the Ku Klux Klan* (Atlanta, Georgia, 1926), 34. F89, Organizational Records, F126, Publications, Kontinental Klan, MF457, MHS.

22. J. A. Orrell to Albert Jones, December 17, 1927, F10, Correspondence, Kontinental Klan, MF457, MHS.

23. Gist, "Secret Societies," 42–43; Hernandez, *The Ku Klux Klan and Freemasonry*, 27–28.

24. *Harlowton Times*, November 25, 1926.

25. Harcourt, *Ku Klux Kulture*, 182–183.

26. Hernandez, *The Ku Klux Klan and Freemasonry*, 29.

27. Hernandez, *The Ku Klux Klan and Freemasonry*, 30.

28. Carnes, *Secret Ritual and Manhood*, 51–55, 151–56; Clawson, *Constructing Brotherhood*, 260.

29. Lewis Terwilliger, Official Circular, October 2, 1929, F167, Publications, Kontinental Klan, MF457, MHS.

30. Lewis Terwilliger, Official Circular, April 9, 1930; May 14, 1929, F167, Publications, Kontinental Klan, MF457, MHS.

31. *Butte Miner*, December 2, 1923; January 13, 1924; July 22, 1921.

32. "Labor and the Ku Klux Klan," *Labor Bulletin* (Butte), April 18, 1924, ACLU Reel 36, Vol 251.

33. For the latest scholarship on D. C. Stephenson, see Egan, *A Fever in the Heartland.*

34. Minutes, Klorero, Missoula, October 20, 1929; and Minutes, Klorero, Great Falls, August 1930, F102 and F103, Organizational Records, Kontinental Klan, MF457, MHS.

35. Terwilliger, Official Circular, January 8, 1931, F168, Publications, Kontinental Klan, MF457, MHS.

36. "Lewis Terwilliger, Pioneer Teacher, Business Man, Dies," *Livingston Enterprise*, October 14, 1948.

Epilogue

Besides the sources listed below, the epilogue is informed by Montana Human Rights Network's executive director Travis McAdam's two presentations on You-Tube: "History of White Nationalism in Montana, 1980–2015" (November 16, 2020) and "White Nationalism in Montana, 2015–Present" (December 7, 2020).

1. Chalmers, *Hooded Americanism*, 305.
2. See, for example, Webb, *Massive Resistance*.
3. For an analysis of the impact of the Vietnam War on what Kathleen Belew calls the white power movement, see chapter 1 in *Bring the War Home*.
4. "Cross Burning Leaves Bridger Teacher Shaken," *Billings Gazette*, May 24, 1979.
5. "KKK-type incident reported," *Great Falls Tribune*, May 5, 1983. The note read: "We have found thee, Rayetta Orr, guilty of harboring a nigger. And openly confronting it to the public. We have judged that thee have six days in which to leave Troy. We the Klan of Montana bestow on thee, Cameron, slavery unless thee flee the great sovereign state of Montana. We the people of Troy Montana judge thee so." [signed] "Nit the wizard, Pen the wizard, and Sam the wizard." Also see "Cross-burning, Assault Bring Tension to Troy," no newspaper or date listed, Merrill G. Burlingame Special Collections, Montana State University.
6. "KKK, Skinheads Vow to Stand Up for Their Beliefs," *Billings Gazette*, March 22, 1993.
7. "City Urged to Actively Fight Hate-Mongering Bigots," *Billings Gazette*, February 11, 1993; "'Hate Flyers' Infiltrate Billings," *Bronc Express* (Billings High School newspaper), February 11, 1993; "Police Chief Urges Action against Hate Groups," *Billings Gazette*, February 18, 1993; "Church Group Wants Others to Adopt Anti-Hate Document," *Billings Gazette*, February 26, 1993.
8. *Montana Quest* c. November 1993, MHRN files.
9. *Montana Quest* c. November 1993, MHRN files; "Billings KKK Targets Network."
10. "Card to Bozeman Business Owner Smacks of Ku Klux Klan Tactics," *Great Falls Tribune*, May 22, 1994; "KKK Targets Two Montana Communities," *Network News*, March 1995; "Community Response to KKK in Red Lodge," *Network News Flash*, no. 2 (December 1993); Greg McCracken, "Racist Material Left in Hardin," *Billings Gazette*, March 21, 1995.
11. "Card to Bozeman Business Owner Smacks of Ku Klux Klan Tactics," *Great Falls Tribune*, May 22, 1994; "KKK Targets Two Montana Communities," *Network News*, March 1995; "Community Response to KKK in Red Lodge," *Network News Flash*, no. 2 (December 1993); Greg McCracken, "Racist Material Left in Hardin," *Billings Gazette*, March 21, 1995; "Response," continued from page one, *Billings Gazette*, March 1, 1993; "KKK, Skinheads Vow to Stand Up for Their Beliefs," *Billings Gazette*, March 22, 1993; "City's Stand on Hate Acts Wins Praise," *Billings Gazette*, September 19, 1993; Wilkinson, "Home, Home on the Range." The Church of the Creator's religious philosophy was based purely on the supremacy of the white

race. They reject Christianity, believing it to be "a lie perpetuated by Jews," and promote RAHOWA (Racial Holy War). Matt Hale was declared the leader of the Church of the Creator in Superior, Montana, in 1996. The movement had begun to splinter by 2009. See "Law Enforcement, Community, and Press Briefing Paper," March 10, 2003, and "Creativity Movement," SPLC Extremist Files.

12. Wilkinson, "Home, Home on the Range"; "Hate Groups Vandalize Jewish Families," *Livingston Enterprise*, December 16, 1993; "Windows with Menorahs Broken by Rock Throwers," *Billings Gazette*, December 16, 1993.

13. "KKK, Skinheads Vow to Stand Up for Their Beliefs," *Billings Gazette*, March 22, 1993.

14. Biggest U.S. Cities, https://www.biggestuscities.com/demographics/mt.

15. Quoted in Kim Murphy (*Los Angeles Times*), "Extremists' Retreat to Northwest Stokes Memories of Ugly Past," *Seattle Times*, February 9, 2012; Holthouse, "High Country Extremism: Patriot Games,"; Lenz, "A Gathering of Eagles."

16. Van Dyke and Soule, "Structural Social Change," 502; Katz and Bailey, "The Militia," 137–138; Also see Barkun's *Religion and the Racist Right*.

17. Wilkinson, "Home, Home on the Range"; Belew, *Bring the War Home*, 187–208.

18. Zeskind, "Montana Freemen Trial May Mark End of an Era"; Zeskind, "Basis of Freemen's Philosophy is Racism"; "Four Montana Freemen Found Guilty"; Neiwert, "Federal Court Sentences Leaders of Montana Freemen to Long Prison Terms." For more on the militia and anti-government movements, see White, "The Current Weirdness in the West," 4–16 and Schlatter, *Aryan Cowboys*, 124–158.

19. Ridgeway, *Blood in the Face*, 109. A new edition, *Blood in the Face: White Nationalism from The Birth of a Nation to the Age of Trump* (Haymarket Books, 2023) will be available July 2023.

20. John Abarr, autobiography (four pages), MHRN files. Abarr has written a longer version, called *Story of a Lone Wolf Klansman: This Is a Story about How John Abarr a Country Kid from Montana and Wyoming Became a Member of the Racialist Movement* (CreateSpace Independent Publishing Platform, 2017).

21. "David Lane," SPLC Extremist Files; "William Pierce," SPLC Extremist Files; Ridgeway, *Blood in the Face*, 109.

22. Ridgeway, *Blood in the Face*, 109. Also, see Belew, *Bring the War Home*, 110–34 on *The Turner Diaries*, Mathews, and the Order.

23. *The Turner Diaries* became "one of the most important pieces of extremist literature in America," inspiring Robert Mathews of the Order and Timothy McVeigh, who blew up the Alfred P. Murrah Federal Building in Oklahoma City. "National Alliance," SPLC Extremist Files; Abarr, autobiography. Mathews remains a hero among white nationalists.

24. "Aryan Nations on Verge of Collapse Following Judgement," SPLC *Intelligence Report*.

25. "The National Alliance Targets Montana."

26. Barrett was inspired by Pat Buchanan's *The Death of the West: How Dying Popula-tions and Immigrant Invasions Imperil Our Country and Civilization* (2002) and said that PLEs were putting Buchanan's vision into action. Barrett, *Pioneer Little Europe (PLE)*, 28; Hatewatch Staff. "Far-right Survivalist and Icon of 'Patriot' Movement Predicts Religious Civil War," SPLC *Hatewatch*.

27. "April Gaede," SPLC, and "Pop-Singing Gaede Twins Renounce Racism," SPLC, *Intelligence Report*. The Order's David Lane, who displayed an unhealthy obsession with Gaede's daughters, died in prison in 2007. He and Gaede were close enough that Lane asked her to dispose of his ashes after cremation. Holthouse, "High Country Extremism: Pioneering Hate." Also see the documentary *Nazi Pop Twins*. Buchanan, "Film of Nazi Pop Twins Highlights Neo-Neo-Nazi Family," SPLC *Intelligence Report*.

28. The quote is from Spencer's speech at the American Renaissance conference, April 2013. See Rivas, "Whitefish Hate Group Representative Makes National Media, Denounced by State and Local Human Rights Activists, Montana."

29. "SPLC Applauds Landmark Ruling Holding White Supremacists Liable in the Charlottesville 'Unite the Right' Civil Trial," November 24, 2021. Integrity First for America, "IFA's Charlottesville Case: *Sines v. Kessler.*"

30. Bassett, "Richard Spencer."

31. Barrouquere, "White Shadow"; "Former Klansman Runs for Montana Legislature," *Montana Human Rights Network News*, February 2002. Duke divided the United States into racially designated areas for whites, Blacks, Jews, and Latinos. See Belew, *Bring the War Home*, 35, 161.

32. Abarr even tried to coopt ideas of inclusivity in 2014 when he announced him-self as leader of the Rocky Mountain Knights, a new kind of Ku Klux Klan that welcomed diversity and opened its membership to all regardless of race, religion, or sexual orientation. The enemy to fight, according to Abarr, was the U.S. gov-ernment, which was plotting to form a "new world order," a charge with clear anti-Semitic overtones. Abarr's veiled attempt to cater to the prejudices that he had once overtly and loudly embraced flew right by the users of Stormfront, who derided his announcement with cutting scorn. Posters on the website ridiculed Abarr ("who?"), and the taunts ranged from sheer disbelief ("the most ridiculous thing I have heard of") to vicious anti-gay slurs ("Even looks like a f—," "Sounds like some pervert . . . who got tired of wearing women's clothing behind closed doors and going to gay bars with fake mustaches.") MHRN, which has tracked Abarr's activities for years, rightfully expressed doubts of Abarr's claim that he was reformed and called his announcement a publicity stunt, hardly a serious attempt at inclusivity. It was also clear, according to MHRN, that Abarr did not have much support and was operating on his own. John Abarr, autobiography. "William Daniel Johnson," SPLC Extremist Files; Neiwert, "Montana Klansman's Idea for 'Inclusive' KKK Elicits Derision," SPLC *Hatewatch*. See also, Kristen Cates, "Many Suspicious of More Inclusive Montana KKK Chapter," *Great Falls Tribune*, November 2, 2014.

33. Most recently, see David Corn, "The Elephant in the Room" and *American Psychosis: A Historical Investigation of How the Republican Party Went Crazy.*

34. Corn, "The Elephant in the Room," 21.

35. Quotes by Andrew Anglin, Brad Griffin, and David Duke in Piggott, "White Nationalists and the So-Called 'Alt-Right' Celebrate Trump's Victory."

36. Gray, "Trump Defends White-Nationalist Protesters."

37. Wehner, "More MAGA Than Ever."

38. "Charlie Kirk and Turning Point USA: Bringing. Minor League Version of White Nationalism to Montana," MHRN, March 2020, 4, 13.

39. "Charlie Kirk and Turning Point USA: Bringing. Minor League Version of White Nationalism to Montana," MHRN, March 2020, 5; Emily Cochrane, "'That's My Kind of Guy,' Trump Says of Republican Lawmaker Who Body-Slammed a Reporter," *New York Times*, October 19, 2018, https://www.nytimes.com/2018/10/19/us/politics/trump-greg-gianforte-montana.html.

40. "MHRN Denounces Proposed Legislation as Part of 'Antifa /Fantasy.'"

41. House Joint Resolution No. 11, Introduced by B. Mitchell, Sixty-Seventh Legislature, Legislative Services Division, link is in "MHRN Denounces Proposed Legislation as Part of 'Antifa /Fantasy,'" https://mhrn.org/2021/02/15/hj11. MHRN, "2021 Legislative Report and Scorecard." Also see Rep. Braxton Mitchell (R) HD-3, https://leg.mt.gov/legislator-information/roster/individual/7563; Danali Sagner, "Columbia Falls Legislator Withdraws Mandatory Fetal Death Certificate Proposal After Extensive Pushback," *Flathead Beacon*, January 18, 2023, https://flatheadbeacon.com/2023/01/18/columbia-falls-legislator-withdraws-mandatory-fetal-death-certificate-proposal-after-extensive-pushback/ and Joshua Margolis, "Bill Banning Minors from Seeing Drag Shows Draws Charged Comments in Helena," NBC Montana, February 9, 2023, https://nbcmontana.com/news/local/bill-banning-minors-from-seeing-drag-shows-draws-charged-comments-in-helena.

42. Marc Racicot and Bob Brown, "Tranel's Life is Marked by Integrity, Hard Work," *Missoulian*, October 22, 2022, https://missoulian.com/opinion/column/marc-racicot-and-bob-brown-tranels-life-is-marked-by-integrity-hard-work/article_9d33dff8-a5c2-5274-b924-01c7df3a0c38.html. Also, see Bob Brown, "Klan's Song is Over but Melody Lingers," *Missoulian*, July 12, 2023, https://missoulian.com/opinion/column/the-klan-in-montana/article_eb78ae7e-16db-11ee-87ed-4f3b416af5c4.html; Anna Phillips and Lisa Rein, "Ryan Zinke Broke Ethics Rules While Leading Trump's Interior Dept., Watchdog Finds," *Washington Post*, February 16, 2022 (updated from February 16, 2022), https://www.washingtonpost.com/climate-environment/2022/02/16/zinke-inspector-general-report/.

43. Terwilliger, Official Circular, December 22, 1928, F166, Publications, Kontinental Klan, MF457, MHS. Schubert, "Montana House Fails to Denounce White Supremacist Groups"; Azi Paybarah, "GOP Senator Says of White Nationalists in the Military, 'I Call Them Americans,'" *Washington Post*, May 10, 2023, updated May 11, 2023. For more on Montana's GOP, see Ken Toole, "Nothing New About the New Montana Republican Party," *Billings Gazette*, April 2, 2023,

https://billingsgazette.com/opinion/columnists/ken-toole-nothing-new-about-the
-new-montana-republican-party/article_8271e88a-cfe8-11ed-be9a-1bc6548cf064
.html.

44. Between 2021 and 2022, anti-Semitic incidents of harassment, vandalism, and assault were up 36 percent, "the highest number on record since Anti-Defamation League began tracking antisemitic incidents in 1979," "Audit of Anti-Semitic Incidents in 2022." Recent national examples of how anti-Semitism has infiltrated the GOP and MAGA include Arizona representative Paul Gosar and Moms for Liberty. See Ramirez, "Paul Gosar's Newsletter Features Website That Calls for Readers to 'Stand up for Hitler.'" Gosar has a history of associating with white nationalists—see Aaron Blake, "GOP Rep. Paul Gosar Appears to Ally with White Nationalists—Again," *Washington Post*, June 29, 2021, https://www.washingtonpost .com/politics/2021/06/29/gop-congressman-appears-ally-with-white-nationalists -again/. Ali Breland, "Who Is Nick Fuentes, and Why Is a US Rep Buddying Up to the Segregationist, Holocaust-Denying Gen Z Influencer?" *Mother Jones*, June 29, 2021, https://www.motherjones.com/politics/2021/06/who-is-nick-fuentes-and -why-is-a-us-rep-buddying-up-to-the-segregationist-holocaust-denying-gen-z -influencer/. "Indiana Chapter of Moms for Liberty Features Hitler Quote in First Newsletter," NPR WFYI Indianapolis, June 22, 2023, https://www.wfyi.org /news/articles/indiana-chapter-of-moms-for-liberty-features-hitler-quote-in-first -newsletter. The quote: "He alone, who OWNS the youth, GAINS the future." Currently Yellowstone County is the only Montana county that has a chapter. https://www.momsforliberty.org/chapters/yellowstone-county-mt/. SPLC has designated Moms for Liberty as a hate group: "Moms for Liberty," SPLC, https:// www.splcenter.org/fighting-hate/extremist-files/group/moms-liberty.

45. Kazin, *The Populist Persuasion*.

46. The quote is from Spencer's speech at the American Renaissance conference, April 2013. See "Whitefish Hate Group Representative Makes National Media, Denounced by State and Local Human Rights Activists," "For Immediate Release," *Montana Human Rights Network*, May 11, 2013.

47. Montana Public Radio, March 3, 2023, https://www.mtpr.org/montana-news/2023 -03-03/at-the-halfway-point-republicans-pass-budget-bills-target-woke-extrem- ism; MHRN, "2021 Legislative Report and Scorecard."

48. Madison, *The Ku Klux Klan in the Heartland*, 189.

49. "The Year in Hate and Extremism: Far-right Extremists Coalescing in Broad-based, Loosely Affiliated Movement," SPLC.

50. Steward Rhodes, head of the Oath Keepers, lived in Montana. See Wilson, "Exclu- sive: Oath Keepers Steward Rhodes' Children Speak"; "Tanya Gersh vs. Andrew Anglin," SPLC. Anglin was also a defendant in *Sines vs. Kessler* (2021). "Andrew Anglin," SPLC Extremist Files.

51. Unfortunately, Twitter is heading in the same direction since Elon Musk assumed control. See, for example, Breland, "White Nationalists Are Big Fans of Elon's 'White Genocide' Tweets."

52. "City urged to actively fight hate-mongering bigots," *Billings Gazette*, February 11, 1993; "Police Chief Urges Action Against Hate Groups," *Billings Gazette*, February 18, 1993; "Church Group Wants Others to Adopt Anti-hate Document," *Billings Gazette*, February 26, 1993; "The Day Billings 'Stood Together,'" *Human Rights Network News*, July 1993.

53. "City's Stand on Hate Acts Wins Praise," *Billings Gazette*, September 19, 1993; Clair Johnson, "'Walk for Unity' begins in Hardin," *Billings Gazette*, August 15, 1995; "Community Response to KKK in Red Lodge," *Network News Flash*, no. 2 (December 1993).

54. Bill Dedman, "Midwest Gunman Had Engaged in Racist Acts at 2 Universities," *New York Times*, July 6, 1999; Smith, "Midwest Shooting Spree Ends with Apparent Suicide of Suspect," CNN.com, July 5, 1999, http://www.cnn.com/US/9907/05/illinois.shootings.02/; McAdam, "History of White Nationalism in Montana, 1980–2015."

55. MHRN Denounces Proposed Legislation as Part of 'Antifa/Fantasy,'" https://mhrn.org/2021/02/15/hj11.

56. Governor Gianforte signed the trans health-care bill into law, and it will take effect in October 2023. Billson, "Brave Zooey Zephyr 'Up and Ready to Work' Despite Being Mocked and Intimidated at Montana State House"; "Montana Rep. Zooey Zephyr Sues Over Her Removal from House Floor." Amy Beth Hanson and Matthew Brown, "Judge Rejects Zooey Zephyr Bid to Return to Montana House," *AP News*, May 3, 2023, https://apnews.com/article/zooey-zephyr-montana-transgender-lawsuit-cce3cfcf6ec2e71abee383b2ad1d4b72.

57. Martin Kidston, "Missoula County Floored by Library Commission's Fears of 'Marxist Lesbian' ALA President," *MissoulaCurrent*, n.d., c. July 22, 2023, https://missoulacurrent.com/missoula-marxist-lesbian/.

58. Meehan and Friedman, "USA: State Laws Supercharge Book Suppression in Schools."

59. Ashley Sloboda, "Northwest Allen County Schools Board Pauses Vote on Library Conference Attendance Request," *Journal Gazette* (Fort Wayne, IN), July 27, 2023, https://www.journalgazette.net/local/schools/northwest-allen-county-schools-board-pauses-vote-on-library-conference-attendance-request/article_7fc6a954-2bdc-11ee-aaf8-63a0222e8b20.html. Also see Devan Filchak, "Rainbow Bracelets from Wells County Library Spark Controversy," *Journal Gazette*, June 8, 2023, https://www.journalgazette.net/local/rainbow-bracelets-from-wells-county-library-spark-controversy/article_dffeb972-059b-11ee-be96-87153a8a91b1.html. Some parents "were alarmed," and one "asked the commissioners to start a fact-finding mission to determine the intent behind the bracelets' purchase."

60. Cullen Peel, "Roundup of Anti-LGBTQ+ Legislation Advancing in States Across the Country." Also see Holly Yan, "Human Rights Campaign Declares a National State of Emergency for LGBTQ+ People."

61. Lavietes, "New House Speaker's Views in LGBTQ Issues Come Under Fresh Scrutiny."

62. Associated Press, "Ex-Officers Plead Guilty to Racist Assault During Raid," *Journal Gazette* (Fort Wayne, IN), August 4, 2023, https://www.journalgazette.net/news/national/ex-mississippi-officers-plead-guilty-to-racist-assault-on-2-black-men-during-raid/article_368ebe2f-25f4-594e-a26e-4191e8b01053.html.

63. Kate Aguilar, "Blocking Black History Is an Attempt to Counter Black Power," *Washington Post*, February 1, 2023, https://www.washingtonpost.com/made-by-history/2023/02/01/desantis-florida-african-american-studies/; Planas, "New Florida Standards Teach Students that Some Black People Benefited from Slavery Because It Taught Useful Skills."

64. See, for example, Marjorie Taylor Greene (@mtgreenee), February 20, 2023, at 8:43 a.m., and other tweets by Marjorie Taylor Greene (@RepMTG), including December 20, 2023, and February 22, 2023, on X. Edwards, "Matt Gaetz: MAGA Will Turn to 'Bloodshed' if Trump's Crimes Exclude Him from Ballot." Also see Alex Cole (@acnewsitics) on X, September 6, 2023, 7:19 p.m., for a video clip of Huckabee warning what could happen if Joe Biden is reelected.

65. The number of transgender people reported murdered almost doubled between 2017 and 2021, mostly by firearms. Brady, "Hate Crimes and Gun Violence."

66. Belew, *Bring the War Home*, 12, 129.

67. Bob Brown, "Klan's Song is Over but Melody Lingers," *Missoulian*, July 12, 2023, https://missoulian.com/opinion/column/the-klan-in-montana/article_eb78ae7e-16db-11ee-87ed-4f3b416af5c4.html. Among other newspapers, Brown's op-ed appeared in the *Helena Independent Record*, the *Billings Gazette*, and the *Valley Journal* (Ronan).

Bibliography

Manuscripts and Archival Sources

Ball State University Archives, Muncie, Indiana
Diocese Scrapbooks, Diocese of Helena, Montana
Jameson Papers, "Ku Klux Klan in Montana," n.d., Jameson Law Library, University of
    Montana School of Law
K. Ross Toole Archives, Mansfield Library, University of Montana, Missoula
Montana Historical Society
    Governors' Papers (Joseph Dixon, John Erickson)
    Knights of the Ku Klux Klan, Kontinental Klan, No. 30 (Butte) 1916–1931
    Knights of the Ku Klux Klan, Wheatland Klan, No. 29 (Harlowton) 1923–1928
    Montana Council of Defense Records, 1916–1921
    Oral History Collection
Montana Human Rights Network
Polk City Directories
Silver Bow Archives, Butte, Montana
Upper Musselshell Museum, Harlowton, Montana

Newspapers

Anaconda Standard
Belle Fourche Bee (South Dakota)
Big Timber Pioneer
Billings Gazette
Butte Bulletin
Butte Evening News
Butte Miner
Choteau Acantha
Columbus News
Daily Missoulian
Examiner (Butte)
Fallon County Times
Flathead Beacon
Glasgow Courier

Great Falls Tribune
Harlowton Times
Helena Independent
Kalispell Times
Lewistown Democratic News
New York Times
Park County News (Livingston)
Producer News (Plentywood)
Ronan Pioneer
Roundup Record
Roundup Tribune
Seattle Times
Spokesman Review (Spokane)
Washington Post

Government Documents

Bureau of the Census. *Religious Bodies: 1926*, vol. 1, Summary and Detailed Tables. Washington, DC: Government Printing Office, 1930.
Bureau of the Census. *Fourteenth Census of the United States: 1920, Population*, vol. 3, Reports by States. Washington, DC: Government Printing Office, 1922.
Bureau of the Census. *Fifteenth Census of the United States: 1930, Population*, vol. 3, Reports by States. Washington, DC: Government Printing Office, 1932.
House Journal of the Twenty-first Legislative Assembly of the State of Montana, January 7, 1929–March 7, 1929. Helena, MT: State Publishing Co.
Montana Highway Commission. *History of the Montana State Highway Department 1913–1942*. Helena, MT: Montana Highway Commission, 1943.
State Department of Agriculture and Publicity. *The Opportunities and Resources of Montana*. Helena, MT: Independent Pub. Co. 1915.

Books and Articles

Aasheim, Magnus. *Sheridan's Daybreak: A Story of Sheridan County and its Pioneers*, vol. 1–3. Great Falls, MT: Blue Print & Letter Co., 1970. Digital Collection, County Histories of Montana.
Abarr, John. *Story of a Lone Wolf Klansman: This Is a Story about How John Abarr a Country Kid from Montana and Wyoming Became a Member of the Racialist Movement*. CreateSpace, 2017.
Albright, Horace Marden. "The Great and Near-Great in Yellowstone." *Montana: The Magazine of Western History* 22, no. 3 (Summer 1972): 80–89.
Alexander, Charles C. "Kleagles and Cash: The Ku Klux Klan as a Business Organization, 1915–1930." *Business History Review* 39, no. 3 (1965): 348–67.
———. *The Ku Klux Klan in the Southwest*. Lexington, KY: University Press of Kentucky, 1965.
Allen, Frederick. *A Decent, Orderly Lynching: The Montana Vigilantes*. Norman: University of Oklahoma Press, 2004.

Ander, Fritiof. "The Swedish American Press and the American Protective Association." *Church History* 6, no. 2 (June 1937): 165–79.

"Audit of Anti-Semitic Incidents in 2022." Anti-Defamation League. March 2023. https://www.adl.org/resources/report/audit-antisemitic-incidents-2022.

Barkun, Michael. *Religion and the Racist Right: The Origins of the Christian Identity Movement*. Chapel Hill: University of North Carolina Press, 1997.

Barnes, Kenneth C. *The Ku Klux Klan in 1920s Arkansas: How Protestant White Nationalism Came to Rule a State*. Fayetteville, AR: The University of Arkansas Press, 2021.

Barrett, H. Michael. *Pioneer Little Europe (PLE) Prospectus*. 2001. http://s3.mediamatters.org.s3.amazonaws.com/static/pdfs/pleprospectus.pdf.

Barrouquere, Brett. "White Shadow: David Duke's Lasting Influence on American White Supremacy." *Hate Watch*, May 17, 2019. Southern Poverty Law Center. https://www.splcenter.org/hatewatch/2019/05/17/white-shadow-david-dukes-lasting-influence-american-white-supremacy.

Bassett, Laura. "Richard Spencer Listed Himself on Bumble as Politically 'Moderate.'" *Jezebel*, June 14, 2022. https://jezebel.com/richard-spencer-bumble-dating-profile-moderate-1849062955.

Basso, Matthew, Laura McCall, and Dee Garceau, eds. *Across the Great Divide: Cultures of Manhood in the American West*. New York: Routledge, 2001.

Bates, J. Leonard. *Senator Thomas J. Walsh of Montana: Law and Public Affairs from TR to FDR*. Urbana: University of Illinois Press, 1999.

Baumler, Ellen. "The Florence Crittenton House: Making a Difference since 1900." *Montana Woman*, March 2005. https://www.florencecrittenton.org/wp-content/uploads/2020/06/Montana-Woman-March-2005.pdf.

Belew, Kathleen. *Bring the War Home: The White Power Movement and Paramilitary America*. Cambridge, MA: Harvard University Press, 2018.

Bi-Centennial Committee of the Big Horn County Historical Society. *Lookin' Back*. Hardin, MT: Big Horn Historical Society, 1976.

"Billings KKK Targets Network," *Human Rights Network News* 2, no. 3 (March 1993).

Billson, Chantelle. "Brave Zooey Zephyr 'Up and Ready to Work' Despite Being Mocked and Intimidated at Montana State House." *PinkNews*, May 2, 2023. https://www.thepinknews.com/2023/05/02/zooey-zephyr-intimidation-montana-state-house/.

Birney, Hoffman. *Roads to Roam*. Philadelphia: The Penn Publishing Co., 1930.

Blee, Kathleen M. "The Geography of Racial Activism: Defining Whiteness at Multiple Scales." In *Geographies of Hate, Discrimination, and Intolerance in the United States*, edited by Colin Flint, 49–68. New York: Routledge, 2004.

———. *Women of the Klan: Racism and Gender in the 1920s*. Berkeley: University of California Press, 1991.

Blumer, Herbert. "Introduction to Social Movements." In *The Sociology of Dissent*, edited by R. Serge Denisoff, 4–20. New York: Harcourt Brace Jovonavich, 1974.

Brady, "Hate Crimes and Gun Violence." Accessed July 7, 2024. https://www.bradyunited.org/fact-sheets/hate-crimes-and-gun-violence.

Breland, Ali. "White Nationalists Are Big Fans of Elon's 'White Genocide' Tweets."
    Mother Jones, July 31, 2023. https://www.motherjones.com/politics/2023/07/twitter
    -elon-musk-white-genocide-nationalist-supremacist-tweets/.

————. "Who Is Nick Fuentes, and Why Is a US Rep Buddying Up to the Segregationist,
    Holocaust-Denying Gen Z Influencer?" *Mother Jones*, June 29, 2021. https://www
    .motherjones.com/politics/2021/06/who-is-nick-fuentes-and-why-is-a-us-rep-buddying
    -up-to-the-segregationist-holocaust-denying-gen-z-influencer/.

Brown, Harwood. "Introduction." *Papers Read at the Meeting of Grand Dragons, Knights
    of the Ku Klux Klan*, First Annual Meeting, Asheville, NC, July 1923.

Buchanan, Susy. "Creativity Movement." Extremist Files. Southern Poverty Law Center.
    Accessed July 7, 2024. https://www.splcenter.org/fighting-hate/extremist-files/group
    /creativity-movement-0.

————. "Film of Nazi Pop Twins Highlights Neo-Nazi Family." *Intelligence Report*,
    October 1, 2007. Southern Poverty Law Center. https://www.splcenter.org/fighting
    -hate/intelligence-report/2007/film-nazi-pop-twins-highlights-neo-neo-nazi-family.

Carnes, Mark C. *Secret Ritual and Manhood in Victorian America*. New Haven, CT:
    Yale University Press, 1989.

Chalmers, David M. *Hooded Americanism: The First Century of the Ku Klux Klan
    1865–1965*. 2nd ed. New York: Doubleday and Company, 1981. First published 1965
    by Doubleday and Company.

Chambers, John Whiteclay II. *To Raise an Army: The Draft Comes to Modern America*.
    New York: The Free Press, 1987.

Chicago, Milwaukee and St. Paul Railway. *Montana, Along the New Line to the Pacific
    Coast*. 1908.

Clark, William Lloyd. *The Story of My Battle with the Scarlet Beast*. W. L. Clark, 1932.

Clawson, Mary Ann. *Constructing Brotherhood: Class, Gender, and Fraternalism*. Prince-
    ton, NJ: Princeton University Press, 1989.

Committee for the Bicentennial, *Furrows and Trails in Judith Basin*, 1976.

Corn, David. *American Psychosis: A Historical Investigation of How the Republican
    Party Went Crazy*. New York: Twelve, 2022.

————. "The Elephant in the Room." *Mother Jones* 47, no. 5 (September–October 2022):
    16–21, 66.

Crew, Danny O., ed. *Ku Klux Klan Sheet Music: An Illustrated Catalogue of Published
    Music, 1867–2002*. Jefferson, NC: McFarland & Company, 2003.

Cuddy, Edward. "The Irish Question and the Revival of Anti-Catholicism in the 1920s."
    Catholic Historical Review 67, no. 2 (April 1981): 236–55.

Dalich, Tony. "Shelby's Fabled Day in the Sun: Dempsey vs. Gibbons Fourth of July 1923."
    Montana: Magazine of Western History 15, no 3 (Summer 1965): 2–23.

Desmond, Humphrey J. *The A.P.A. Movement*. Washington: The New Century Press,
    1912. Reprint, New York: Arno Press, 1964.

Dissly, Robert L. *History of Lewistown*. News-Argus Printing, 2000.

Donovan, Roberta. *The First Hundred Years: A History of Lewistown, Montana*. Lew-
    istown: Central Montana Publishing Co., 1994.

Dumenil, Lynn. *The Modern Temper: American Culture and Society in the 1920s.* New York: Hill & Wang, 1995.

———. "The Tribal Twenties: 'Assimilated' Catholics' Response to Anti-Catholicism in the 1920s." *Journal of American Ethnic History* 11 (Fall 1991): 1–14.

Edwards, David. "Matt Gaetz: MAGA Will Turn to 'Bloodshed' if Trump's Crimes Exclude Him from Ballot." *Raw Story,* September 7, 2023. https://www.rawstory.com/matt-gaetz-maga-will-turn-to-bloodshed-if-trump-s-crimes-exclude-him-from-ballot/.

Egan, Timothy. *A Fever in the Heartland: The Ku Klux Klan's Plot to Take Over America and the Woman Who Stopped Them.* New York: Viking, 2023.

Emmons, David M. *The Butte Irish: Class and Ethnicity in an American Mining Town, 1875–1925.* Urbana: University of Illinois Press, 1989.

———. "The Orange and the Green in Montana: A Reconsideration of the Origins of the Clark-Daly Feud." *Arizona and the West* 28, no. 3 (1986): 225–45.

Erickson, Christine K. "'Come Join the K.K.K. in the Old Town Tonight': The Ku Klux Klan in Harlowton, Montana, during the 1920s." *Montana: The Magazine of Western History* 64, no. 3 (November 2014): 49–64, 89–92.

———. "'Kluxer Blues': The Klan Confronts Catholics in Butte, Montana, 1923–1929." *Montana: The Magazine of Western History* 53, no. 1 (Spring, 2003): 44–57.

Evans, Hiram Wesley. "The Klan's Fight for Americanism," *North American Review* 223, no. 830 (Spring 1926): 33–63.

———. "The Menace of Modern Immigration," Address delivered on Klan Day of the Texas State Fair, October 24, 1923. Atlanta: Knights of the Ku Klux Klan, 1924.

Fergus County Bi-Centennial Heritage Committee. *The Heritage Book of the Original Fergus County Area.* 1976.

Ferguson, Charles W. *Fifty Million Brothers.* New York: Farrar & Rinehart, 1937.

Fisher, Arthur. "Montana: Land of the Copper Collar," *Nation* 117, no. 3037 (September 19, 1923): 290–92.

Flint, Colin, ed. *Spaces of Hate: Geographies of Discrimination and Intolerance in the U.S.A.* New York: Routledge, 2004.

Fox, Craig. *Everyday Klansfolk: White Protestant Life and the KKK in 1920s Michigan.* East Lansing: Michigan State University Press, 2011.

Frink, Brenda D. "'God Give Us Men!': Manliness, the American Protective Association, and Catholicism in San Francisco, 1893–1896." *Ex Post Facto* (San Francisco State University) 11 (2002): 49–63.

Gates, Paul W. "Homesteading in the High Plains, 1876–1936." *Agricultural History* 51, no. 1 (January 1977): 109–133.

Gerlach, Larry R. *Blazing Crosses in Zion: the Ku Klux Klan in Utah.* Logan: Utah State University Press, 1982.

Gist, Noel P. "Secret Societies: A Cultural Study of Fraternalism in the United States." *University of Missouri Studies* 15 (1940).

Goldberg, Robert A. *Hooded Empire: The Ku Klux Klan in Colorado.* Urbana: University of Illinois Press, 1981.

Gordon, Linda. *The Second Coming of the KKK: The Ku Klux Klan of the 1920s and the American Political Tradition*. New York: Liveright Publishing Corporation, 2017.

Grand Lodge of Ancient Free and Accepted Masons. *1924 and 1925 Proceedings of the Grand Lodge of Ancient Free and Accepted Masons of the State of Montana*.

Gray, Rosie. "Trump Defends White-Nationalist Protesters: 'Some Very Fine People on Both Sides.'" *The Atlantic*, August 15, 2017. https://www.theatlantic.com/politics/archive/2017/08/trump-defends-white-nationalist-protesters-some-very-fine-people-on-both-sides/537012/.

Gutfeld, Arnon. *Montana's Agony: Years of War and Hysteria, 1917–1921*. Gainesville: University of Florida Press, 1979.

Hanson, Amy Beth, and Matthew Brown. "Judge Rejects Zooey Zephyr Bid to Return to Montana House." *AP News*, May 3, 2023. https://apnews.com/article/zooey-zephyr-montana-transgender-lawsuit-cce3cfcf6ec2e71abee383b2ad1d4b72.

Harcourt, Felix. *Ku Klux Kulture: America and the Klan in the 1920s*. Chicago: University of Chicago Press, 2017.

Hargreaves, Mary. *Dry Farming in the Northern Great Plains 1920–1990*. Lawrence: University Press of Kansas, 1993.

Harlowton Woman's Club. *Yesteryears and Pioneers*. Harlowton, MT: Western Printing and Lithography, 1972.

Hatewatch Staff. "Far-right Survivalist and Icon of 'Patriot' Movement Predicts Religious Civil War." *Hatewatch*, January 3, 2019. Southern Poverty Law Center. https://www.splcenter.org/hatewatch/2019/01/03/far-right-survivalist-and-icon-patriot-movement-predicts-religious-civil-war.

Hernandez, Miguel. *The Ku Klux Klan and Freemasonry in 1920s America: Fighting Fraternities*. London: Routledge, 2020.

Higham, John. *Strangers in the Land: Patterns of American Nativism 1860–1925*. 2nd ed. New Brunswick, NJ: Rutgers University Press, 1988.

History of Park County, Montana. Taylor Publishing Co., 1984.

Holthouse, David. "High Country Extremism: Patriot Games." *Media Matters*, 2011. https://www.mediamatters.org/diversity-discrimination/high-country-extremism-patriot-games.

———. "High Country Extremism: Pioneering Hate." *Media Matters*, 2011. https://www.mediamatters.org/diversity-discrimination/high-country-extremism-pioneering-hate.

Horowitz, David A., ed. *Inside the Klavern: The Secret History of a Klu Klux Klan of the 1920s*. Carbondale: Southern Illinois University Press, 1999.

Hougardy, Beulah C., Hazel Spidel, Alice B. Graves, and Frances Spek, eds. *Horizons O'er the Musselshell*. Musselshell Valley Pioneer Club, 1974.

House Joint Resolution No. 11. Introduced by B. Mitchell. "A Joint Resolution of the Senate and the House of Representatives of the State of Montana Calling for the Designation of Antifa as a Domestic Terrorist Organization." 67th Legislature. Legislative Services Division, January–April 2021, 1–2.

Hunt, Robert V., Jr. "The Heyday of the Denver American Protective Association, 1892–1894." *Journal of the West* 35 (October 4, 1996): 74–81.

Huppert, Arnold. *Looking Back.* Livingston, MT: The Park County News, n.d.

Integrity First for America. "IFA's Charlottesville Case: *Sines v. Kessler.*" 2021. https://www.integrityfirstforamerica.org/our-work/case/charlottesville-case.

Jackson, Kenneth T. *The Ku Klux Klan in the City, 1915–1930.* Oxford, NY: Oxford University Press, 1967.

Jacobson, Matthew Frye. *Whiteness of a Different Color: European Immigrants and the Alchemy of Race.* Cambridge, MA: Harvard University Press, 1998.

Katz, Rebecca S., and Joey Bailey. "The Militia, a Legal and Social Movement Analysis: Will the Real Militia Please Stand Up? Militia Hate Group or the Constitutional Militia?" *Sociological Focus* 33, no. 2, Special Issue: White Supremacy and Hate Crimes (May 2000): 133–51.

Kazin, Michael. *The Populist Persuasion: An American History.* Rev. 2nd ed. Ithaca, NY: Cornell University Press, 1995.

Kennedy, Lawrence W. "Pulpits and Politics: Anti-Catholicism in Boston in the 1880s and 1890s." *Historical Journal of Massachusetts* 28 no 1 (2000): 56–75.

Kidston, Martin. "Missoula County Floored by Library Commission's Fears of 'Marxist Lesbian' ALA President." *MissoulaCurrent,* n.d. Accessed July 6, 2024. https://missoulacurrent.com/missoula-marxist-lesbian/.

Kinzer, Donald. *An Episode in Anti-Catholicism: The American Protective Association.* Seattle: University of Washington Press, 1964.

Knapp, Norman C. "Abstract, Devil's Basin Oilfield, Musselshell County, Montana." Billings Geological Society: Guidebook: Seventh Annual Field Conference, August 16–18, 1956. https://archives.datapages.com/data/mgs/mt/data/0007/0126/0126.html.

Lavietes, Mike. "New House Speaker's Views on LGBTQ Issues Come Under Fresh Scrutiny." NBC, October 26, 2023. https://www.nbcnews.com/nbc-out/out-politics-and-policy/mike-johnson-house-speaker-lgbtq-views-scrutiny-rcna122317.

Lay, Shawn., ed. *The Invisible Empire in the West: Toward a New Historical Appraisal of the Ku Klux Klan of the 1920s.* Urbana: University of Illinois Press, 1992.

Lenz, Ryan. "A Gathering of Eagles: Extremists Look to Montana." *Intelligence Report,* Winter 2011. Southern Poverty Law Center. https://www.splcenter.org/fighting-hate/intelligence-report/2011/gathering-eagles-extremists-look-montana.

Livingston Enterprise. *Centennial Scrapbook: Livingston 1882–1982.* Livingston, MT, 1982.

Loewen, James W. *Sundown Towns: A Hidden Dimension of American Racism.* New York: The New Press, 2005.

MacLean, Nancy. *Behind the Mask of Chivalry: The Making of the Second Ku Klux Klan.* New York: Oxford University Press, 1994.

Madison, James H. *The Ku Klux Klan in the Heartland.* Bloomington: Indiana University Press, 2020.

Mahon, John K. *History of the Militia and the National Guard.* New York: Macmillan Publishing Co., 1983.

Malone, Michael P. *The Battle for Butte.* Seattle: University of Washington Press, 1981.

Malone, Michael P., Richard B. Roeder, and William L. Lang. *Montana: A History of Two Centuries.* Rev. ed. Seattle: University of Washington Press, 1991.

Manfra, Jo Ann. "Hometown Politics and the American Protective Association, 1887–1890." *Annals of Iowa* 55, Issue 2 (Spring 1996): 138–166.

Margolis, Joshua. "Bill Banning Minors from Seeing Drag Shows Draws Charged Comments in Helena." NBC Montana, February 9, 2023. https://nbcmontana.com/news /local/bill-banning-minors-from-seeing-drag-shows-draws-charged-comments -in-helena.

McAdam, Travis. "History of White Nationalism in Montana 1980–2015." YouTube. Accessed July 5, 2024. https://www.youtube.com/watch?v=ioSPp9C6now.

———. "White Nationalism in Montana 2015–Present." YouTube. Accessed July 5, 2024. https://www.youtube.com/watch?v=EVXvsh5a1Ds.

McDonald, Verlaine Stoner. *The Red Corner: The Rise and Fall of Communism in Northeastern Montana.* Helena: Montana Historical Press, 2010.

Meehan, Kasey, and Jonathan Friedman. "USA: State Laws Supercharge Book Suppression in Schools." *Pen America,* 2023. https://pen.org/report/banned-in-the-usa-state -laws-supercharge-book-suppression-in-schools/.

Merz, Charles. "Sweet Land of Secrecy: The Strange Spectacle of American Fraternalism." *Harper's Magazine* 154 (February 1927): 329–34.

Meyers, Rex C. "Homestead on the Range: The Emergence of Community in Eastern Montana 1900–1925." *Great Plains Quarterly* 10, no. 4 (Fall 1990): 218–27.

"Moms for Liberty," Southern Poverty Law Center. Accessed July 7, 2024. https://www .splcenter.org/fighting-hate/extremist-files/group/moms-liberty.

Montana Historical Society. *Not in Precious Metals Alone: A Manuscript History of Montana.* Helena, MT: Montana Historical Society, 1976.

Montana Human Rights Network. "2021 Legislative Report and Scorecard." n.d. https:// www.mhrn.org/.

———. "Billings KKK Targets Network." *Human Rights Network News* 2, no. 3 (March 1993).

———. "Charlie Kirk and Turning Point USA: Bringing a Minor League Version of White Nationalism to Montana." March 2020.

———. "Community Response to KKK in Red Lodge." *Network News Flash,* no. 2 (December 1993).

———. "The Day Billings Stood Together." *Human Rights Network News,* July 1993.

———. "Former Klansman Runs for Montana Legislature." *Human Rights Network News,* February 2002.

———. "KKK Targets Two Montana Communities." *Network News,* March 1995.

———. "MHRN Denounces Proposed Legislation as Part of 'Antifa /Fantasy.'" February 15, 2021. https://mhrn.org/2021/02/15/hj11.

———. "The National Alliance Targets Montana." *Human Rights Network News* 14, no. 3, November 2004.

"Montana Rep. Zooey Zephyr Sues Over Her Removal from House Floor." NPR. May 1,
    2023. https://www.npr.org/2023/05/01/1173079450/montana-rep-zooey-zephyr-sues
    -over-her-removal-from-house-floor.
Monteval, Marion [Edgar I. Fuller]. *The Klan Inside Out.* Claremore, OK, 1928. Reprinted,
    New York: Negro Universities Press, 1970.
Morris, Richard B. *Encyclopedia of American History.* New York: Harper and Brothers,
    1953.
Morsanny, Mary, Phyllis Adolph, and Annie Larsen. *Roundup on the Musselshell.*
    Billings, MT: Reporter Printing and Supply, 1974.
Murphy, Mary. "Bootlegging Mothers and Drinking Daughters: Gender and Prohibition
    in Butte, Montana." In *Montana Legacy,* edited by Harry Fritz, 177–200. Helena:
    Montana Historical Society Press, 2002.
———. *Mining Cultures: Men, Women, and Leisure in Butte, 1914–41.* Urbana: University
    of Illinois Press, 1997.
Neiwert, David. "Federal Court Sentences Leaders of Montana Freemen to Long Prison
    Terms." *Intelligence Report,* 1999. Southern Poverty Law Center. https://www.splcenter
    .org/fighting-hate/intelligence-report/1999/federal-court-sentences-leaders-montana
    -freemen-long-prison-terms.
———. "Montana Klansman's Idea for 'Inclusive' KKK Elicits Derision." *Hatewatch,*
    November 17, 2014. Southern Poverty Law Center. https://www.splcenter.org
    /hatewatch/2014/11/17/montana-klansman's-idea-'inclusive'-kkk-elicits-derision.
    July 6, 2024.
Peel, Cullen. "Roundup of Anti-LGBTQ+ Legislation Advancing in States Across the
    Country." Human Rights Watch, May 23, 2023. https://www.hrc.org/press-releases
    /roundup-of-anti-lgbtq-legislation-advancing-in-states-across-the-country.
    July 2024.
Pegram, Thomas R. *One Hundred Percent American: The Rebirth and Decline of the Ku
    Klux Klan in the 1920s.* Chicago: Ivan R. Dee, 2011.
Piggott, Stephen. "White Nationalists and the So-Called 'Alt-Right' Celebrate Trump's
    Victory," *Hatewatch,* November 9, 2016. https://www.splcenter.org/hatewatch/2016
    /11/09/white-nationalists-and-so-called-alt-right-celebrate-trumps-victory.
Planas, Antonio. "New Florida Standards Teach Students that Some Black People
    Benefited from Slavery Because It Taught Useful Skills." NBC News. July 20, 2023.
    https://www.nbcnews.com/news/us-news/new-florida-standards-teach-black-people
    -benefited-slavery-taught-usef-rcna95418.
Progressive Men of the State of Montana. Chicago: A. W. Bowen & Co., 1902.
Ramirez, Nikki McCann. "Paul Gosar's Newsletter Features Website That Calls for
    Readers to 'Stand Up for Hitler': Report," *Rolling Stone,* July 24, 2023. https://www
    .rollingstone.com/music/music-news/paul-gosar-newsletter-antisemtic-racist-pro
    -hitler-website-links-1234794315/.
Raymer, Robert G. *Montana: The Land and its People,* vol. 2. The Lewis Publishing
    Co., 1930.

Rice, Tom. *White Robes, Silver Screens: Movies and the Making of the Ku Klux Klan.* Bloomington: Indiana University Press, 2015.

Richard, Mark Paul. *Not a Catholic Nation: The Ku Klux Klan Confronts New England in the 1920s.* Amherst: University of Massachusetts Press, 2015.

Ridgeway, James. *Blood in the Face: The Ku Klux Klan, Aryan Nations, Nazi Skinheads, and the Rise of a New White Culture.* Revised and updated. New York: Thunder's Mouth Press, 1995.

Rivas, Rachel Carroll. "Whitefish Hate Group Representative Makes National Media, Denounced by State and Local Human Rights Activists." Montana Human Rights Network. May 11, 2013.

Rodriquez, Alicia E. "'No Ku Klux Klan for Kern': The Rise and Fall of the 1920s KKK in Kern County, California." *Southern California Quarterly* 99, no. 1 (Spring 2017): 5–45.

Roy History Committee. *Homestead Shacks over Buffalo Tracks: History of Northeastern Fergus County.* 1990.

Rustebakke, Dorothy, and Bob Southland. *Millennium Memories: Historical Highlights of Daniels, Sheridan, and North Valley Counties.* 2000.

"'Saving Girls': Montana State Vocational School for Girls." Women's History Matters. 2014. https://montanawomenshistory.org/saving-girls-montana-state-vocational-school-for-girls/.

Schaertl, Richard L. *Echoes of the Past: An Immigrant Family History.* Edmonds, WA, 1989.

Schlatter, Evelyn A. *Aryan Cowboys: White Supremacists and the Search for a New Frontier 1970–2000.* Austin: University of Texas Press, 2006.

Schmidt, Alvin J. "Fraternal Organizations." *The Greenwood Encyclopedia of American Institutions.* Westport, CT: Greenwood Press, 1980.

Schubert, Keith. "Montana House Fails to Denounce White Supremacist Groups." *Missoula Current,* February 25, 2021. https://missoulacurrent.com/montana-white-supremacy/.

Shepherd, William G. "Ku Klux Koin." *Colliers* 82 (July 21, 1928).

Small, Lawrence F. *A Century of Politics on the Yellowstone.* Billings, MT: Rocky Mountain College, 1983.

Smith, Benjamin Nathaniel. "Midwest Shooting Spree Ends with Apparent Suicide of Suspect." CNN.com. July 5, 1999. http://www.cnn.com/US/9907/05/illinois.shootings.02/.

Southern Poverty Law Center. "Active Ku Klux Klan Groups." *Intelligence Report,* March 3, 2015. https://www.splcenter.org/fighting-hate/intelligence-report/2015/active-ku-klux-klan-groups.

———. "Andrew Anglin." Extremist Files. Accessed July 4, 2024. https://www.splcenter.org/fighting-hate/extremist-files/individual/andrew-anglin.

———. "April Gaede." Extremist Files. Accessed July 4, 2024. https://www.splcenter.org/fighting-hate/extremist-files/individual/april-gaede.

———. "Aryan Nations on Verge of Collapse Following Judgement." *Intelligence Report*, December 6, 2000. https://www.splcenter.org/fighting-hate/intelligence-report/2000 /aryan-nations-verge-collapse-following-judgment.

———. "David Lane." Extremist Files. Southern Poverty Law Center. Accessed July 3, 2024. https://www.splcenter.org/fighting-hate/extremist-files/individual/david -lane.

———. "Four Montana Freemen Found Guilty." *Intelligence Report*, September 15, 1998. https://www.splcenter.org/fighting-hate/intelligence-report/1998/four-montana -freemen-found-guilty.

———. "National Alliance." Extremist Files. Accessed July 7, 2024. https://www.splcenter .org/fighting-hate/extremist-files/group/national-alliance.

———. "Pop-Singing Gaede Twins Renounce Racism." *Intelligence Report*, November 15, 2011. https://www.splcenter.org/fighting-hate/intelligence-report/2011/pop-singing -gaede-twins-renounce-racism.

———. "SPLC Applauds Landmark Ruling Holding White Supremacists Liable in the Charlottesville 'Unite the Right' Civil Trial." November 24, 2021. https:// www.splcenter.org/presscenter/splc-applauds-landmark-ruling-holding-white -supremacists-liable-charlottesville-unite.

———. "Tanya Gersh v Andrew Anglin." Accessed July 6, 2024. https://www.splcenter .org/seeking-justice/case-docket/tanya-gersh-v-andrew-anglin.

———. "William Daniel Johnson." Extremist Files. Accessed July 4, 2024. https://www .splcenter.org/fighting-hate/extremist-files/individual/william-daniel-johnson.

———. "William Pierce." Extremist Files. Accessed July 4, 2024. https://www.splcenter .org/fighting-hate/extremist-files/individual/william-pierce.

Spiro, Jonathan Peter. *Defending the Master Race: Conservation, Eugenics, and the Legacy of Madison Grant*. Burlington: University of Vermont Press, 2009.

Spritzer, Don. *Roadside History of Montana*. Missoula, MT: Mountain Press Publishing Company, 1999.

Stearns, Harold Joseph. *A History of the Upper Musselshell Valley (to 1920)*. Harlowton, MT: Times Clarion Publishers, 1966.

Steele, Volney. *Wellington Rankin, His Family, Life and Times*. Bozeman, MT: Bridger Creek Historical Press, 2002.

Stevens, Albert C. *The Cyclopedia of Fraternities*. 2nd ed. New York: E. B. Treat & Co., 1907.

Stout, Tom. *Montana: Its Story and Biography*, vol. 3. Chicago: The American Historical Society, 1921.

Strong, Josiah. *Our Country*, ed. Jurgen Herbst. Cambridge, MA: Belknap Press, 1963. First pub. in 1886, revised edition 1891.

Svingen, Orlan J. "Jim Crow, Indian Style." *American Indian Quarterly* 11, no. 4 (Autumn 1987): 167–202.

Thomson, Janet D. *News about Our Families Who Lived in Harlowton, Montana, 1908–1939: Husband, Thomson, Boifeuillet, Lunney, Gaines, and Knudson Families*. Great Falls, MT. 2003.

Toole, K. Ross. *Twentieth-Century Montana: A State of Extremes.* Norman: University of Oklahoma Press, 1972.

Toy, Eckard V. "Robe and Gown: The Ku Klux Klan in Eugene, Oregon."

Van Dyke, Nella, and Sarah A. Soule. "Structural Change and the Mobilizing Effect of Threat: Explaining Levels of Patriot and Militia Organizing in the United States." *Social Problems* 49 no. 4 (November 2002): 497–520.

Waldron, Ellis L. *Atlas of Montana Elections.* Missoula: University of Montana Press, 1978.

Wallace, Les. *The Rhetoric of Anti-Catholicism: The American Protective Association, 1887–1911.* New York: Garland Pub., 1990.

Walter, Dave. "KKK: White Hoods Under the Big Sky." *Montana Magazine,* no. 147 (January–February 1998): 71–76.

Webb Clive, ed. *Massive Resistance: Southern Opposition to the Second Reconstruction.* New York: Oxford University Press, 2005.

Wehner, Peter. "More MAGA Than Ever." *The Atlantic,* November 10, 2022. https://www .theatlantic.com/ideas/archive/2022/11/midterms-trump-desantis-dobbs-republicans /672068/.

Wheeler, Burton. *Yankee from the West: The Candid, Turbulent Life Story of the Yankee-born U.S. Senator from Montana.* Garden City, NY: Doubleday, 1962.

White, Richard. "The Current Weirdness in the West." *Western Historical Quarterly* 28, no. 1 (Spring, 1997): 4–16.

"Why They Join the Klan." *New Republic* 36 (November 21, 1923): 321.

Wilkerson, Bill. "Lines West Memories." Harlowton, MT: MT: Times Clarion Publishers, 1992.

Wilkinson, Todd. "Home, Home on the Range, Where the Neo-Nazis and Skinheads Roam," *High Country News,* June 27, 1994, 1, 8–11.

Wilson, Gary A. *Honky Tonk Town: Havre's Bootlegging Days.* 10th anniversary edition. Havre, MT: High-Line Books, 1995.

Wilson, Jason. "Exclusive: Oath Keepers Steward Rhodes' Children Speak." *Hate Watch,* Southern Poverty Law Center. May 12, 2022. https://www.splcenter.org/hatewatch /2022/05/12/exclusive-oath-keepers-leader-stewart-rhodes-children-speak.

Writers Project of Montana. *Copper Camp.* Helena, MT: Riverbend Publishing, 1943, 2002.

Wyss, Marilyn. *Roads to Romance: The Origins and Development of the Road and Trail System in Montana.* Helena: Montana Department of Transportation, 1992.

Yan, Holly. "Human Rights Campaign Declares a National State of Emergency for LGBTQ+ People." CNN. June 2, 2023. https://www.cnn.com/2023/06/06/us/hrc -lgbtq-emergency-declared/index.html.

"The Year in Hate and Extremism: Far-right Extremists Coalescing in Broad-based, Loosely Affiliated Movement." Southern Poverty Law Center. February 5, 2021. https://www.splcenter.org/news/2021/02/05/year-hate-and-extremism-far-right -extremists-coalescing-broad-based-loosely-affiliated.

Zellick, Anna, with Florence Kettering. *Anna: A Memoir, April 21, 1927–March 3, 2002.* Montana Memory Project. https://mtmemory.recollectcms.com/nodes/view/3617.

———. "'Fire in the Hole': Slovenians, Croatians, and Coal Mining in the Musselshell." *Montana: The Magazine of Western History* 40, no. 2 (Spring 1990): 16–31.

———. "Patriots on the Rampage: Mob Action in Lewistown, 1917–1918." *Montana* 31, no. 1 (Winter 1981): 30–43.

Zeskind, Leonard. "Basis of Freemen's Philosophy is Racism." *Intelligence Report,* June 15, 1998. Southern Poverty Law Center. https://www.splcenter.org/fighting -hate/intelligence-report/1998/basis-freemen's-philosophy-racism.

———. "Montana Freemen Trial May Mark End of an Era." *Intelligence Report,* June 15, 1998. Southern Poverty Law Center. https://www.splcenter.org/fighting-hate /intelligence-report/1998/montana-freemen-trial-may-mark-end-era

Index

INDEX 197

Evans, Hiram Wesley, 2, 3, 30, 35–41, 45, 48, 106; lecture tour (1930), 68; presidential election of 1928, 63, 67; Terwilliger appointment, 6, 17, 18; Texas speech, 50–51, 107

"exalted womanhood," 97, 105

Examiner (APA), 11, 13, 14, 31, 33, 74

Fellowship Forum, 41–42, 64–65

Fergus County, Mont., 20. *See also* Lewistown, Mont.

Fisk, Robert, 102

Florida, 135, 136

Follet, Charles G., 61

fraternal orders, 18, 22, 26–28, 73–74, 80, 86–87, 117–18. *See also* Knights of Columbus; Masons; Royal Riders of the Red Robe

fraudulent documents, 12

Freemasons. *See* Masons

Gaede, April, 128, 176n27

Gaetz, Matt, 136

Galen, Albert J., 68

gay and lesbian people. *See* LGBTQ people

Georgia, 106, 136, 169n19, 171n72

Gianforte, Greg, 130, 135, 179n36

Gibbons, Tommy, 82

Gilmore, Robert P., 101

girls' correctional schools, 61–63

Glasgow, Mont., 20, 21, 103

Glendive, Mont., 45

Gordon, Linda, 3

Grant, Madison: *The Passing of the Great Race*, 50, 153n14

Great Falls, Mont., 21; Abarr, 129; cross burnings, 49, 107; Evans lecture, 68; Prohibition, 53; Stanton, 164n70

Great Falls Tribune, 16, 19–20, 100

Great Northern Railroad, 19, 52, 86

Greene, Marjorie Taylor, 136

Griffin, Brad, 120

Griffith, D. W.: *The Birth of a Nation*, 16

Hale, Matt, 133–34, 175n11

Hamilton, Mont., 2, 20, 99, 108

Hampton, Shelton, 42

Hardin, Mont., 53, 60, 99, 112

Harlowton, Mont., 9, 10, 19–24, 34, 49, 53–55, 84–92, 169n30; Francis Harrison, 99; public schools, 14. *See also* Wheatland Klan

Harlowton Brotherhood, 90

Harlowton Times, 15, 16, 58, 64, 86, 88, 97

Harrison, Francis, 99

Harrison, John C., 99, 169n30

Hassett, Dan, 134

Hathaway, Maggie, 105

Havre, Mont., 20, 21, 52

Hayden Lake, Idaho, 126, 129

Helena, Mont., 20, 22, 86, 97–98, 103; Catholic Diocese, 12; Crittenton Home, 62; House of Good Shepherd, 61–63; Oak Street Methodist Church, 103, 107; Prohibition, 53–54; State Vocational School for Girls, 61, 62

Helena Independent, 58, 97–98

Hernandez, Miguel, 117

hoaxes and pranks, 106–10, 118

Hokanson, Ann Scally, 101–2

homesteading, 9–10, 78, 84

homophobia, 123–24, 129, 135, 136, 176n32

Hoover, Herbert, 65, 67

horses, 18, 52; Klan riders, 2, 20, 98–99

House of Good Shepherd, Helena, 61–63

Huckabee, Mike, 136

Huppe, Charles F., 93–96, 168n15

Husband, W. C., 87, 89, 90

Idaho, 125, 126, 128

immigrants and immigration, 9–10, 12, 50, 51, 55; Butte, 51, 72; Harlowton, 84; Roundup, 78, 80

Immigration Act of 1924, 38, 51, 68, 119

South Dakota, 45
Southern Poverty Law Center (SPLC), 127, 131, 132–33
Spencer, Richard, 128–29, 132
Squires, Howard, 88, 169n30
state legislatures: anti-LGBTQ bills, 135; Louisiana, 129. *See also* Montana state legislature
State Vocational School for Girls, 61, 62
Stephenson, David C., 38, 118–19, 121
Stevensville, Mont., 100, 108
Stewart, Sam V., 54, 165n88
Stoddard, Lothrop: *The Rising Tide of Color*, 50, 81, 153n14
Stormfront, 128, 176n32
Stout, Tom, 56
Strong, Josiah, 13
sundown towns, 80–81, 164n59
Superior, Mont., 99, 133–34, 175n11

Taylor, Elizabeth, 16
Terry, Mont., 45
Terwilliger, Lewis, 2–9, 17–69, 93, 96–97, 98, 111–21; anti-Catholicism, 5, 27, 29, 39, 48–49, 61–63, 66, 67; Butte, 76, 77; Clare Rawlings and, 105–6; frugality, 104; Knights of Pythias, 86–87; secret fraternalism and, 26–46; W. C. Husband and, 87; "white civilization shall be maintained," 131
Texas State Fair: "Klan Day," 50–51
Thompson Falls, Mont., 112
Thurston, L. H., 82
Tighe, Stephen, 30–31, 81, 90, 94–95
Toole, Ken, 125, 133, 144n49
Tranel, Monica, 131
transgender people, 134–35, 136, 180n65
Trochmann, John, 125
Troy, Mont., 122, 174n5
Trump, Donald, 129–33

Tuberville, Tommy, 131
Turner Diaries, The (Macdonald [Pierce]), 127, 175n23
Turning Point USA (TPUSA), 130

unions, 96, 122
Unite the Right rally, Charlottesville, Va., 2017, 128, 130
University City Klan, 53, 98, 104, 110
University of Montana, 109–10, 118

Vicars, Joe, 80, 81, 83, 95
vigilantism, 15, 97, 100–102, 108
voting rights, Native American, 59–60

Walkerville, Mont., 74, 76
Walsh, Thomas J., 54, 56, 57, 59, 68
Wehner, Peter, 130
Wheatland County, Mont., 11, 14, 15, 49, 53, 55, 166n105. *See also* Harlowton, Mont.
Wheatland Klan, 4, 11, 19, 23, 58, 59
Wheeler, Burton, 54, 65
Whitefish, Mont., 128, 133
Whitehall, Mont., 77, 171n71
White Sulphur Springs, Mont., 109
"wokeness," 132
womanhood, exalted. *See* "exalted womanhood"
Woman's Christian Temperance Union, 55
World Court, 68
World War I, 9, 11, 14–15, 79, 82, 85
Wyoming, 3, 45, 49, 129

Yellowstone National Park, 99

Zellick, Anna, 78, 84
Zephyr, Zooey, 134
Zinke, Ryan, 131

.